TIME WARPS

Ashis Nandy

TIME WARPS

*Silent and Evasive Pasts
in Indian Politics and Religion*

HURST & COMPANY, LONDON

First published in Great Britain in 2002
by C. Hurst & Company (Publishers) Ltd,
38 King Street, London WC2E 8JZ
Copyright © 2002 Ashis Nandy
This edition published by arrangement with the original publisher,
Permanent Black, New Delhi
For sale only outside South Asia

A British Library Cataloguing-in-Publication Data
record for this book is available on request from the British Library.

ISBN 1-85065-479-4 (cloth)
ISBN 1-85065-484-0 (paper)

Printed in England

Introduction

Most of these essays try to bypass a past that can be formalised and exhausted by the idea of history. Indeed, they defy the idea of history as a museum—authoritative, passing final judgements—'a substitute for medieval cathedrals.' The past, in the following pages, is an open-ended record of the human predicaments of our times. For one interested in cultural and political psychology, the past is not only the objective history of a person or a group but a record of marks left in the form of memories, experiences, scars and adaptive resources within personalities. In a clinical case-history, reconfigured memories are the stuff of contemporary subjectivity, and a theory of the past is actually a prognosis of the future; the patient's self mediates between the past and the future and pilots the time travel between the two. Diagnosis, thus, becomes an attempt to read the past as an essay on human prospects, and health as the ability to live with one's constructions of the past and deploy them creatively.

This idea of the past has some curious implications. First, a study of the past becomes not merely a conversation with archives, but also the creation of new and unique dialogues with those who live with their distinctive pasts. To put it aphoristically, though the past lives only in the present, it is that part of the self on which the present does not have a stranglehold. As in all creative ventures into the future—made by visionaries and hardboiled futurists—time travel to the past too is a play with the boundaries of self. This is more so in societies where nonhistoricised pasts—myths, legends, epics and unofficial memories—predominate, and where clues to the future lie scattered in diverse pasts created by human ingenuity. In such societies, cultural politics does not remain a matter of cognitive puzzle-solving or intellectual virtuosity. It involves mobilising the inner resources and technologies of the self to rework personal and collective biographies, to fathom the present resilience and future potentialities of our selves.

The inner resources of people and cultures which rework these personal or collective biographies include analytic frames and categories tinged with the experiences of those who bear the brunt of the social and political pathologies of our times. Through a neo-Brahminic sleight of hand, we may have delegitimised these frames and categories or converted them into data to protect our favourite social theories. But a large part of the world continues to use its unhistoricised pasts as life-defining. Even among those who are seemingly immersed in contemporary ideologies and fully share contemporary historical sensitivities, there is often the awareness of another world of knowledge that refuses to die—comprising non-conventional systems of healing, non-formal modes of education, deviant theories of ethnic or communal violence and amity, and so on. Many who live with these alternatives are in constant dialogue with their pasts, not defensively, but as a way of accessing their own tacit knowledge. They believe that the pathway to the future may be through aspects of our pasts that survive as our undersocialised or less-colonised selves. The best studies of the future are also often studies of the past.

In paying respect to these other ways of negotiating time, these essays do not presume to speak on behalf of the victims of history: they seek to clear a political path for the overawed to speak and the silenced to be heard. 'We have written enough about the victims,' someone has said, 'now let them speak for themselves.' This is easier said than done. For these new voices are often, to our chagrin, a negation of our own voices. They carry the intimations of alternative formulations about our times and passions.

If there is no 'real' or immutable past, and all constructed pasts and all history are ways of coping with hopes, ambitions, fears and anxieties in the present, so are the visions and fantasies of the future. The technologies of the mind that we employ to grapple with the future are not essentially different from the ones with which we cope with the past. Only, in the case of the future, our constructions regularly turn out to be self-destructive. All important projections about the future go wrong, because they project the future by changing human consciousness. It is an indicator of the power of George Orwell's *1984* that the year of that name passed us tamely by. Orwell's novel contributed to that tame passage.

This way of looking at time has, I believe, a better chance of subverting the global mass culture's massive dependence on the ego defence of 'denial'. Once seen as a relatively primitive defence, associated more with psychoses than neuroses, denial has now escaped from the psychiatrist's clinic and contaminated the core of our public life. Suffering and unhappiness are being increasingly subjected not merely to reification and rationalisation, they are being handled like the minor ailments of a few hypochondriacs. Institutionalised denial has given contemporary global culture an element of heartlessness which verges on psychopathy. Unsteadily perched on a global structure of denial, we protect ourselves against all strange knowledge lest it breach our faiths and ideologies.

The certitudes that guard the imperium of denial in our times constitute a second line of defence. The dominant global culture has honed certain analytic tools that have become, in practice, entities beyond history and culture, too sacred to be demystified. Theoretically they may be falsifiable, particularly if they have pretensions to being scientific, but in practice they are sacrosanct until, with the retirement or death of their protagonists or a change in fashion, they fall from grace. As a result, even the mainstream schools of social criticism have not been able to dismantle, or even threaten, the structures of denial on which today's self-congratulatory public culture is perched.

A tacit neo-Leibnitzian belief—that we live in the best of all possible worlds—strengthens our defences. So does a certain fear of the people which has gradually come to constitute the underside of important global theories of democratic culture. Such theories are willing to give everyone the right to vote, but not the right to bring their odd cultural ideas and morality into the public sphere. Very few of these theories offer any space to popular theories of politics and public life.

All these factors have together begun to limit the play with self-definitions, ego boundaries and identity fragments that is needed to unleash the potentialities of a culture of participatory democracy. Perhaps one can extend the insights of psychological studies into individual creativity to larger aggregates, to claim that social creativity requires, among other things, some capacity to play with one's past-as-a-part-of-one's-self. That capacity becomes crucial in situations where 'the past' is not conveniently dead, but is often stealthily historicised and pushed back artificially into the realms of the dead. Many living communities are 'dead' in academic texts and in public documents in the Southern world; policy-makers and scholars talk about them in the past tense even when they are a few feet away, perhaps just on the other side of the road. We exile these communities to history, so that we can safely bemoan their death, and thus dismiss all who remain concerned with them as incurable romantics.

In such a world, an ability to play with the past is a necessary counterpoint to the dredging of the past that has become a standard marker of official enquiry commissions all over the world. It is not perhaps a terrible liability that, in South Asia, though the future may not always look open, the past rarely looks closed. I believe that social and political creativity requires this capacity for play. As the intellectually accessible universe expands, and as we confront disowned cultures and states of consciousness about which the presently dominant global middle-class culture of knowledge knows nothing, we need more than ever our capacity to recognise the alternative realities that we are daily coerced to bury. These essays are blatantly partisan to the extent that they try—alas, they can only try—to look beyond the structure of denial that, through concepts such as development, progress and history, narrow our world.

Like most of my other books, this one too is a series of explorations in the politics of awareness. The subjects and contexts have shifted, so have the time frames. But the main concern has remained the same: the rediscovery of everyday life and ordinariness as sources of and clues to human potentialities.

A democratic order, I used to think, could not be anything but a celebration of this ordinariness. I was mistaken. Such ordinariness in developed mass societies—and, hence, in the mainstream social sciences—smacks of predictability, psychopathologies of everyday life, and the throttling of human creativity through the production of media-managed conformity. Unfortunately for those brought up on a staple diet of scepticism towards the banality of everyday in fully industrialised societies, democratic polities outside the temperate zone often confront societies that are not yet massified, where communities may be under threat but are not yet dead, and where the political élite, petrified by the diversity of recalcitrant peoples given citizenship, console themselves by talking of 'unity in diversity', 'integration into the mainstream' and middle-class nationalism in sports and entertainment. The sense of nationhood in most Afro-Asian countries is built on the dream of bringing these cussed citizens within the domains of such worthy global processes as development, secularisation, integration, and progress.

These developing countries—that is how these countries now style themselves—can have no visions of the future. They are forbidden to have such visions. For that requires a defiant assertion of intellectual autonomy and sense of mastery over one's fate. Visions of the future are now the monopoly of the powerful and the wealthy. They have taken patents on all visions of the future and it will be an infringement of intellectual property rights if anyone in the southern world is ungrateful or unethical enough to poach in the area. Officially, the South is only allowed the luxury of time-travel to the past. So that when it does, it can be accused of being backward-looking and prescribed a larger dose of the official ideology of the state. Southern intellectuals usually conform dutifully to this regime, playing the game of dissent by re-envisioning what has already been envisioned by their elders and betters. As a result, today, the local power-élite's idea of the future of their own society is nothing more than an edited version of contemporary North America and West Europe. For that matter, their idea of the present state of their societies is often no different from what they have read of pre-modern Europe in their school texts.

This book is a book on distinctiveness and an attempt to, as Ziauddin Sardar may put it, 'rescue all our futures' by celebrating the ordinariness of India, created by a different kind of clash of civilisations.

Politics in our times, Mohandas (alias Mahatma) Gandhi believed, yielded *yugadharma* or codes of conduct appropriate for our times. His search for self-realisation, therefore, led him not to mysticism, but to social and political activism. These essays are interrelated by being case diaries of a personal search for—and an articulation of—this yugadharma in a language accessible to those who fear this odd meaning of politics. When Gandhi thus defined politics, he had in mind not so much conventional politics, but the politics of awareness—that liminal world where you create through civil disobedience a space for critical self-awareness, while venturing outer-directed social criticism. You test your categories of knowledge when trying to dismantle the categories of others. For those like myself, who concentrate on the nastier side of life, this is one of the few checks on self-righteousness.

This emphasis on the politics of awareness involves time-travel to the past and the future in culturally and psychologically distinctive ways. It makes the construction of the-here-and-the-now a statement of self-identity that links existing, lost, recessive, retrievable and possible future selves. This is the other plane on which these essays try to negotiate time outside the domain of history. Such constructions of the contemporary—through self-definitions that span times that many think are safely past or fortunately inaccessible—are not merely part of politics, they also constitute, I believe, the heart of the discipline of political psychology. It is a political psychology that balances the psychology and culture of politics with the politics of psychology and culture as systems of knowledge.

The first two essays in the book are direct introductions to the political culture of contemporary India, particularly to the crises and contradictions in the culture of the Indian state. They try to conceptualise the democratic process as a series of contestations, not merely among communities and organised socio-political formations, but also among worldviews and forms of consciousness. I have tried to tell this part of the story without forgetting the insights that a galaxy of scholars have produced over the decades, but I have also been forced to depend on less conventional sources like newspapers, formal and informal enquiry reports, and news bulletins of social and political activists of various hues. Though only the second essay concentrates on public expectations and anxieties about the state, both recognise the space that the modern state now occupies in the culture of Indian politics and in public consciousness to shape the diverse concepts of citizenship and participatory democracy.

The next four essays return to a subject that has been with me through nearly two decades—the role of religion in the culture of Indian politics and its relationship with the problem of violence. The first two of them, 'The Politics of Secularism' and 'Coping with the Politics of Faiths and Cultures,' analyse the changing role of the ideology of secularism in Indian public life and the strange, cumbersome baggage it has to carry, as a badge of correct political socialisation and, unknown to its protagonists, as a projective test for those committed to it. The ideology now tells more about the persons propagating it than about the people who are supposed to benefit from it. For the latter, the ideology has become either a distant, inscrutable official slogan or a principle of exclusion. Once touted as the final marker of progress and as a crucial component of the theology of the Indian state, it continues to guide ritual performances in the temple of progress and instrumental rationality, but has gradually begun to display many of the standard features of a state-sponsored ideology. You can virtually get away with anything in the name of secularism, and even the most flamboyant religious or ethnic nationalists now claim to be genuine champions of the ideology, while calling others pseudo-secularists. On the other hand, non-state actors and movements fighting for secularism are being drawn into a sterile debate on who is genuinely, objectively or practically a secularist, and who is not.

In the meanwhile, a huge majority of the citizens continue to lead their lives without the benefit of even knowing what secularism means. When the chips are down, they resist religious and ethnic violence and, when they fail to resist them, they cope with the consequences of such violence with the help of their traditional, rickety repertoire of ideas and skills derived from experiences of co-survival from everyday morality and everyday religion. One of the essays makes the point that even India's politicians, belonging to virtually every party, are well aware of the limits of the ideology of secularism and, though they may not admit it, have constantly tried to adapt it to political and social situations in ways that flout the canons of the ideology. Strangely they do so not merely to unleash or take political advantage of ethno-religious strife but also to fight it.

The next two essays, 'A Report on the Present State of Health of the Gods and Goddesses in South Asia' and 'Time Travel to a Possible,' go a little further. Instead of entering the debate on secularism, they explore the range and limits of the repertoire that Indians bring to bear upon their concept of religious and ethnic tolerance and inter-subjectivity. One of them is an attempt to engage with the traditional armoury of psychological skills and cultural tools that

Indians have brought to bear upon not merely religious conflicts but also a wide range of public issues. It grapples with the world of gods and goddesses in the region who, refusing to be chained to a standard pantheon, enter and exit from the everyday lives of citizens like so many impossible, unpredictable, troublesome house-guests. Negotiating these recalcitrant gods and goddesses, the essay tacitly argues, is a way of coping with or rearranging fragments of one's own self. That is why, in the whole of South Asia, gods and goddesses cut across territorial, historical, ethnic and religious boundaries. To supplement many refurbished, gentrified, high-brow, distant gods and goddesses—who may divide by demanding zealous allegiance—there are also low-brow gods and goddesses who can unite, be playful and accessible, sometimes even establishing their accessibility by being somewhat disreputable and venal.

'Time Travel to a Possible Self,' written in the form of an introductory case report on the mind of a city, is a tentative, incomplete psychogeography of Cochin. It tries to identify the mythic Cochin on which the reality of today's Cochin is delicately balanced. The bonding between that mythic Cochin and attitudes, beliefs, values, prejudices and stereotypes with which the Cochinis now live is the main theme of the essay. The nature of that bonding shows that Cochin's ethno-religious hospitality is as much dependent on its cross-cutting ethnic and communal dislikes as on its inter-caste and interreligious amity.

The last essay in the collection is only apparently discontinuous with the rest. It addresses the larger global issues of violence and its representation that serve as a backdrop to the politics of identities in India. It does so by examining the creative responses of a writer and thinker who, along with Gandhi, has most deeply influenced Indian intellectual life—Rabindranath Tagore. It seeks to reclaim Tagore from the persistent efforts to locate him within the Enlightenment vision of Europe as a Brown Encyclopaedist. *That* Tagore, stuck in the heat and dust of India, also wrote poetry and songs, presumably to drown his sorrows at being part of a defeated civilisation, being forced by global forces to retool itself as an acceptable, fully transparent modern nation-state. (The sun smiles in the morning, Ernest Gellner once told me, because it knows that it will be in the West by the evening.) The Tagore invoked here has a complex, tacit, civilisational theory of violence in our times and this theory gradually pushes him, towards the end of his life, to develop a hesitant but full-fledged critique of modernity, and, through his intellectual encounters with Gandhi, a critique of the legitimacy that exists in the Enlightenment vision for a particular style of assembly-line violence that has now acquired epidemic proportions.

The seven essays in the book, therefore, traverse a trajectory. They seek to identify and mark out the landscape of Indian political culture and its elusive psychological contours. They then offset these against elements of the culturally embedded knowledge systems that are supposed to fight the growing, free-floating, mostly anomic violence that has come to mark the public spheres in India in recent decades, and the armoury of psychological traits and interpersonal skills that stand unsteadily against that violence. The book ends with an essay that examines this resistance through the more organised creativity of a larger-than-life literary figure whose journey, from the past to the future to the past, has given the contemporary in India the touch of an active, time-transcending witness. Once again, such time-travel reshapes the past and the future, to hold them up as mirrors to the present. If you allow me the right to my own cliché, even the notorious Indian fatalism assumes that the past in India is open-ended and so is the future, if properly handled through the magical technologies of mind; it is only the present that pretends to be determined. The mediating role that the contemporary plays in this time travel is the running theme in these essays, not any historical propriety or historiographic convention. If any history has inadvertently slipped into a narrative, I apologise for the mishap. As I have said in the beginning, this is a book on case histories, not history.

Some of these essays have had earlier incarnations and bear *karmic* imprints of their past. 'Contending Stories in the Culture of Indian Politics' was first presented at a conference on contemporary India organised by the Fondazione Giovanni Agnelli at Turin in 1996. It is actually another attempt to systematise a reading of India's political culture that has been with me for more than two decades. I leave it to the reader to judge if this attempt is any better than the earlier ones. 'Democratic Culture and Images of the State' was written for a conference on the State in India at Kyoto University in December 1999. It grew out of a keynote address at the conference on Democracy and the Problematique of Culture in Contemporary Asia, organised by Hokkaido University in 1998. The essay also draws upon my M.S. Mehta Memorial Lecture delivered earlier, under the auspices of Sewa Mandir, Udaipur. Earlier versions of two of the essays, 'Coping with the Politics of Faiths and Cultures' and 'Time Travel to a Possible Self', were specifically written for a collaborative project initiated by Neelan Tiruchelvam at the International Centre for Ethnic Studies, Colombo. Another version of 'Time Travel' was published in *The Japanese Journal of Political Science*. 'The Politics of Secularism' is a revised version of an essay published in *Alternatives*.

'A Report on the Present State of Health of the Gods and Goddesses in South Asia' began as an informal, extempore presentation at a *samskriti shivira* (workshop on cultural studies) on gods and goddesses organised by Ninasam, Heggodu, Karnataka, in 1995. K.V. Akshara and his associates painstakingly transcribed the lecture, and D.R. Nagaraj insisted that I turn it into something resembling a proper essay. The resulting version was delivered as a keynote address at the American Academy of Religion, New Orleans, in 1996, and published in *Manushi* in 1997. The present revised and expanded version was delivered as the Regents' Lecture at the University of California, Department of History, in 1997, and published in *Postcolonial Studies.* 'Violence and Creativity in the Late Twentieth Century' was delivered as a keynote address to the conference on 'Home and the World: Rabindranath Tagore at the End of the Millennium', organised by the University of Connecticut at Storrs in 1998. It was rewritten for a book being edited by Patrick Hogan and Lalita Pandit.

All the essays in the present book have gained immensely from the comments, criticisms and help of friends, associates, collaborators, listeners and critics, and some of them would not have been written but for my encounters or arguments with thinkers, public intellectuals and some rather obstreperous editors. I would especially like to thank the following for provocations, insights and help: M.N. Srinivas, U.R. Anantha Murthy, Vinay Lal, Ziauddin Sardar, D.R. Nagaraj, Charles Long, Ivan Illich, Michio Araki, Nur Yalmin, V.R. Krishna Iyer, S. Sreekala, M. Hussain, T.Y. Vinod Krishnan, Ashutosh Varshney, Neelan Tiruchelvam, Tamotsu Aoki, R.L. Kumar, Madhu Kishwar, Kageaki Kajiwara, Masaaki Kimura, T.N. Madan, Darini Rajasingham, Shalva Weil, Chandrika Parmar, Giri Deshingkar, Rustum Roy, Kayoko Tatsumi, and Imtiaz Ahmed.

CHAPTER 1

Contending Stories in the Culture of Indian Politics

Traditions and the Future of Democracy

The young are given to analysis; they love to sift every issue threadbare with passionate scepticism and eager competence. The elderly tell stories. Fortunately for the latter, in recent years stories have become respectable in the social sciences, more so after some people have cleverly begun to call them narratives. However, listening to Indian stories can be trying, even in these post-modern days. Most of them lack a proper ending—this is no longer a crime, I am told—but they are also often not new, which is still an unforgivable sin in the global culture of knowledge. As with classical plays and ritual narrations of epics and sacred myths, these stories create their own surprises in the process of being re-told. So I need not apologise if you find my story is not new and lacks a proper ending; I shall apologise only if you find that I have not told it right.

This is actually a story about stories. It begins with the awareness that in ancient societies like China and India, which possess resilient cultural traditions, there is a certain ambivalence towards democratic politics. While drawing sustenance from traditions, democratic politics is also expected to alter and update such societies for the contemporary world. These countries have reportedly fallen behind in the race that all countries these days breathlessly run to stay where they stand in the global Olympiad of nation-states. One enters this race not just with a political style which reflects specific cultural traditions, but also with a political process seeking to become a legitimate force of cultural change and promising to mediate between hope and experience, inherited fears and acquired ambitions. The contending stories of politics and traditions frame this process. They contain the ambivalence and anxieties associated with democracy in those afflicted by both, and they help construct the past in a way that makes possible meaningful political choices in the present.

Such stories also have shelf lives. They are born and they die; some after a long and glorious life, others after a brief, inglorious tenure. For instance, scholars of Indian political culture have, off and on, ventured the story of a stable culture facing an alien political order and, on the whole, unable to make much sense of it.[1] Their idea of Indian politics as a straightforward reflection of Hindu culture and personality now looks jaded not because of the passage of time and academic fashions, but because a different political situation has now gripped the public imagination—that of a culture being literally bombarded by new global challenges and trying to maintain its identity in the face of these. Likewise, the competing stories that others have produced—of cultural and psychological forces as epiphenomena, and of Indian politics as a

[1] The most famous of the works along these lines is Max Weber, *The Religion of India: The Sociology of Hinduism* (Glencoe: Free Press, 1958). However, the more typical of the changing temper of our times are those influenced by the post-War culture-and-personality studies or the economic-development-and-cultural-change literature. For instance, P. Spratt, *Hindu Culture and Personality* (Bombay: Manaktalas, 1966); and K.W. Kapp, *Hindu Culture, Economic Development and Economic Planning* (New York: Asia, 1963). Readers who think that such summary trials of South Asian cultures is a now-defunct fashion may like to consult Dor Bahadur Bista, *Fatalism and Development: Nepal's Struggle for Modernisation* (Hyderabad: Orient Longman, 1991).

sequence of modern economic forms vanquishing traditional structures of behaviour and ideas in order to establish the supremacy of a historically superior order—have not survived well either. The global resurgence of religion and ethnicity has taken better care of such economic determinism than have their academic opponents.[2] In both cases, the truth or falsity of such stories is of secondary importance; more important is the fact that neither rings true in the present global context.

I shall talk here of four persistent stories that seem to have survived the vicissitudes of time and continue to frame the relationship between politics and traditions in India. These paradigmatic stories can be read not so much as realistic descriptions of the styles of response to the changing relationship between society and politics—the global and the local, the personal and the collective—but as attempts to search out an 'appropriate' construction of Indian culture for contemporary purposes. As these purposes have changed, the stories have also changed, though not beyond recognition.

I

In all four stories political style not only has a history, it is 'history'. For it includes a construction of the Indian self as it has emerged from its encounters with the outside world. The first story, fabricated towards the beginning of the nineteenth century, mirrors the early impact of the colonial system, which began to bring with in politics a social order organised more around religion and culture than around its polity. Not that India did not know politics, but colonial politics was a different kettle of fish. It denied the

[2] For instance, see A.R. Desai, *Social Background of Indian Nationalism* (Bombay: Popular Prakashan, 1959); D.D. Kosambi, *Myth and Reality: Studies in the Formation of Indian Culture* (Bombay: Popular Prakashan, 1962); and *Introduction to the Study of Indian History* (Bombay: Popular Prakashan, 1975).

autonomy of culture and, despite an official ideology of non-interference in society, prescribed a different lifestyle as the basis of politics.

The appeal of this story, which still dominates the consciousness of the more settled, established sections of the urban, Westernised middle class, is a major source of modern India's self-esteem.
It draws heavily upon the experience of India's early exposure to the
Raj. That exposure had a few notable features. First, the colonial
political economy favoured the Brahminic castes in government
appointments and in the modern professions which it opened up
around the middle of the nineteenth century. The traditional skills
of these castes helped them to reconcile work, worldview and selfhood by reinterpreting traditions—which was their prerogative as
well as specialisation—and by ascribing acceptable meanings to
exogenous bureaucratic, political, and judicial forms.

This was also the time when the colonial bureaucracy was socially non-interfering and the initiatives for social reform came mainly from Indians. Till about 1830—that is, for nearly seventy-five
years—the colonial legal system was built on the customary laws of
various Indian communities, though its points of reference in social
matters were Brahminic and élite North Indian Muslim cultures.
The educational system relied mainly on Sanskrit, Persian and the
vernaculars, not English. Christian evangelism, to the chagrin of
missionaries, was discouraged. All this favoured the upper castes
and made them less defensive about the new political economy. To
them, Westernisation looked like a relatively painless form of dissent, and any resistance to it irrational and cussed. Though their
prominence in trade and commerce ended once business became a
matter of entrepreneurial acumen rather than ideology, style or
patronage, the upper-caste domination of public life lasted till the
1930s while that of the professions and bureaucracy still continues.[3] This long dominance, though consolidating the older caste

---

[3] Perhaps the most appropriate symbol of the first change was the collapse
of the business empire of Dwarkanath Tagore, grandfather of Rabindranath.
Dwarkanath founded his business empire on jute, shipping and banking, and

hierarchy, has induced significant changes in the self-definition of the Brahminic sector.[4] Those belonging to it have learnt to live with a dissociation between their new means of livelihood—a secular incentive system having forced them to re-earn their élite status—and the older cultural norms. They do not view the demands of work-life as negating their private values. Nor do they expect the latter to interfere with the former. Neither is difficult in a culture that does not overdo the demand for internal consistency and encourages the accretion of new cultural elements, rather than the substitution of the old. This 'controlled split' has now become the marker of a distinctive style of political adaptation.

A deeper penetration of Western norms in the second half of the nineteenth century, along with growing British chauvinism and commitment to Europe's civilising mission, further damaged Indian self-esteem. The earlier style of adaptation now split into two, to cope with middle-class anxieties. One sought salvation in aggressive modernisation, the other in an odd form of reactive

---

failed in all three. It must have taken a very special kind of enterprise to fail in the very three industries that were to become the backbone of the modern Indian economy within a short time.

On the changing nature of the dominance of the traditional élite castes, see D.L. Sheth, 'Castes and Classes in India: Social Reality and Political Representations', in V.A. Pai Panandikar and A. Nandy (eds), *Contemporary India* (New Delhi: Tata-McGraw-Hill, 1999), pp. 337–63.

[4] This can be considered the modern counterpart of the thesis of J.C. Heesterman, *The Inner Conflict of Tradition: Essays in Indian Ritual, Kingship and Society* (New Delhi: Oxford University Press, 1985). On the aggressive syncretism of the *babus*, one of the best descriptions is in Bengali, Sivanath Shastri, *Ramtanu Lahiri O Tatkalin Banga Samaj* (1909) (Calcutta: New Age, 1957). But there are good discussions in Denis Dalton, *Indian Idea of Freedom* (Gurgaon: Academic, 1982); David Kopf, *British Orientalism and Bengal Renaissance: The Dynamics of Indian Modernization* (Berkeley: University of California Press, 1969); and Tapan Raychaudhuri, *Europe Reconsidered* (New Delhi: Oxford University Press, 1988). There is also a charming invocation of such ecumenism in Jawaharlal Nehru, *An Autobiography* (London: Bodley Head, 1936).

Westernisation which wore the garb of cultural nationalism, to help crystallise the second story of politics and culture in modern India. The former survives today as the primary source of Indian liberalism as well as radicalism, the latter as the sire of Hindu nationalism and revivalism. If one is proudly and aggressively modern (and hence dismissive of most things native), the other is proudly and aggressively 'Hindu' (while rejecting all existing Hindus as a degenerate version of ancient Hindus—who now look, in retrospect, like a cheap, Eastern edition of India's imperious, Western rulers). Between them these offer the small but growing middle class two models of social change and two collective identities.

However, as the first group grew out of the reformism of the earlier phase, and as the era ended up favouring reactive nationalism, the second remains more typical of the period. Riding the growing political participation and exposure to new forms of communication, both of which had been effectively deployed for social reform in the earlier generation, cultural nationalists soon became a significant presence in Indian public life. They were the first Orientalists that the Orient itself produced in defence of the Orient. They depended mainly upon the knowledge that nineteenth-century Europe produced about India, and on their revaluation of the country's martial past. This they legitimised with the help of new and more this-worldly interpretations of some sacred texts, mainly the *Gita*—which had been earlier read usually as a text on non-dualist spiritualism—and by marginalising the more ecumenical upanishadic base of social reforms, so clearly a part of the first story. The response was underwritten by the British rediscovery of Kshatriyas as the true Indians, and the country's surviving princely class as the natural leaders of the masses (and incidentally as markers of the nobility of the noble savage). The Kiplingesque antipathy towards Anglicised, city-bred, effeminate babus was now not entirely unacceptable to the modern Indian.[5]

[5] Some examples of the internalisation of the British estimate of babus, and the resulting brutal self-denigration, are Bankimchandra Chattopadhyay,

The third story crystallised with the emergence of Mohandas Karamchand Gandhi in Indian politics, though some of the changes associated with him were probably inevitable and would have come about in any case. Beginning in the 1920s, while the upper castes could still cling to the leadership of the freedom movement—thanks to their Western education, Western-style nationalism, skills in modern communication, and the ability to forge solidarities on the basis of their Sanskritic/Brahminic identity—the attempts to mobilise larger support unintentionally unleashed other forces. More accessible cultural symbols had now to be invoked, entrenched social divisions had to be negotiated, the vernacular and the indigenous had to be rediscovered at the expense of the Sanskritic and the imported, and traditions in turn had to be reinterpreted so that they could be made palatable to modernists and could span the country's immense diversity. Gandhi was a response to these demands. He pushed the earlier, culturally less defensive first response to the margins, as an odd, indigenous form of political liberalism; and the more defensive second response towards a militant—some might say self-destructive—form of nationalism which tried to change the fate of the country through armed means. To the former, Gandhian mobilisational politics looked ideologically impure, a self-seeking demagogy or a Mephistophelean compromise with traditions. To the latter, it looked effeminate, unrealistic, disorganised, anti-statist and, above all, divisive in relation to Hindus. To both, the new politicians began to look de-ideologised, crude, rustic, sanctimonious, often given to ruthless power politics.

Gandhian politics did something more to Hindu nationalism.

'Babu' (1873) in *Rachanabali* (Calcutta: Sahitya Samsad, 1954), vol. II, pp. 10–12; Michael Madhusudan Dutt, *'Ekei ki Bole Sabhyata'* (1860) in *Rachanabali* (Calcutta: Sahitya Samsad, 1965), pp. 241–54; Ramanbhai M. Nilkantha, *Bhadrambhadra* (1900) (Ahmedabad: Suryaprakash, 1932); and Saratchandra Chattopadhyay, *Srikanta*, in *Sahityasamagra* (1917) (Calcutta: Ananda, 1986), vol. 1, esp. part I, pp. 268–324. Though written from a

Exactly as Hindu nationalism had split the earlier 'syncretic' style into both a creative, ecumenical approach to the West and a mainstream culture of collaboration, mimicry and self-hatred, Gandhian politics split Hindu nationalism into both a creative, if defensive, return to traditions (as in Bankimchandra Chattopadhyay, Vivekananda and Brahmabandhav Upadhyay) and a mainstream culture of collaboration, mimicry and self-hatred which sought to re-engineer Hindus into better Hindus according to European ideas of nationality and nationalism.[6] It is certainly no accident that all three attempts on Gandhi's life in India, the last of which succeeded, were made by Hindu nationalists.

The fourth story can be construed as a gift of India's democratic revolution. After independence in 1947, there is now much less need to 'sell' politics as the pure pursuit of a cause. Politics has become a vocation. Like other vocations, it ensures economic and social mobility. Adult franchise favours previously peripheral groups willing to take advantage of their numbers (to challenge older hierarchies, paradoxically by allowing caste-based bargaining and competition); mass politics has become decisively non-Brahminic; and the literati, once so conspicuous in public life, has been virtually banished from politics.[7] Naturally, the brown version of the white man's burden, which has for long been a ruling principle in Indian

---

different point of view, the emergence of religious nationalism and its links with existing religious traditions in India are neatly captured in T.N. Madan, *Modern Myths, Locked Minds: Secularism and Fundamentalism in India* (Delhi: Oxford University Press, 1997).

[6] For the moment, I am ignoring the analogous process within South Asian Islam. For an example, see Rafiuddin Ahmed, *Bengal Muslims 1871–1906: Quest for Identity* (New Delhi: Oxford University Press, 1981).

[7] On the politics of this process, see Edward Shils, 'Influence and Withdrawal: The Intellectual in Indian Political Development', in D. Marvick (ed.), *Political Decision-makers* (Glencoe: Free Press, 1961), pp. 29–59; and D.L. Sheth, 'The Great Language Debate: Politics of Metropolitan *versus* Vernacular India', in Upendra Baxi and Bhikhu Parekh (eds), *Crisis and Change in Contemporary India* (New Delhi, Sage, 1995), pp. 187–215.

politics, has also suffered decline. Once, the Brahminic self-concept of the scholar-politician had projected into politics a demand for Platonic—often Fabian or Marxist—*acharya*-kings. Now, it has made the *acharyas* the first victims of mass politics and thrown into further relief professional, de-ideologised politicians. As power seeps through the fingers of the older élite, they are becoming more open to an anomic, almost nihilistic politics of desperation. But even that has not yielded them much political dividend. Extremist politics, too, has ebbed, and though it has staged a partial comeback as the marginal politics of revivalism and militant separatism, it is obviously trying to adjust to long-term trends in Indian politics. (It is doubtful if the support that the Hindu nationalist parties get— roughly one-fifth of the votes polled—has much to do with their ideology; and, despite popular belief, separatism has never probably involved more than 25 million in a country of about one billion.)

Likewise, despite the entry of neo-Gandhian ideas into public life through a number of powerful grassroots movements, even the 'saintly' politics of the Gandhians has been contained and its major expositors turned into lonely messiahs or activist-thinkers with limited political appeal.[8] (This of course is no guarantee that some, like environmentalist Sundarlal Bahuguna, Anna Hazare, Medha Patkar or Vandana Shiva will not emerge in the future as rallying points of powerful new political formations.) For those telling, or

---

[8] The consensual decision-making style of many vernacular communities, dependent on a highly specified system of allocation of rights, duties, and responsibilities—and what many see as the widespread Indian tendency to prefer harmony over abstract justice—survives in many neo-Gandhian pleas for a non-competitive, party-less polity, and in certain forms of voluntarism. M.N. Roy, *Power, Parties and Politics* (Calcutta: Renaissance, 1960); and J.P. Narayan, 'Organic Democracy', in S.P. Ayar and R. Srinivas (ed.), *Studies in Indian Democracy* (Bombay: Allied, 1965) pp. 325–44. Narayan was the last Gandhian to lead a successful pan-Indian movement within mainstream politics along Gandhian lines.

living by, this story, Gandhi himself is an unattainable ideal, though he is not subjected to the hostility and ridicule to which the carriers of the first two stories are subjected.

Of the four stories, the first one is complete and can be considered the only one with 'global' ambitions. It dominates not merely Indian but also non-Indian perceptions of Indian politics. The story is well written and it has penetrated the higher rungs of modern education and 'official' historical consciousness in India. The second story dominates the consciousness of the newly urbanised and modernised and, especially, those among them who belong to the traditional élite confronting the loss of power. It has now penetrated some sections of India's power élite and constitutes a psychological substratum in some areas of popular culture. The third and fourth stories still remain half-articulate; they are now being written.[9] Like folklore and epics in oral cultures, however, they crucially

---

However, within the 'one-party dominance system' that ruled the Indian polity for nearly three decades, decision-making depended not so much on a consensus of programme, ideology, or mutual gain, but on a subtler dynamics growing out of modes of demand articulation, expectations about desirable interpersonal behaviour, styles of conflict-resolution, and images of the 'true' leader as a faction-managing consensus builder. Rajni Kothari, *Politics in India* (Boston: Little Brown, 1970).

The shift from the first and second stories to the third and the fourth is politically more interesting and hence it has generated some of the earliest studies of political culture in India. For example, W.H. Morris-Jones, 'Behaviour and Idea in Political India', R.N. Spann (ed.), *Constitutionalism in India* (Bombay: Asia, 1963), pp. 74–91; and Myron Weiner, 'India: Two Political Cultures', in L.W. Pye and S. Verba (eds), *Political Culture and Political Development* (Princeton: Princeton University Press, 1965), pp. 199–244; Kothari, *Politics in India,* ch. 9.

[9] This may sound a strange proposition when one of the stories is associated with Gandhi, but actually most stories of Gandhi in India have been written

inform the public consciousness of a sizeable section, probably a majority, of India's citizens. They do so while the modern educational system and public discourse oscillate between the first two stories and modern Indians live out their lives fully convinced that they can master the intricacies of Indian culture within the format of the first two stories.

II

The four stories—and the corresponding political styles—give some clues as to how the Indian literati, perhaps even India's functioning politicians, have at different times read the various cultural themes in Indian politics, as well as their origins and uses. The stories are also four modes of political adaptation and communication. You can enter public life riding any of them, though your success will depend on which particular strand dominates politics at the time. Let me now give two examples of highly resilient and apparently immutable cultural themes to show how their meaning and political use run through the four stories. I shall choose examples that not only inform popular stereotypes, but are also the implicit focii of scholarly debates on how Indian culture has fared in modern times.

There is a long tradition of scholarship which claims that the nucleus of the culture of Indian politics is a pervasive tendency to

---

as a part of the first story and a few as that of the second. A partially successful recent attempt to break out of the straitjacket is Bhikhu Parekh, *Colonialism, Tradition and Reform: Analysis of Gandhi's Political Philosophy* (New Delhi: Sage, 1989). However, one of the most exciting recent works that relocates Gandhi in Indian political culture is D.R. Nagaraj, *The Flaming Feet: A Study of the Dalit Movement in India* (Bangalore: South Forum and ICRA, 1992). For a brief, synoptic view of Gandhi's fate in contemporary Indian public life, see Ashis Nandy, 'Gandhi After Gandhi: The Fate of Dissent in Our Times', *The Little Magazine*, May 2000, pp. 38–41.

ignore history and the linear process of time.[10] The Indian seems
to live with a concept of 'cyclical' time where the present, past, and
future blend into a static 'timeless' absolute, and where progress
and material well-being bear no direct relationship to progression
in time. The result is submissiveness, passivity, and—if literary
reflections are to be trusted—unbridled fatalism.[11] To many, this
aspect of the Indian cosmology is the least tolerable; it seems to go
with inadequate control over human affairs and nature, and to
smack of a reification of reality, a global and 'besetting passion for
metaphysics and philosophising', and 'abstraction of time, history
and person'.[12]

This theme is particularly fascinating because of the discomfort
it causes to many Indians, though that discomfort varies with the
four stories. The first two stories treat the traditional Indian concept of time as a metaphysical liability that must be exorcised from
Indian life for India to emerge as a historically self-conscious
society, able to extract its civic values from history rather than from
the sacred texts and epics. For the second story especially, while

---

[10] S.J. Samartha, *The Hindu View of History: Classical and Modern* (Bangalore: Christian Institute for the Study of Religion and Society, 1959).

[11] Some examples are G.M. Carstairs, *The Twice-Born* (Bloomington:
Indiana, 1957), esp. pp. 137–69; Dhirendra Narayan, 'Indian National
Character in the Twentieth Century', *The Annals of the American Academy of
Political and Social Science,* March 1967 (370), pp. 124–32, esp. p. 130; and
N.C. Chaudhuri, *Autobiography of an Unknown Indian* (London: Macmillan,
1951).

Often this has also shaped the external popular imagination of India. For
instance, W.S. Maughum, *The Summing Up* (New York: Doubleday 1943);
T.S. Eliot, 'Burnt Norton', *Four Quartets* (London: Faber and Faber, 1959),
p. 13; and J.B. Priestly, *Man and Time* (London: Aldus, 1964), pp. 171–3.

[12] H. Zimmer, *Philosophies of India* (London: Pantheon, 1951); Albert
Schweitzer, *Indian Thought and its Development* (New York: Beacon, 1959);
R.N. Dandekar, 'Brahmanism', W.T. de Bary, *et al.* (eds), *Sources of Indian
Tradition* (New York: Columbia University Press, 1958) pp. 1–36; and R.E.
Hume, *The Thirteen Principal Upanishads* (London: Oxford University Press,
1958), pp. 32–42, 52–7.

timelessness may or may not have been an aspect of Indian cosmology, it certainly has been a liability for contemporary Hindus.
Their ahistoricity has made them ignore the historical wrongs done
to them by 'outsiders' and not allowed them to develop a proper
sense of national dignity or pride. It has also discouraged them from
organising and militarising themselves.

According to the first story, Indian attitudes to time and history,
early in the colonial period, helped consolidate the stereotype of
India as radically different from colonising societies. The stereotype probably did something more. It spared the new participants
in the modern sector of inhibitory or incapacitating anxiety by
assigning a certain amount of inevitability to British rule and the
global dominance of the modern West. It spared them this anxiety
by encouraging the belief that the alien government would ultimately have to give way due to the inexorable logic of destiny, and
by allowing a passive acceptance of history at a time when active
intervention seemed impossible.[13] Thus, the story goes, the Indian
theory of time, by default, helped legitimise a newly emerging way
of life and a style of scholarship in the West from which neither
India nor the West has as yet broken free. Later scholars have claimed that this cultural strand has helped integrate different religions
and castes, first within a single national movement and then within
a nation-state.[14] At least one scholar has held the Indian concept of
time responsible for an unconcern with worldly suffering in the
country, with the ability to postpone explosive consumption demands of the kind that help planned development through a con-
tainment of consumption.[15]

[13] For instance, this theme runs through what is arguably the most
important political novel ever written in India, Bankimchandra Chattopadhyay,
Anandamath (1876–8), in *Rachanabali*, vol. I; also Swami Vivekananda,
Modern India (Almora: Advaita Ashram, 1913).

[14] D.E. Smith, *India as a Secular State* (Princeton: Princeton University
Press, 1963), p. 40.

[15] K.W. Kapp, *Hindu Culture, Economic Development and Economic
Planning* (New York: Asia, 1963).

The first two stories also recognise that, even in a benighted ahistorical society like India, political mobilisation and competitive politics have eroded the stoicism and patience of the underprivileged. There is now growing historical consciousness and a refusal to accept the available as the fated. Apparently, resignation and apathy in many are clashing with hope and self-confidence, and at least some of the previously powerless are trying to change the 'fated' actively, through self-created roles.[16] Even the Gandhian strand has transformed the idea of renunciation which Indians are reportedly saddled with, made the 'saintly' style a criterion of charisma in mass politics, and introduced the ideas of active pacifism and directed asceticism.[17]

I am not here making the point that sacred texts can be interpreted in various ways or that traditional stereotypes can be broken. I am proposing that, rather than the theme itself, it is the debate and the use of the theme that defines politics *and*, more than the debates on the truth or falsity of such themes, it is their systematic re-interpretation from the viewpoints of the competing stories that shapes India's political culture.

My other example is the idea of hierarchy which, students of Louis Dumont know, is encrypted in the concept of dharma, codes of conduct or duty.[18] Often acting as the final source of temporal

[16] The paradigmatic work on the nature of this change is M.N. Srinivas, *Caste in Modern India and Other Essays* (Bombay: Asia, 1962). It was probably written as a part of the first story but has managed to cross frontiers and enter the third and fourth stories.

[17] D.M. Dutta, 'Political Legal and Economic Thought in Indian Perspective', C.A. Moore (ed.), *Philosophy and Culture, East and West* (Honolulu: University of Hawaii), pp. 569–93.

[18] Louis Dumont, *Homo Hierarchicus: The Caste System and Its Implications* (Delhi: Oxford University Press, 1988). However, perhaps more immediately relevant to political culture is the brief comparative picture of hierarchy

power in India, dharma has influenced the organisation and legitimacy of political power, decision-making authority, and law. An impersonal, trans-moral sense of duty seems to supersede personal morality and equates inner detachment with freedom, from the sense of good as well as evil. Traditional socialisation, the extended family, caste, and village ties validate it.[19]

In the first story, dharma strengthens family and caste allegiances and, thus, limits individual autonomy, initiative and public responsibility. It reduces free-floating power, status, and resources and narrows political, social and occupational choices. The belief in a highly individualised path to salvation tends to hold each person responsible for his or her own worldly status, and gives him/her the power to acquire a new status in another life. Some scholars have gone so far as to diagnose dharma, not monism, as *the* final source of Indian narcissism and the Indian tendency to perceive politics as an amoral, clinical, ruthless pursuit.[20]

The second story is wary about the consequences of dharma. Those who live by the story are all too aware that it can cut two ways. It can be a potent symbol but also a practical hindrance in unifying Hindus and converting them into a cleanly defined, predictable nationality or ethnic grouping. In fact, this tension between the two faces of dharma has been a running theme in Hindu nationalist texts. In the fourth story, too, dharma sanctions social diversity and dissent, assumes that rightness and goodness vary with caste, occupation, age and sex, and grants intrinsic legitimacy to diverse goals

---

supplied by Alan Roland, *In Search of Self in India and Japan: Toward a Cross-Cultural Psychology* (Princeton: Princeton University Press, 1988).

[19] The term dharma is almost impossible to translate. However, there is a good discussion of it in P.V. Kane's *History of the Dharmashastra* (Poona: Bhandarkar Oriental Research Institute, 1946), vol. 3, pp. 241, 825–9. It also informs works like Irawati Karve, *Hindu Society: An Interpretation* (Poona: Deccan College, 1961); and P.H. Prabhu, *Hindu Social Organisation* (Bombay: Popular Prakashan, 1954), pp. 215–98.

[20] For instance, Dutta, 'Political, Legal and Economic Thought', pp. 571–3; also Spratt, *Hindu Culture and Personality.*

and criteria espoused by persons or communities. Dharma in this story neutralises dissent and radical innovations by accommodating them in a larger consensual system.

In the third story, the principle of hierarchy has a different role. To mobilise wider support, the freedom movement had to fight against all forms of sectarianism.[21] Not only did it challenge the caste-specific concept of dharma, it revalued many caste professions previously considered dirty or contaminating. Both the attributes have uncomfortable associations in contemporary Indian politics at a time when the traditional élite, handicapped by a participatory democracy, have begun to see all politics as dirty, corrupting and ill-informed—with the possible exception of some forms of authoritarian or ethno-chauvinist politics; whereas to many numerically strong, traditionally low-status communities, politics has become *the* means of rising in the social hierarchy. Indian politics is still grappling with this asymmetry. First, while the changing hierarchical relations and status-hunting supply a part of the ideational basis of competitive politics, this cannot be acknowledged and has to be camouflaged in conventional ideological terms. Caste leaders are sometimes treated as reactionaries, sometimes as ideologues, though everyone seems to know that they are both at the same time. The growing self-esteem of the upwardly mobile castes and their vernacular, non-Brahminic style, on the other hand, get justified in the new culture of politics as a more 'hard headed' and 'down-to-earth' ideology.

Secondly, as some of the older skills of 'lower' castes have become functional, they have acquired more political clout and have consolidated their new-found status by a second reinterpretation of sacred texts, remembered pasts and caste *puranas*. Simultaneously, as the traditional skills of some other castes have become

[21] On segmentation see Morris-Jones, 'Behaviour and Idea', pp. 82–3. Segmentation as reinforcing the distinction between the functions of political and religious authorities and strengthening secularism, see Smith, *India as a Secular State*, pp. 153–246.

dysfunctional or obsolete in the modern sector, they have lost status and have been, in some cases, pushed to destitution or extinction. In sum, while political changes have validated caste identifications, broadened the basis of caste ties, and politicised caste associations, they have, by these very means, changed the nature of caste and undermined many of its normative assumptions.[22] Castes now compete, cooperate or fall apart in a manner that explicitly invalidates the older hierarchy.[23] As a result, the previously disprivileged Shudra castes now occupy a significant sector of India's expanding middle class.[24]

Of all the so-called cultural immutables in Indian politics, the first story says, the idea of hierarchy as enshrined in the concept of dharma has shown the greatest resilience. Even the much vaunted Indian tolerance is framed in hierarchy; the accepted style of handling heterodoxy has been to bring the latter within the hierarchical order and thus neutralise it.[25] Authority in India may traditionally have been open to some degree of competition, pressures and fear of dislodgement, but it also has its 'natural, substantially hereditary seats' and cannot be subverted without modifying the entire structure within which it operates.[26] Undoubtedly, the new occupational opportunities and work relations have allowed traditional, emerging, and functional hierarchies to operate at cross-purposes, but they have not weakened the principle of hierarchy.

---

[22] Srinivas, *Caste in Modern India*, esp. ch .1; see also Lloyd and Susanne Rudoph, *The Modernity of Tradition: Political Development in India* (Chicago: University of Chicago, 1967), part I.

[23] The reader may notice that the link between dharma and ahimsa (nonviolence), so conspicuous in India's epic culture, especially in the Mahabharata, has not played that conspicuous a role in this story. Gandhi is respected and his memory venerated, but he is also often shelved as a symbol of unattainable heights of political morality and propriety.

[24] Sheth, 'Castes and Classes In India'.

[25] Ibid., esp. pp. 87–97, 112–19.

[26] W. H. Morris-Jones, *Parliament in India* (London: Longman, 1957).

Thus, Western education, while it encourages individual mobility, also creates new status relations. Not only has it become crushingly hierarchical itself, it now even confers upper-caste status.

Nonetheless, escaping the format of the first story, India's long tradition of heterodoxy does give a unique cultural basis to democracy. Indications of this are the legitimacy and the disproportionately important role assigned to leaders of the Opposition till 1967 (when the election results provided them with a formal basis), the ability to make large-scale political compromises (which contributes to the image of sanctimonious yet purchasable Indian leaders), and the ideological catholicity all parties try to acquire or to publicly project when they move closer to power.

III

Both examples show that, though many elements of Indian political culture have their classical and non-canonical antecedents, they have been developing new referents. Indian political values now have more significant symbolic than psychological and social continuities. But the flux is not infinite either; the four stories set a limit to their variations.

It is also obvious that the apparently canonical Brahminic norms—in their pure or diluted forms—though still a formidable presence in the culture of Indian politics, have begun to play a more modest and ambivalent role. At one time, Sanskritisation and the Savarna or upper-caste identity endorsed the entire modern package, including liberal democracy. Now, as democracy has acquired wider cultural meaning, they endorse a certain scepticism towards the democratic process and towards those who have come to dominate it. This is despite the fact that in recent years, politics is becoming more elections-dominated or psephocratic, and parties are becoming essentially electoral machines. Both have allowed the pan-Indian middle class and the modern media to stage a dramatic comeback, giving a new lease of life to the Brahminic heritage and its old bonding with modernity.[27] On the whole, however, democratic values have begun to derive strength from the more pragmatic, non-canonical cultures and the everyday life of ordinary Indians.

In this respect, the absence of a perfect accord among cultural norms, individual selfhood, and the political process has been a source of creative tension in Indian society. It has given India's traditional plurality a different kind of psychological basis, and it has given a new life to culture as a political reality. Instead of being a burden in contemporary times, culture has become a means of monitoring politics.

I have outlined four stories of the relationship between politics and culture floating around in modern India. This is not the way modern Indians, and certainly not the hard-boiled modernists, tell the stories. They prefer to tell one story to the exclusion of others; for them, these competing stories are only forms of false consciousness and distorted or conspiratorial constructions of history which can be better explained with the help of categories derived from one's favourite political or psychiatric theory. I shall now end by reflecting on how this narrative—which tells the four stories simultaneously—helps our understanding of Indian politics. I shall do so with a few broad propositions about the three main legacies of the double-edged role of modernity in Indian politics. After all, the first two stories are about the modernisation of India (even though in the second story the formation of nationality and nationalism are given primacy). These two stories also tell us how, as a means of coping with the confrontation between two complex cultures,

[27] This is part of a larger syndrome, which includes the rediscovery of culture as a globally marketable commodity. See for instance the papers in Carol A. Breckenridge (ed.), *Consuming Modernity: Public Culture in a South Asian World* (Minneapolis: University of Minnesota, 1995).

Indian modernity has not only determined the exogenous elements that could be culturally integrated, but also the selection, redefinition, and rejection of traditions in a manner that would create a space for a modern nation-state in an ancient society.[28]

Firstly, over the entire nineteenth century, modernity conceptualised political authority as a stabilising, liberal instrument that could be used for social reform. The pro-British sentiments of the Indian élite in the last century were not so much due to the crumbs from the table of colonial exploitation they were collecting, though that is the way some narratives of the Indian nation-state go. These sentiments also grew out of the overlap or bonding between the Utilitarian sense of mission in sections of the British rulers and the Brahminic sense of mission in many Indians. True, this mutually reinforcing sense of a 'cause' was gradually destroyed by the supercilious arrogance of the rulers spawned by the quickening tempo of industrial and scientific changes in the West, the entry of culturally less secure and more defensive British middle-class elements into the ruling structures in India, and the consequent feelings of inferiority among Indians. Nonetheless, the old expectation that the state should be the major agent of social change persists. Much of Indian radicalism, led by Westernised upper- and middle-class ideologues, can be seen as a by-product of the vision of working with, and through, the colonial state towards a more humane society. Such radicalism has not betrayed the hopes of Indian liberal reformers of the nineteenth century whose support for, and expectations from, the state were often total.

Otherwise too, through the intermittent affairs with socialist, centralised models of social engineering, and by bringing charismatic authority within the government through people like Jawaharlal Nehru and Vallabbhai Patel, Indian politics has partly neutralised the Gandhian emphases on voluntary, non-governmental,

[28] Ashis Nandy, Shikha Trivedi, Achyut Yagnik and Shail Mayaram, *Creating a Nationality: The Ramjanmabhumi Movement and Fear of the Self* (New Delhi: Oxford University Press, 1995).

reformist politics. This decline in voluntarism has been hastened by a psephocratic model of democratic participation where power is relinquished to 'elected kings', and the gradual emergence of professional politics dominated by previously marginalised social groups. Gandhi's voluntarism, on the other hand, has in recent decades found powerful self-expression outside party politics.

The entire enterprise of constructing an acceptable, central, political authority in India can be said to be related to the four strands of political culture—the four narratives of cultural politics—that seem to be rooted in four strata of Indian personality.

The first narrative invokes a period witnessing a growing awareness of the incipient Indian nation-state as a field of expanding economic and occupational opportunities for the traditional élite. One's deeper concepts of authority, hierarchy and power persisted but combined with an acquired taste in the white man's magic, including the totems of a proper nation-state, a homogenised national culture, and modern science and technology.

The second narrative binds feelings of personal or collective inferiority by projecting one's unacceptable self outwards—on to cultural and religious minorities, but even more importantly, towards the ordinary citizens seen as unworthy of the great civilisation they have by default inherited. To borrow the language of psychoanalysis, a major element in the style is the imagery of a motherland, by identifying with whose might one restores one's sense of infantile omnipotence. Deriving strength from some of the cultural myths centring around the mother, mother goddesses, and the feminine principle in the cosmos, this narrative serves as a defence against the ambivalence towards the first and only intimate, powerful, authority the traditional Indian has to cope with in a traditional Indian family, to construct paradoxically a hyper-masculine modern political authority system. One suspects that this narrative is doomed to chauvinist millennialism whenever the self-system is under pressure.

The third narrative is profoundly Gandhian, though its best

example is not Gandhi but two sets of his followers. One set seeks to tackle political problems as moral problems, sometimes showing doctrinaire, cramped conformity to pacifism and impulse-control, or searching for political potency through various forms of visible renunciation. The more the personal feelings of shame about 'impulse indulgence' that participation in the modern sector induces, the more the attempt to define political participation as a pursuit of moral goals. The style is mobilisational, emphasising conquest of the self and self-realisation and, ultimately, mobilisation of one's ideal self. (Ethno-nationalism is trying today to hijack a part of this narrative, too, though without any conspicuous success, partly because of the presence of strong androgynous elements in it.) The other set of followers builds on Gandhi but is not restrained overmuch by his historical presence. It works broadly within a Gandhian frame, but the specifics of ideology and strategies of intervention this set has forged are uniquely contemporary.[29]

The fourth narrative is closely linked to organisational skills, professional politics, and competitive mass politics. It demands a certain interpersonal competence and appeals to one's needs for achievement, competition and power. It taps a stratum of Indian personality not yet fully acceptable to either the traditional or the modern élite. For it rejects both ideological purism and social in-flexibility and refuses to convert politics into a morality play. In fact, at times, it looks as if this narrative would like to do away with all the four narratives, to thereby unburden Indians of all shared memories that encumber 'pure' politics. Remembered pasts are relevant in this tradition only to the extent that they contribute to the pragmatics of contemporary life. However, what looks like cultivated amorality or 'peasant cunning' is often a desperate attempt to acquire and hold on to political power, seen as the only means of improving one's life chances, or for holding on to what looks like one's fragile middle- or upper-class status.

[29] Nandy, 'Gandhi After Gandhi'.

No story about India can end unambiguously, not even this one. Many would like read the culture of Indian politics as an unfolding of the forces of modernisation and progress, as the consolidation of constitutional processes and citizenship. I think my narrative has made clear that the same culture can be read another way—as a record of the continuous updating of Indian traditions, and of their reappearance at the centre of Indian politics as a symbol of the political rights of a forgotten majority. This reading carries with it the awareness that there is an uneasy, if not inverse, relationship between democracy and modernisation in this part of the world. This is because of the way modernity has entered South Asia, riding piggyback on an oppressive colonial society to establish lasting bonds with the traditional stratarchies in society. But for that very reason, democratic politics in the region has broken loose from its European bonds with modernity, capitalism, and even the Enlightenment in order to become the highest court of appeal against the forms of injustice and indignity that come packaged in our times both as age-old cultural values and as new secular theories of emancipation.

CHAPTER 2

Democratic Culture and Images
of the State
India's Unending Ambivalence

Of the various instruments of democracy that the non-Western world borrowed from the West, one of the most problematic has been the modern nation-state. I sometimes suspect that many Afro-Asian and South American activist-scholars just do not know what to make of the state. Some think that the absence in their context of a proper state, modelled after the European nation-state, was the reason for the humiliation of non-Western societies in colonial times. Others think that without radical changes in the concept of the state they cannot negotiate contemporary social problems. Still others believe that the state itself has become the root of all problems in third world societies: unless these societies learn to disengage themselves from the state, no creative initiative can be taken in public life that would make sense, culturally, to citizens. Simultaneously, a deep chasm has grown between those who think that the state should have priority over culture in society as well as the right to re-tool the culture for the state's purposes, and those who think that culture should have priority over the state, for, after all, the state is supposed to protect a lifestyle and not empty territory.[1] In societies like India, these diverse opinions have little to do with the contemporary debate on

[1] I have discussed these issues at length elsewhere. Ashis Nandy, 'Culture, State, and the Rediscovery of Indian Politics', in Patrick C. Hogan and Lalita Pandit (eds), *Literary India: Comparative Studies in Aesthetics, Colonialism,*

economic globalisation and the state's role in it. Indeed, the opinions frame the debate and make Indian attitudes to globalisation more ambiguous and incomprehensible to many outsiders.

A few societies in Asia have apparently bypassed these problems, perhaps because they were never directly colonised. I have occasionally met Japanese scholars who find it difficult to think of the state as dissociated from society and politics. The Japanese state, too, sometimes seems to be a part of a single seamless cultural and socio-political process. However, even if this is true—and it does not always seem so—Japan is one among very few exceptions. Usually, in the non-Western world, there is a constant ambivalent affair with the modern state, even among those who hate everything Western. During the last hundred years we have seen the odd spectacle of virtually every major revivalist movement seeking to capture the state—by which I mean capture the standard nation-state— and use it for ethno-chauvinist or fundamentalist projects. Few of these movements have seriously tried to return to the traditional ideas of the state in Asia or Africa. Fundamentalists and revivalists seem equally comfortable with the conventional nation-state as they seem with modern technology when it comes to jihad, holy war or *dharmayuddha*. They usually only want to capture the nation-state, not alter it. In the process, they end up legitimising the nation-state even within societies that are the least comfortable with it.

The culture of the state, therefore, is often the crucial clue to the way democracy functions or does not function in an Afro-Asian context. No study or analysis of long-term cultures of politics in this part of the world is complete unless expectations and anxieties over the state within the political leadership and among ordinary citizens are systematically explored. I try in this essay to use the example of India, where this ambivalence towards the state has reached a

and Culture (New York: The State University of New York, 1995), pp. 255–74; and 'The Political Culture of the Indian State', *Daedalus*, Fall 1989, 118(4), pp. 1–26.

particularly high level during the last thirty years. This is a country where the intellectual culture and traditions of political analysis can be divided into two parts. One comprises those who think that the state is a major instrument of social and political change and must be given primacy in social life; the other comprises those who think that, for civil society to thrive, the state must be contained and redefined.[2] I have come to suspect that many of the pathetic, often violent attempts to introduce hardboiled, mechanomorphic, ultra-positivist, socialist ideologies into the third world were actually half-hearted attempts to redefine and make more acceptable the nineteenth-century European nation-state. After all, that was the only kind of European state which the first generation postcolonial Asian and African leaders had really known, first-hand, during the colonial period. The attempts can be read as counterparts of the tacit, unwitting project of the revivalists that I have already mentioned.

I

Let me now turn to the story of the Indian state. During the last 150 years, the popular culture of Indian politics has been dominated by

[2] For instance, Pranab Bardhan, 'The State against Society: The Great Divide in Indian Social Science Discourse', in Sugata Bose and Ayesha Jalal (eds), *Nationalism, Democracy and Development* (New Delhi: Oxford University Press, 1998). This paper, however, uses the slightly different political-cultural distinction that Ali Mazrui draws between those deliberately or unwittingly caught in the intrinsic logic of one of the most dangerous and seductive political innovations of our times, the sovereign state, and those self-consciously resisting the projects of the state. Mazrui's analysis recognises that many who begin by fighting the oppressive presence of the Frankenstein state, end up by internalising that logic; those who capture the state invariably end up by being captured by the state. No wonder, in the southern hemisphere at least, states have successfully crushed most social movements. Ali Mazrui, 'The Frankenstein State and Unequal Sovereignty', in D.L. Sheth and Ashis Nandy (eds), *The Multiverse of Democracy: Essays in Honour of Rajni Kothari* (New Delhi: Sage Publications, 1996), pp. 50–77.

three images of the Indian state. These images have sometimes supplemented each other; sometimes they have acted as competing stereotypes; sometimes they have encroached on each other. The interplay of these images has linked the Indian state to the culture of Indian politics, and even shaped most analyses of the linkage. There is some evidence that the images also dominate the political cultures of most non-Western societies with a colonial past. For there is something vaguely inescapable about the emergence of these images in societies where the traditional idea of the state has a hoary career but the idea of a modern nation-state is often a new acquisition.

The first of the three images is that of *the state as a protector.* The Indian state is expected by many Indians, to protect society against arbitrary oppressors and marauding outsiders. As in most societies in the southern world, large sections of Indian society, too, have lived for ages with experiences of domination and victimisation that seem *prima facie* inescapable. These sections have often seemed more comfortable with predictable, rule-bound injustice; they have preferred predictable oppression to less but more arbitrary governance. This is understandable: non-arbitrary governance gives its victims more room. It gives more scope for finding loopholes and devising means of survival. Arbitrary or random oppression is more difficult to contain. Parts of Indian society, those which have been at the receiving end of the Indian and global political economy, primarily expect the Indian state to eliminate, control, make rule-bound or manageable the second kind of oppression.

As a corollary, the state is expected to protect native lifestyles. Indian ultra-nationalists bemoan the frequency with which Indians have collaborated with foreign political authorities throughout history, and ultra-Hindus lament the fact that Hindus have often sung, at the slightest provocation, paeans to their non-Hindu rulers. Neither seems fully sensitive to the widespread expectation in ordinary Indian citizens that state authority, in exchange for demonstrative political loyalty, should try to leave its subjects culturally alone and protect their everyday life. Indians seem willing to tolerate a certain amount of low-level, predictable violence of which they have—or think they have—learnt to take out the edge to avoid a total onslaught on their lifestyle.

During the colonial period, rulers recognised this expectation from the state as part of its 'mandate' and reaped the benefits.[3] Even an ardent nationalist like Bankimchandra Chattopadhyay (1838–94) suggested, in his novel *Anandamath*, that British rule protected Indians from the country's erstwhile Muslim rulers who, during the last days of Mughal rule, were unable to provide even minimal cultural and personal security.[4] Attempts have been made to explain this attitude either as sectarianism or as a cover for the novel's anti-British tone. Attempts have also been made to debate whether the last days of Mughal empire were really as bad, and to argue that apologists of the Raj promoted the stereotype. The fact remains that the expectation of state protection was widespread throughout the colonial period and has survived the demise of colonialism.

The colonial administration tried to live up to this expectation the hard way. In the case of virtually every major social or religious reform, the British-Indian government supported reform, through administrative or legislative action, only after decades of pressure from Indian leaders. Instances of this are the movements against sati, infanticide, human sacrifices and child marriage. Likewise, missionary activities in India were banned for the first sixty-five years of the Raj, English laws were not introduced until the mid-1820s, English education until about the same time, and the

---

[3] Queen Victoria's proclamation, while taking over as the ruler of India from the East India Company in 1857, is ample evidence of this. In that proclamation the British were trying, belatedly, to go back to the first phase of colonialism when the culture of the ruled was respected and even feared.

[4] One can give similar examples from the writings of religious and social reformers like Dayanand Saraswati (1825–83) and Keshab Chandra Sen (1838–84).

Western medical system was not introduced until the 1830s. These policy choices, justified or otherwise, do give an idea of the extent of state protection of culture in the first phase of colonialism. There *were* specific political considerations behind each British refusal to interfere in Indian culture. Nonetheless, there was a general belief in the rulers that large parts of Indian society expected rulers to ensure, against some protection payment, that Indian lifestyles were not going to be unduly disturbed. That this strategy did not in the end protect lifestyles, and managed only to increase the protection payment to unacceptable levels, is beside the point.

In our times, many of the arguments for a hard state in India, given by both liberal democrats and neo-Bismarckians, derive their appeal from this image of a state that will first ensure security to its citizens. First, there must be a proper state authority, they argue, before secondary needs such as democratic freedom and cultural authenticity are met. Weak and gullible Indians require a strong state and the kind of governance that such a state can supply before being granted the luxury of full-fledged participatory democracy.[5] Also, the Indian state must provide security to Indians first, before providing it to others. Therefore, if such security can be ensured by turning a blind eye to violence abroad, or even to the export of violence, exploitation and authoritarianism into the neighbourhood— as done by 'advanced' and powerful democratic societies elsewhere—the Indian citizen should be so protected. The same argument is applied to sub-national groupings. Today, statists in India feel fully justified in being ruthless with ethnic groups and peripheral cultures to protect the 'mainstream' in the event that such

[5] This ideology has been blatantly proclaimed in the writings of many Asian leaders, especially by the late Ferdinand Marcos of Philippines, Mahathir Mohammad of Malaysia, and Lee Kuan Yew of Singapore. For a while Prime Minister Indira Gandhi picked up the same rhetoric, but then left it to her hangers-on to articulate. For instance, B.K. Nehru, *Western Democracy and the Third World* (London: Third World Foundation, 1980), monograph 8.

groups or cultures stand in the way of the authority of the state.[6] The official concern with the fate of oppressed cultures and races elsewhere in the world is now matched by a deep fear of, and readiness to suppress, the self-assertion of ethnic minorities within India.

The second image of the Indian state dominates the politics of India's modern élite, though it is also now becoming a feature of the urban middle classes as a whole. It is the image of the *state as a moderniser or liberator.* Traditional Indian culture and modernity are seen here as antonyms, and it is presumed that the state's main function is to introduce Indian society to the modern world. Though some elements of Indian culture are seen as compatible with modernity, it is assumed that much of the culture is not. The expectation is that traditions incompatible with modernity will be eliminated by enlightened statecraft, and the modern Indian state will thus gradually create a modern Indian culture in order to sustain a modern polity. Even during the non-interventionist phase of the Raj there were thinkers and political leaders who attacked the regime for not interfering, as opposed to those who saw the British as good rulers because they did not interfere with religion and society. In the early years of the Raj, Rammohun Roy (1772–1833) entered into virulent theological disputes with Christian missionaries but also forged a coalition with them to fight official non-interference in culture. In the last days of the Raj, Jawaharlal Nehru

[6] Three important publications that came out at the same time in the mid-1980s illustrate this point neatly. Sunanda K. Datta Ray, *Smash and Grab: Annexation of Sikkim* (New Delhi: Vikas, 1984); Luingam Luthui and Nandita Haksar, *The Nagaland File: A Question of Human Rights* (New Delhi: Lancer International, 1984); and Amiya Rao, Aurobindo Ghose, Sunil Bhattacharya, Tejinder Singh Ahuja and N.D. Pancholi, *Report to the Nation: Oppression in Punjab* (Delhi: Citizens for Democracy, 1985). In recent years, the argument has been articulated by the likes of K.P.S. Gill, the police officer who helped crush the Punjab militancy, with accusations of human rights violations ringing in his ears; and Arun Shourie, the journalist-politician.

(1890–1964), while attacking the destructive role of the colonial state, also held it against the Raj that it had left the country mired in unchanging, oppressive traditions.

Today, all along the ideological spectrum are Indians to whom the main function of the Indian state is to change Indian culture and personality to liberate under-privileged, under-developed Indians. Capturing and using the state to direct social change, and for that reason seeing the state as the nerve centre of the Indian polity, are important parts of this image. As a result, transferring control to the state, be it in the matter of industrial units or of the performing arts, was for a long time an end in itself, for the nation-state was seen as the ultimate principle of social creativity in India. (In the case of industries, nationalisation may no longer be fashionable; in education, sports and culture, it continues to be so.) Predictably, Indian society has thrown up an entire sector that lives off its control over the state, often in the name of distributive justice. This sector sees itself not as a privileged class thrown up by the new role of the state in society, but as a declassed vanguard working for the future liberation of the Indian people.

Like the first image of the state, this image too is wedded to a dualist vision of politics. If the state is the phalanx or tool of progress and culture an object waiting to be re-tooled, rebuilt, renovated or repaired, the latter is bound to become psychologically associated with retrogression and obscurantism. And it becomes justifiable then to retain, somehow or the other, some access to state power, even if that means ideological or moral compromises. Many who change loyalties overnight after the fall or rise of a regime, notably within the bureaucracy and the intelligentsia, and many radicals who are willing to adorn the smallest offices of power under regimes they themselves attack as reactionary, justify themselves through this widely shared image of state and culture. They may look like seedy opportunists and turncoats, but they believe they follow what was once a grand and romantic strategy for altering the civilisational face of India. They feel that, by somehow being close to power, they contribute to good governance and radical social transformation.

Not surprisingly, in recent years this image of the state has become a major means of justifying state violence and bureaucratic centralism in India. During the colonial period many Indian leaders saw the Indian steeped in his culture as a child weighed down by childish superstition, yet they did not see it as the bounden duty of the political or social leadership to drive citizens like cattle towards a better future. It is only after the introduction of participatory democracy in free India, and only when facing more determined resistance to the modern élite as the ultimate social pace-setters, that a touch of 'repressive development-alism' and some patriarchal versions of 'conscientisation' begin to look like unavoidable minor hazards on the way to a new Indian society.

Finally, there is the image of the Indian state as a small but significant and well-defined part of Indian society and politics. This image sees the Indian *state as an arbiter* and the sphere of the state as an area where social relationships can be renegotiated. The state in this image is theoretically delimited—the image has obviously something to do with the frequently observed marginality of organised politics in traditional Indian lifestyle—and is seen to provide a bargaining table or market place where new power relationships among social aggregates can be worked out.

Such an image can be both creative and otherwise. For instance, when the politics of mass mobilisation first entered Indian society in the 1920s, it did, in three or four decades, things which one and half centuries of social reform had not done. Within the Hindu social order, mass politics consummated changes initiated in the early nineteenth century, unleashing forces comparable in strength to the *bhakti* movement. Social mobility-patterns changed dramatically. The traditional unit of social mobility in India was caste, not the individual. But such mobility generally took decades, sometimes even centuries. Participatory politics speeded up the process. It is true that the image of a static, backward-looking

Indian society was a caricature produced for middle-class consumption by colonial progressivist discourse, but it is also true that mass politics established a more creative and open relationship between citizenship, ethnicity and vocation. Overtly, this underscored traditional caste divisions because the unit of mobility still remained caste. Covertly, it opened up the social order. After all, what is so traditional about a competition for power between, say, the Brahmans and the Shudras, when they compete on the basis of numbers, without reference to their centuries-old unequal ritual or cultural status?

On the negative side, the image of the state as a delimited market place for the re-negotiation of traditional social relationships has made the Indian state exactly that: a market place. Those who have entered politics for the first time, usually the less privileged and less exposed, have a weaker commitment to the rules and conventions which define the limits of statecraft in society. They thus contribute to the classical picture of political decay in which political participation outstrips the institutionalisation of politics and the growth of system legitimacy. The decay has pushed the Indian polity towards a situation of limitless politics or *matsyanyay*—the ancient term for the condition in which big fish eat the little fish. Such politics does not allow one to build even a new basis for alternatives because both support to and dissent from the system are seen from a cynical, Machiavellian vantage ground. The strengthening of the image of the state as a market place has also generated in recent years a deep hostility towards the growing self-assertion of social aggregates seeking to express their politics through an adversarial relationship with the state. Such self-assertion, even when it takes place within the bounds of the culture of Indian politics, is seen as something that requires ruthless repression by the state.[7]

[7] Ashis Nandy, 'Indira Gandhi and the Culture of Indian Politics', in *At the Edge of Psychology: Essays in Politics and Culture* (New Delhi: Oxford University Press, 1980), pp. 112–30; and 'Culture, State and the Rediscovery of Indian Politics'.

In postcolonial societies, living with self-doubts about their own ability to run a proper nation-state, the two processes cannot but constitute a vicious circle. The more the participation, the more the hostility towards new participants as threats to the system. More the threat perception, more the hostility towards those who take on the state in areas such as civil rights and cultural survival.

II

The balance among the three images once gave the culture of Indian politics its distinct flavour. The imbalance among them explains much of the fluidity in the political culture of the country now. A crucial aspect of this imbalance is the inadequate legitimacy for the last image of the Indian state—of the state as an area within the public realm where terms for new transactions among old social grouping are settled—as compared to the first two images. This has distorted and split the third image. The pathology of the state as a market place in India has overshadowed the creative use of the state as a means of cultural self-renewal through the open renegotiation of social relationships. It is possible that the demands of the first two images have brought the worst out of the third image.

This is not a convoluted denial of the creative role of the first two images. During the last 150 years, these images have often been justifiably salient at the expense of the third. The idea of the postcolonial state as a defender of culture and society had to be re-emphasised during the colonial period, when the state had become, for most Indians, an alien entity. Likewise, the idea of the state as a liberating force powered social reform movements during the last century and social changes brought about through legislative and judicial actions in this century. However, politics in India has reached a stage when the state's role as a protective agency and as a catalyst of social change confronts the scepticism of those fighting for survival through a basic transformation of power relations in society. To these sceptics, all emphasis on the protective and emancipatory roles of the Indian state has now become an overemphasis, if not a ploy to subvert dissent and underwrite a national consensus tilted in favour of the dominant ideology of the Indian state. Strangely, scepticism towards the Indian state within its critics often does not translate into scepticism towards the ideas of the modern nation-state. One peculiarity within Indian political culture is that the most strident critics of the Indian state are also sometimes those that protest most vociferously when one suggests any limit on the role of the state in Indian society.

The reasons for this scepticism are obvious. First, the image of the state as a protector of Indian civilisation has consistently justified the right of the state to reorder that civilisation for purposes of the state. This has gradually removed all cultural and normative restraints on the state and allowed it to set the standards for judging all aspects of Indianness. The demands of the state are no longer conditional in India; they have become absolute. This has taken away the primacy of cultural life, in which the moral order of Indian society is encoded, creating in turn large-scale normlessness in the public realm.

On the other hand, evaluations of the state from the point of view of culture or lifestyle—when such evaluations are admitted into public discourse in modern India—are mostly conditional. They are supposed to accept the primacy of the state and strengthen it further through 'informed criticism'. Thus, even an entirely corrupt, totally inefficient, ruthlessly exploitative and authoritarian state is supposed to deserve the allegiance of all Indians, because even such a state supposedly protects Indian civilisation from destruction by dedicated enemies outside. If in the process the civilisation itself is altered beyond recognition or annihilated, that is not the concern of the state or of the statists. Echoing the feelings of that clever American army officer who saved a Vietnamese village from the enemy by destroying it, many Indian politicians, bureaucrats, intellectuals and journalists are willing to say that to protect Indian culture and society, and for that matter Indians, it may be necessary to abolish them altogether.

The reach of the protective image of the Indian state is best exemplified by India's foreign policy which, to protect Indian interests, now lives with a vague fear of anything which smacks of Indian culture. For that matter, any invocation of culture looks like empty moralism to India's politically articulate middle classes. The culture of the Indian state no longer has a built-in critique of the dominant style of international politics; Indian foreign policy is now squarely a part of what the Indian élite sees as the only possible style of handling international relations. India's ruling élite now looks back on the earlier idealism of the nationalist movement and that of the immediate post-Independence period as a Gandhian or Nehruvian voodoo that has fortunately been lifted. Consequently, the 'play' that Indian foreign policy once had, by being less than predictable in conventional terms, has diminished. The principles of foreign policy are now seen as universal and fixed. India's hard-eyed foreign policy is less and less a reflection of India's political traditions; rather it increasingly shapes the culture of the country's national élite.[8] The nuclear tests of 1998 can be seen as a direct product of this re-tooled culture of politics.

Simultaneously, the dominant global culture of international politics is being hawked within India as the 'state of the art' in politics and as an indicator of mature statecraft. For the modern Indian, there is no longer any *Indian* foreign policy. There is only a foreign policy of the nation-state called India, which has taken upon itself the full responsibility of protecting gullible Indians not merely from a devious, scheming, external world but from their own soft, effeminate, ill-defined self, and from the threats to their survival that this self poses. This is of course very different from the days of Jawaharlal Nehru who, ignoring all accusations of faint-hearted sanctimony and woolliness, and despite his own Eurocentric worldview and Edwardian whimsies, did attempt to bring into international politics something of the civilisational perspective of

[8] Cf. Giri Deshingkar, 'Civilisational Concerns', *Seminar*, December 1980 (257).

Indian society. Large parts of the Indian élite that have ritually sworn by Nehru, in order to be close to the dynasty he founded, have shown little sensitivity to the nature of the enterprise. They have made it possible to analyse the vicissitudes of India's foreign policy—trying to shed its earlier cultural sensitivity as a liability in the world of *realpolitik*—as the vicissitudes of the foreign policy of a national security state.[9]

Likewise, many aspects of India's bureaucratic socialism or state capitalism can be directly traced to the overuse of the image of the Indian state as a protector and liberator. Legitimised as a form of socialism, such state ownership left the content of an industry or an institution intact; it merely brought the unit under the control of the state and within easy reach of the tertiary sector. Whatever the original vision, socialising the means of production in practice meant nationalising red-tapism, giganticism, inefficiency and corruption—mainly to cater to the small but vociferous urban middle class, to neutralise a noisy and middle-class-based public opinion. It meant sustaining and pampering the middle-class belief that the choice was one between state and private ownership and could never be one among different forms of decentralised public ownership, or between them and socially responsible forms of private ownership.

The system merely took advantage of the idea that had gradually gained ground in the middle-class culture of Indian politics that nationalised corruption, giganticism and bureaucracy were better than their privatised versions. In retrospect, one can hypothesise that the ills of state capitalism in India were actually its goals, and the egalitarian ideology that went with it was paradoxically a successful legitimation of an unequal order. Institutions were designed so that they would not perform their stated function but meet other needs. The images of the state as a protector and a liberator merely used the ideologies of liberal and Leninist democratic centralism in

---

[9] For instance, Bharat Wariavwallah, 'Indira's India: A National Security State', *Round Table*, July 1983.

India to contain full-scale political participation—and what soci-ologist Edward Shils used to call the dispersal of charisma. If the masses are definitionally ignorant, or devoid of revolutionary con-sciousness, and the state has the responsibility of bringing them into the modern world, then there has to be some limit to the poli-tics of those without historical sensitivities. Such a state, has to have a special dispensation for the willing teachers of the masses—the secular rationalists, the scientifically-minded, the 'declassed' intel-lectuals with their superior cognition of history, and the myriad ex-perts on national security with their deeper understanding of India's external and internal enemies. In each case, the attempt is to curtail the legitimacy of the collective political choices of those who refuse to grant centrality to the nation-state in Indian life. Indians as a politically underdeveloped, ahistorical, less-than-rational collectivity—which for that reason is particularly vulner-able in international politics—is a stereotype that constitutes the underside of the images of the Indian state as the liberator, moderniser and protector of the Indian people. The stereotype has successfully dissociated large parts of the analysis of Indian politics from the categories used by a majority of the citizens to understand that politics.

III

The obverse of this disjunction is the tension between the image of the state as a market place and the protective and emancipatory images of the state among the middle classes.

During the last two decades, in public discourse the Indian state has retained and strengthened its image as a protector and a pace-setter. Yet, in terms of its functions and accessibility, it has less resemblance to the moderate, liberal nation-state to which many in the articulate, urban middle classes give their allegiance.[10] The

[10] Rajni Kothari, 'The Decline of the Moderate State', in *The State Against Democracy: In Search of Humane Governance* (Delhi: Ajanta, 1988), pp. 13–36.

legitimacy granted to the Indian state by large parts of the bureau-cracy, the media, the professions and academia is now mostly an allegiance to a shadowy, idealised state. Like the smile of the Cheshire cat, what lingers in the air is the legitimacy of the Indian nation-state built by the nationalist movement and the first genera-tion of India's post-Independence leaders. That legitimacy survives mainly in the media, textbooks and middle-class consciousness. The present instruments and institutions of the state, rightly or wrongly, do not have the capacity to elicit or hold the allegiance of Indians outside this charmed circle. What looks like allegiance to the state is really an allegiance to democracy. As a result, many of those who live with the older culture of modern politics in India, though they perceive themselves as tough-minded realists, are in effect what the sociologist Bharat Wariavwalla, echoing Iris Mur-doch, calls 'romantic realists'. Their realism derives from the exist-ing literature on the modern nation-state, not from the existent Indian state.

The Indian state may have outwardly grown stronger, thanks to its growing coercive might and its technological and industrial sup-port base. But it has become, over the years, less legitimate among the ruled as a reasonably just arbiter among different religious, ethnic and regional entities, as a protector of the weak and the poor, and as a reasonably—only reasonably—incorruptible pace-setter of desirable social changes. This is a dramatic change from the days when the modern Indian nation-state, though legitimised in terms of keywords such as security, development and science, derived power from its role as a new moral arbiter in society.

The overemphasis on the state's role as a protector and liberator of society has unleashed three processes that have become increas-ingly salient over the last decade. (1) It has endorsed the dominance of the tertiary sector—from which political analysts and political theorists mostly come—creating a vested interest in perpetuating the split between the *principles of legitimation* used by Westernised Indians and the rest of society. (2) It has made successive regimes more dependent on theatrical science and spectacular organisational feats as the new opiates of the middle classes; it has made them more inclined to use the rhetoric of national security and development to mobilise political support; and more inclined to exploit, for electoral and other secular political purposes, religious and ethnic conflicts.[11] (3) It has contributed handsomely to the criminalisation of the apparatus of the Indian state during recent years. To use an imperfect indicator, allegedly one-fifth of India's state legislators have criminal police records; in some states, the proportion goes up to about half.[12]

[11] If this seems too harsh a judgement, there is a series of reports by civil rights groups and other independent bodies on issues involving development, science, national security and ethnic relations. These studies show that issues such as development, science, national security and secularism have now entered the political lexicon as new justifications of large-scale violence, corruption and environmental vandalism. These slogans are now gradually displacing older justifications of violence and domination, such as religion, language, caste and kinship. For instance: People's Union of Democratic Rights and People's Union of Civil Liberties, *Who are the Guilty? Report of a Joint Inquiry into the Causes and Impact of the Riots in Delhi from 31 October to 10 November* (Delhi: PUDR and PUCL, 1985); S.M. Sikri, Badrud-din Tyabji, Rajeshwar Dayal, Govind Narain and T.C.A. Srinivasvardan, *Delhi, 31 October to 4 November: Report of the Citizens' Commission* (Delhi: Citizens' Commission, 1985); Justice Srikrishna Commission, *Report on Bombay Riots, 1992–3* (Bombay: Srikrishna Commission, 1998). For a discussion of the clear break between the old and new forms of ethnic violence, see Ashis Nandy, 'An Anti-Secularist Manifesto', *India International Centre Quarterly*, 1995, 22(1).

[12] A large mass of data and insights has accumulated on the subject, thanks often to those who reject the thrust of their own writings. E.g. Amnesty International, 'India: Some Reports Concerning Deaths in Police Custody Allegedly as a Result of Torture or Shooting During 1985' (London: Amnesty International, 1986), ASA 20/03/86, mimeo; A comprehensive work is A.R. Desai (ed.), *Violation of Democratic Rights in India* (Bombay: Popular Prakashan, 1986), vol. I. The experience, however, is not unique to India. It is shared, in different degrees by a number of democratic polities—notably, Italy, Nigeria, Columbia, Pakistan, Bangladesh, the USA and Japan.

The last process needs more detailed comment. It is not as if the Indian state was a perfectly moral entity that has suddenly turned criminal. However, the nature of the link between crime and politics has changed. Previously, a few criminals supported politicians and sought protection in exchange. Now, in many cases, large numbers of criminals operating outside or at the borderlines of law have entered public life. They protect themselves and sell protection to others.

To give a few lovable examples, some years ago the queen of illicit distillation in Bihar became a respected member of the ruling party in the Bihar state assembly, and in 1978 the hijacker of an Indian Airlines plane was elected a member of the Uttar Pradesh state assembly on the ticket of the Indian National Congress. Both were naturally protected by the privileges of the legislatures. Likewise, a gun-running guru was for a decade the person closest to the family of Prime Minister Indira Gandhi. At least three members of the 1998 central cabinet of the Bharatiya Janata Party are facing charges of directly fomenting communal riots. And if this looks just natural to a Hindu nationalist government, the main opposition, the Indian National Congress, also included in its cabinet two ministers who had taken leading parts in a communal riot. Some state governors and party presidents have in recent years been involved in nepotism and theft; others in direct attacks on the press. The police, in many states, have been involved in major criminal enterprises—from drug trafficking to smuggling, from rape to robbery. For a while, the boss of a coalmines mafia was the closest friend of a prime minister; and, as if to prove that ideology was no barrier in 'real' politics, a now-deceased minister of the West Bengal's leftist government who had an illustrious criminal record publicly threatened to shoot political opponents even while he was a minister. A few years ago, the police burnt two newspaper presses in Ahmedabad and killed well-known civil rights activists in Andhra, and the number of deaths from officially justified fake encounters staged by the police in Uttar Pradesh, Punjab, Andhra, Maharashtra and Kerala runs into thousands. If these look like the misadventures of lower-level functionaries, two prime ministers of India have been accused of theft.[13]

One suspects that middle-class political culture, so protective about the Indian state, is pegged to a state already more accessible to criminals than to the state's ideologues within the middle classes. Of this Indian state, which for a number of years now has been run as the private business venture of a new class, the romantic realists have no clue. They neither understand the nature of the business nor exercise any influence over its fate, except as post-facto legitimisers, minor beneficiaries and ineffective critics.

Two features identify these romantic ideologues of the state. First, when they talk of strengthening the state, they never speak of strengthening all the institutions of the state equally. They never speak, for instance, of strengthening the judiciary or parliament; they mostly speak of strengthening the military or the police, intelligence and counter-intelligence, the prime minister or the prime minister's secretariat. Second, when they admit the criminalisation of the Indian state, they absolve of responsibility those who have presided over the state during the period—as if the present state of Indian politics were *sui generis*, or perhaps an accidental by-product of social change.

It is thus fair to argue that more realistic analysts of the Indian state today are the criminalised elements in the polity. They are in close touch with the state and can get the best out of it. This political counter-community includes a proportion of the displaced traditional élite, but it primarily includes uprooted, anomic sections that have found access to the state through their socio-economic and political mobility.

---

[13] Nothing is more revealing than an insider's report to the government on the nexus between criminals and politicians, written by a home secretary as the head of an official committee that included the Directors of the Intelligence Bureau and the Central Bureau of Investigation. The report was submitted in 1993. See N.N. Vora, *Vora Committee Report and Right to Information* (New Delhi: Lok Shakti Abhiyan, 1997).

There is a reason why the term 'counter-community' is particularly apt. During the last twenty-five years, the concept of counter-culture has been often used to describe the fringe of Western society which has been forced out—or which has itself opted out—of mainstream politics. Such countercultures have in the West often been moved by utopian visions of the state, which, for the counter-cultures, are not so much realisable goals but intellectual and moral critiques of the existing state.

That relationship has been reversed in India. Unlike the West, in India mainstream middle-class culture and a majority of the intellectuals brought up within its confines are loyal to a shadow state—an imagined state, a state as it ought to be rather than as it is—while the counter-community owes allegiance to and understands the workings of the present Indian state better than the ordinary, law-abiding citizen and the establishment intellectual. This counter-community has not merely greater access to and control over the state, it is also more realistic and hard-headed about Indian politics.

Here, too, the images of the state as protector and liberator play a role. They allow many Indian intellectuals, especially political analysts, to maintain double ledgers. Many of them have rather clear-cut ideas about the nature of the present Indian state. But the more they see the state deviating from the norms of democratic governance and 'managing' dissent at the peripheries of the society through force, and the more the state uses the languages of national security, science, and development to cover up its criminalisation, the more desperately they cling to the state as a protector and redeemer. The more destruction and violence the state produces, the more they point to all-round destruction and violence as the reason why the Indian state deserves the unqualified support of all Indians.

Underlying these paradoxes is a deeper problem: the images of the state as a protector and liberator encourage most urban middle-class Indians to see the Indian state as the key to the fate of Indian civilisation. These Indians are neither capable of redefining the

Indian nation-state from the point of view of Indian civilisation, nor able to escape the existing grid of rationality, which prompts them to see their own form of statism as scientific, rational and, therefore, sagacious and practical. The main concepts of the statist ideology—national security, strong centre, national mainstream, national interest, military preparedness, constant vigilance against foreign conspiracy, nuclear weaponry, hard state and hard choices, central authority—all these have now acquired sanctity and become ends in themselves. Instead of being an instrument of the larger goals of Indian society and a temporary compromise with the demands of 'normal' statecraft in an imperfect world, this cluster of concepts has now become the *raison d'etre* of Indian civilisation.

To some this is a matter of sorrow, to others of pride. Many Indians are happy that an unwieldy Indic civilisation is now being squeezed into a proper, modern nation-state. For such people, those who do not accept the absolute primacy of the Indian nation-state are woolly-headed idealists or the stooges of foreign powers.

All this is a long-winded way of saying that the first two images of the state have been taken over by that part of the Indian public consciousness which has accepted the absolute primacy of the state and which sees salvation in India becoming a true copy of the 'advanced' nations of the world. The ideologues of the system justify their politics mainly by referring to that core assumption. To an increasingly vocal minority of Indians, in turn, these statists look like vandals in league with the counter-community, trying hard to turn the country into a second-class imitation of the modern West, sacrificing Indians who culturally and politically resist their project.

IV

Let me now sum up my arguments by teasing out some of their implications. One, the images of the state-as-a-protector and the state-as-a-liberator have cornered the image of the state-as-an-arbiter in

India. (The last is a somewhat misleading description of the third image but I must request the reader to bear with it for the moment.) As a result, the third image has fractured, and that part of it which finds expression in unlimited pure politics has freer play than the part which finds expression in the use of the state to politically re-negotiate relationships among various social aggregates.

Two, the pursuit of social justice, human rights and cultural sur-vival, which could have been facilitated through the open political process in India, have become, for participants in the mainstream culture of politics, the prerogative of the state—the state seen as the protector and liberator of the Indian people. Yet, given the nature of the state, actualisation of these values through the state has become more, not less, difficult. On the other hand, pursuing these values outside the domain of the state remains illegitimate or looks utopian to the high culture of Indian politics.

Three, the fragmentation and decline of the third image have paradoxically set the context to a state that neither protects nor libe-rates. It legitimises a state that endorses the new hierarchies defined by modern institutions such as the bureaucracy, the development community, the technocracy and the security establishment. All these institutions articulate on behalf of the citizen state-oriented millennial ideologies of the left and the right, and help vest all hope in the emancipatory role of the state. In the meanwhile, the citizen's access to the Indian state and its major institutions diminishes further.

Four, despite the unrestrained, pure politics it has endorsed, some aspects of the third image have retained the capacity to under-write an open polity and, perhaps, the capacity to underwrite a new equation between open politics and Indian traditions. At the mo-ment, while India has a surfeit of politics, that politics is of a special kind. There is ample scope for politics organised around the state and for dissent that accepts the absolute primacy of the state, but the space for politics that challenges the existing definition of the state has shrunk over the last forty years. Those who find their politics thus restricted are, therefore, increasingly forced to seek alternative means of political self-expression.[14]

Five, the emphasis on its protective and emancipatory roles is pushing the Indian state to become more and more independent of the political process in the country. The legitimacy of the political order now partly depends on the performance of sectors outside the political system, but related to the state. Thus, the state has to often find legitimacy through the spectacular feats of scientists, technocrats, sportsmen; through the successful organisation of international cultural and art events; even through the performance of individual expatriates.

This analysis has a lesson even for the avowed statist. If such a statist does not happen to be allergic to all criticisms of the idea of the modern state and does not view the idea as a space-and-time-defying entity, he or she may have to seriously consider if the survival of the Indian state itself does not now demand (1) a less absolute idea of the state and a more attenuated role for it in society, (2) more institutional and political efforts to avoid overloading the state, and (3) a greater play for the politics of cultures to provide the basis for new forms of political imagination and political intervention. A generation ago, most political analysts would have considered such formulations a sure prescription for national suicide or a

---

[14] Perhaps for the first time in India, the slogans of the ruling parties have become predominantly nonpolitical and noneconomic: computers, modern management and 'futuribles'. A large proportion of ultra-élites in the system has begun to come from the worlds of showbiz, advertising and public relations. Even membership of the Indian Planning Commission, the major instrument of development in the country, has begun to reflect the same shift away from economists and politicians—scientists and managers are now often in a majority in the Commission.

plea for old-style conservatism. Gradually and painfully many of them have come to realise that both modern India and the Indian state have 'made it'; neither needs unqualified support from the citizen, and the social violence associated with the modern sector in India has gradually overtaken the violence organised around traditions. There is also the realisation that India needs a new social critique of the idea of the nation-state, for the idea now provides an institutional and ideological axis for the growing violence in the modern sector.

Such an attenuated role for the state is not unknown to Indians. Throughout the colonial period, they lived with the image of a 'distant' state. True, that distance was imposed, and Indians had the right, on attaining political freedom, to give a more central place to the state in public life. But they have over-corrected the distance, and by over-extending the state have narrowed the scope and the concept of politics. Only that which centres on the state and its formal structures is considered politics now. As a result, the struggles of child labourers, women's movements and environmentalism, even the politics of trade unions and landless agricultural labourers, look less political these days than defections and factional realignments in parties.

Perhaps the definition of politics in India is becoming more open-ended, even in the Indian middle classes. The foibles of politicians who cannot survive without access, or promise of access, to the state has already begun to pall. However, it is unlikely that the pathologies of the Indian state will immediately induce a fundamental rethinking of the role of the state. It is more likely that, as in other postcolonial societies, in the coming decades the state will be forced to exercise some restraint on itself. Presumably, that process will be quickened by the withdrawal of the absolute legitimacy previously given to the state by large sections of citizens.

To express that hope is also to recognise that many of the baroque theories of political praxis, imported through the university system and the global media, have already become disjunctive with

Indian life. Given this, it may be useful to remember the *Yoga Vashishtha,* which claims that while knowledge with action is superior to knowledge without action, knowledge without action is superior to action without knowledge.

I can put it differently—and more conservatively—for those who may find my argument as reified as the reification it criticises. A political analysis could be for fellow-analysts; it could be for those trying to express their vague, disorganised experiences of Indian politics in communicable terms but failing. This failure in turn can be for many reasons, but if it is because the experiences which the victims of the system are trying to express are not communicable within the existing conceptual frames, it becomes our responsibility to create a new language or borrow it from the victims. The victims are under no obligation to fit their experiences within our models.

CHAPTER 3

The Politics of Secularism and the Recovery of Religious Tolerance

I. Faith, Ideology and the Self

A significant aspect of postcolonial structures of knowledge in the third world is a peculiar imperialism of categories. Within this form of imperialism, a conceptual domain is hegemonised by a concept produced and honed in the West, hegemonised so effectively that the original domain vanishes from awareness. Intellect and intelligence become IQ, oral cultures become the cultures of the non-literate or the uneducated, the oppressed become the proletariat, social change becomes development. After a while, people begin to forget that IQ is only a crude measure of intelligence and that someday someone else may think up another kind of index to assess the same thing; that social change did not begin with development and will not stop once the idea of development dies a natural or unnatural death.

In the following pages, I seek to provide a political preface to the recovery of a well-known domain of public concern in South Asia—ethnic and, especially, religious tolerance—from the hegemonic language of secularism popularised by Westernised intellectuals and the middle classes in this part of the world. This language, whatever its positive contributions to humane governance and to religious tolerance earlier, has increasingly become a cover for the complicity of modern intellectuals and the modernising middle classes of South Asia with the new forms of religious violence that have entered the Asian scene. These are forms in which the state, the media and the ideologies of national security, development and modernity—propagated by the modern intelligentsia and the middle classes—play crucial roles.

To provide that political preface, I shall first describe four trends that have become clear in South Asia during this century, particularly after the Second World War.

The first and most important of these trends is that each religion in our part of the world has been split into two: faith and ideology. Both are inappropriate terms, but I give them specific private meanings to serve my purpose in this essay. By faith I mean religion as a way of life, a tradition which is definitionally non-monolithic and operationally plural. I say 'definitionally' because, unless a religion is geographically and culturally confined to a small area, religion as a way of life has in effect to turn into a confederation of a number of ways of life, linked by a common faith and with some theological space for heterogeneity.

By ideology I mean religion as a sub-national, national or cross-national identifier of populations contesting for or protecting non-religious, usually political or socioeconomic, interests. Such religions-as-ideologies usually get identified with one or more texts which, rather than the ways of life of believers, then become the final identifiers of the pure forms of the religions. The texts help anchor the ideologies in something seemingly concrete and delimited and, in effect, provide a set of manageable operational definitions.

The two categories are not mutually exclusive; they are like two axes on which the state of contemporary religions can be plotted. One way of explaining the difference between the two is to conceive of ideology as something that, for individuals and people who believe in it, needs to be constantly protected, and faith as something that the faithful usually expect to protect them. For a faith always includes a theory of transcendence and usually sanctions the experience of transcendence, whereas an ideology tends to bypass or fear theories and experiences of transcendence, except when they could be used for secular purposes.[1]

The modern state always prefers to deal with religious ideologies rather than with faiths. It is wary of both forms of religion but it finds ways of life more inchoate and, hence, unmanageable, even though it is faith rather than ideology which has traditionally been more pliable and catholic. It is religion-as-faith which prompted 200,000 Indians to declare themselves Mohammedan Hindus in the census of 1911; and it was catholicity of faith which prompted Mole-Salam Girasia Rajputs to traditionally have two names for every member of the community, one Hindu and one Muslim.[2] It is religion-as-ideology, on the other hand, which prompted a significant proportion of Punjabi-speaking Hindus to declare Hindi their mother tongue, thus underlining the differences between Sikhism and Hinduism and sowing the seeds for the creation of a new minority. Likewise it is religion-as-ideology which has provided a potent tool to the Jamaat e Islami to disown traditional, plural forms of Islam in the Indian subcontinent and, by separating official religion from everyday life, producing a pre-packaged Islam for Muslims uprooted and decultured by processes of engineered social change in the region.

Second, during the last two centuries or so there has grown a tendency to view the older faiths of the region through the eyes of post-medieval European Christianity and its various off-shoots—

[1] It should be obvious that I am not talking of ideology here in Mannheimian or Marxian sense. The meaning of the term is closer to the definition of ideology in standard social and political psychological literature.

[2] Shamoon T. Lokhandwala, 'Indian Islam: Composite Culture and Integration', *New Quest*, March–April 1985 (50), pp. 87–101.

such as the masculine Christianity associated with nineteenth-century missionaries like Joshua Marshman and William Carey in South Asia, or its mirror image in the orthodox modernism vended by the likes of Frederich Engels and Thomas Huxley. Because this particular Eurocentric way of looking at faiths gradually came to be associated with the dominant culture of the colonial states in the region, it subsumes a set of clear polarities: centre versus periphery, true faith versus its distortions, civil versus primordial, and great traditions versus local cultures.

It is a part of the same story that, in each of the dyads, the second category is set up to lose. It is also a part of the same story that, once the colonial concept of state was internalised by the societies of the region through nationalist ideology—in turn heavily influenced by Western theories of state and statecraft[3]—the nascent nation-states of the region took upon themselves the same civilising mission that colonial states had once taken upon themselves *vis-à-vis* the ancient faiths of the subcontinent.

Third, the idea of secularism, an import from nineteenth-century Europe into South Asia, has acquired immense potency in the middle-class cultures and state sectors of South Asia, thanks to its connection with and response to religion-as-ideology. Secularism has little to say about cultures—it is definitionally ethnophobic and frequently ethnocidal, unless of course cultures and those living by cultures are willing to show total subservience to the modern nation-state and become ornaments or adjuncts to modern living—and the orthodox secularists have no clue to the way a religion can link up different faiths or ways of life according to its own configurative principles.

To such secularists, religion is an ideology in opposition to the ideology of modern statecraft and, therefore, needs to be contained. They feel even more uncomfortable with religion-as-a-faith, claiming to have its own principles of tolerance and intolerance, for that

[3] For instance, Partha Chatterjee, *National Thought and the Colonial World: A Derivative Discourse?* (New Delhi: Oxford University Press, 1986).

claim denies the state and the middle-class ideologues of the state the right to be the ultimate reservoir of sanity and the ultimate arbiter among different religions and communities.[4] This denial is particularly galling to those who see the clash between two faiths merely as a clash of socioeconomic interests, not as a simultaneous clash between conflicting interests and a philosophical encounter between two metaphysics. The Westernised middle classes and literati of South Asia love to see all such differences as liabilities and as sources of ethnic violence.

Fourth, the imported idea of secularism has become increasingly incompatible and, as it were, uncomfortable with the somewhat fluid definitions of the self with which many South Asian cultures live.[5] Such a self, which can be conceptually viewed as a configuration of selves, simultaneously shapes, invokes and reflects the configurative principles of religions-as-faiths. It also happens to be a negation of the modern concept of selfhood acquired partly from

[4] Jyoti Ananthu has drawn my attention to the inadequacy of the term 'tolerance', used more than once in this essay because it is itself a product of the secular worldview. She gives the example of Kakasaheb Kalelkar, distinguished freedom fighter and Gandhian, who used to talk of *samanvaya* (crudely synthetism), which cannot be based only on tolerance. Trilokinath Madan ('Secularism in Its Place', *The Journal of Asian Studies*, 1987, 46(4), pp. 747–59) has used the term 'understanding' which seems less demanding than Kalelkar's. Paulos Mar Gregorios rejects the term tolerance even more sharply. 'Understanding based on mutual respect' is the expression preferred by him. Paulos Mar Gregorios, 'Speaking of Tolerance and Intolerance', in *India International Centre Quarterly*, Spring 1995, 22(1), pp. 22–34. I reluctantly retain the expression 'tolerance' for the moment because it presumes least from the ordinary citizen by way of knowledge and empathy, though I have begun to use it in conjunction with the idea of hospitality used in Madhu Suri Prakash and Gustavo Esteva, *Grassroots Postmodernism: Remaking the Soil of Cultures* (London: Zed, 1998).

[5] Though I am speaking here of cultural selfhood, this description is perfectly compatible with psychoanalytic studies of self and separation, particularly ego boundaries, in India. For a recent example, see Alan Roland,

the Enlightenment West and partly from a rediscovery of previously recessive elements in Indian traditions. Religion-as-ideology, working with the concept of well-bounded, mutually exclusive religious identities, on the other hand, is more compatible with and analogous to the definition of the self as a well-bounded, individuated entity clearly separable from the non-self. Such individuation is taking place in South Asian societies at a fast pace and, to that extent, more exclusive definitions of the self, too, are emerging in these societies as a by-product of secularisation.[6]

A more fluid definition of the self is not merely more compatible with religion-as-faith, it also has—and depends more upon—a distinctive set of the non-selves and anti-selves (a neologism analogous to anti-heroes). At one plane, these anti-selves are similar to what psychotherapist Carl Rogers used to call, not very felicitously, the 'not-me'—and to what some others call rejected selves. At another plane, they, the anti-selves, are counterpoints without which the self just cannot be defined in the major cultures of this part of the world. It is the self in conjunction with its anti-selves and its distinctive concept of the non-self that define the domain of the self. Religion-as-faith is more compatible with such a complex self-definition; secularism has no inkling of this distinct, though certainly not unique, form of self-definition in South Asia. This is because secularism is, as T.N. Madan puts it, a gift of Christianity, by which he presumably means a 'gift of post-medieval, European Christianity.[7]

It is in the context of these four processes that I shall now discuss the scope and limits of the ideology of secularism in India and its

---

'Psychoanalysis in India and Japan: Toward a Comparative Psychoanalysis', *The American Journal of Psychoanalysis*, 1991, 51(1), pp. 1–10.

[6] Cf. Donald F. Miller, 'Five Theses on the Question of Religion in India Today: A Response to Ashis Nandy's "An AntiSecularist Manifesto" ', paper presented at the Conference on 'What's Happening to India?', Melbourne, December 27, 1986.

[7] T.N. Madan, 'Secularism in Its Place'.

relationship with the new forms of ethnic violence we have been witnessing.

II. The Fate of Secularism

I must admit at this point that I am no secularist. In fact, I can be called an anti-secularist. I say this with some trepidation because, in the company in which I move, this is not a fashionable position to take. Fortunately, such is the pull of the ideology of secularism in India today that, recently, when I wrote an anti-secularist manifesto, many interpreted the article to be a hidden homage to secularism.

I call myself an anti-secularist because I feel that the ideology and politics of secularism have more or less exhausted their possibilities. And we may now have to work with a different conceptual frame that is already vaguely visible at the borders of Indian political culture.[8]

When I say that the ideology and politics of secularism have exhausted themselves, I have in mind the standard English meaning of the word 'secularism'. As we know, there are two meanings of the word current in modern and semi-modern India and, for that matter, in the whole of this subcontinent. One of the two meanings is easily found in dictionaries. The other is a non-standard, local meaning which, many like to believe, is typically and distinctively Indian or South Asian. As we shall see, it also has a Western tail, but that tail is now increasingly vestigial.

The first meaning becomes clear when people talk of secular trends in history or economics, or when they speak of secularising the state. The word 'secularism' has been used in this sense in the

---

[8] My position in this respect is close to that of Ansar Hussain Khan who says that: 'Of all the words that can be applied to India, the word "secular" is the most unwanted. It is totally irrelevant and indeed offensive to most Indians.' Ansar Hussain Khan, *The Rediscovery of India: A New Subcontinent* (Hyderabad: Orient Longman, 1995), p. 253.

West for more than 300 years. This secularism chalks out an area in public life where religion is not admitted. One can have religion in one's private life; one can be a good Hindu or a good Muslim within one's home or at one's place of worship. But when one enters public life, one is expected to leave one's faith behind. This ideology of secularism is associated with slogans like 'we are Indians first, Hindus second', or 'we are Indians first, then Sikhs'. Implicit in the ideology is the belief that managing the public realm is a science which is essentially universal, that religion, to the extent that it is opposed to the Baconian world-image of science, is an open or potential threat to any modern polity.

In contrast, the non-Western meaning of secularism revolves around equal respect for all religions. This is the way it is usually put by public figures. Less crudely, this idea of secularism implies that while public life may or may not be kept free of religion, it must have space for a continuous dialogue among religious traditions and between the religious and the secular. That is, in the final analysis, each major faith in the region includes *within* it an in-house version of the other faiths both as an internal criticism and as a reminder of the diversity of the theory of transcendence.

Ali Akhtar Khan has drawn attention to the fact that George Jacob Holyoake, who coined the word secularism in 1850, advocated a form of secularism that could accommodate religion, one that would emphasise diversities and coexistence in the matter of faith. His contemporary Joseph Bradlaugh, on the other hand, believed in a secularism that rejected religion and made science its deity. Most non-modern Indians (that is, Indians who would have reduced the late Professor Max Weber to tears), pushed around by the political and cultural forces unleashed by colonialism still operating in Indian society, have unwittingly opted for the accommodative and pluralist meaning; whereas India's Westernised intellectuals have consciously opted for the abolition of religion from the public sphere.

In other words, the accommodative meaning is more compatible with the meaning a majority of Indians, independently of Bradlaugh, have given to the word 'secularism'. This meaning has always disconcerted the country's Westernised intellectuals. They have seen such people's secularism as adulterated, as compromising true secularism. This despite the fact that the ultimate symbol of religious tolerance for modern Indians, Gandhi, obviously had this adulterated meaning in mind on the few occasions when he seemed to plead for secularism. This is clear from Gandhi's notorious claim that those who thought religion and politics could be kept separate understood neither religion nor politics.

The saving grace in all this is that, while the scientific, rational meaning of secularism has dominated India's middle-class public consciousness, the Indian people and, till recently, most practising Indian politicians depended on the accommodative meaning. The danger is that the accelerating process of modernisation in India supports the first meaning. As a result, there is now a clearer fit between the declared ideology of the modern Indian nation-state and the secularism that fears religion and ethnicity. Sociologist Imtiaz Ahmed euphemistically calls this fearful, nervous secularism the new liberalism of the Indian élite.[9]

Associated with this—what South Asians perceive as the more scientific Western meaning of secularism—is a hidden political hierarchy. I have spelt out this hierarchy elsewhere but I shall, nevertheless, have to restate it to make the rest of my argument. This hierarchy makes a four-fold classification of the political actors in the subcontinent.

At the top of the hierarchy are those who are believers neither in public nor in private. They are supposed to be scientific and rational, and they are expected not only to rule this society but also

[9] Imtiaz Ahmed, 'Muslims and Boycott Call: Political Realities Ignored', *The Times of India*, 14 January 1987.

dominate its political culture. An obvious example is Jawaharlal Nehru. Though we are now told with a great deal of embarrassment that he believed in astrology and tantra, Nehru rightfully belongs to this rung because he always made modern Indians a little asham- ed of their religious beliefs and ethnic origins. He convinced them that he himself had the courage and rationality to neither believe in private nor in public. By the common consent of the Indian middle classes, Nehru provided a perfect role model for twentieth-century citizens of the flawed cultural reality called India. It is the Nehruvian model which informs the following charming letter, written some years ago by a distinguished former ambassador, to the editor of India's best-known national daily:

> M.V. Kamath asks in his article 'Where do we find the Indian?' My dear friend and colleague, the late Ambassador M.R.A. Beg, often used to say: 'Don't you think, old boy, that the only Indians are we wogs [Westernised Oriental Gentlemen]?' However quaint it may have sounded 30 years ago, the validity of this statement has increasingly become apparent over the years.[10]

On the second rung are those who choose not to appear as believ- ers in public despite being devout believers in private. I can think of no better example of this type than Indira Gandhi. She was a genuine non-believer in her public life (after all she died at the hands of her own Sikh guards rather than accept the advice of her security officers to change guards) but in private she was a devout Hindu who had to make her seventy-one—or was it sixty-nine?— pilgrimages. Both the selves of Indira Gandhi were genuine and together they represented a sizeable portion of the Indian mid- dle classes. A number of rulers in this part of the world fit this category—from Ayub Khan to Lal Bahadur Shastri to Sheikh Mujibur Rahman. Though the Westernised literati in South Asian societies have never cared much for this model of religious and eth- nic tolerance, they have usually been willing to accept the model as

[10] Gurbachan Singh, 'Where's the Indian?', *The Times of India*, 21 Sep- tember 1986.

a reasonable compromise with the 'underdeveloped' cultures of South Asia.

On the third rung are believers in public who do not believe in private. This may seem an odd category, but one or two examples will make clear its meaning and also partially explain why this category includes problematic men and women. To me the two most illustrious examples of this type from our part of the world are Mohammed Ali Jinnah, who was an agnostic in private life but took up the cause of Islam successfully in public; and V.D. Savarkar, an atheist in private life, who declared Hinduism his political ideology. When Bhimrao Ambedkar converted to Buddhism, he probably entered this category from the first.

Such people can sometimes be dangerous because religion is a political tool for them, a means of fighting one's own, and one's community's, sense of cultural inadequacy. Religion to them is not a matter of piety. Their private denial of belief only puts the secularist off guard. He cannot fathom the seriousness with which the Jinnahs and the Savarkars take religion as a political instrument. On the other hand, their public faith puts the faithful off-guard, because the latter never discern the contempt in which such heroes hold the common run of the faithful. Often, these heroes invoke the classical versions of their faiths to underplay, marginalise or even delegitimise the existing ways of life associated with their faiths. The goal of those holding such an instrumental view of religion has always been to homogenise their co-believers into proper political formations and, for that reason, to eliminate those parts of religion which smack of folkways and which threaten to legitimise diversities, inter-faith dialogue, and theological polycentrism.

At the bottom of the hierarchy are believers in private as well as in public. The best and most notorious example is Gandhi, who openly believed both in private and in public, and gave his belief spectacular play in politics. This category has its strengths and weaknesses. One may say that exactly as the category manifests its strength in people like Gandhi, Khan Abdul Gaffar Khan and Maulana Bhasani, it shows its weakness in others like Ayatollah

Khomeini in Iran or Jarnail Singh Bhindranwale in Punjab. The category can even throw up grand eccentrics. Sixty years ago Chaudhuri Rehmat Ali used to stand on Fridays outside the King's College gate at Cambridge and chant like a street hawker, 'come and buy Pakistan—my earth-shaking pamphlet'.[11]

The four categories are not neat and in real life they rarely come in their pure forms. Often, the same person can move from one category to another. Thus, Rahi Masoom Raja, being a scriptwriter for commercial Hindi films and being at home with spectacular changes of heart, comfortably oscillates between the first two categories: 'This Babari Masjid and Ram Janambhoomi temple should be demolished . . . We as Indians are not interested in Babari Masjid, Rama Janambhoomis . . . as secular people we must crush the religious fanatics.'[12]

Only ten months earlier Raja had, with as much passion, said: 'I, Rahi Masoom Raja, son of the late Mr Syed Bashir Hasan Abidi, a Muslim and one of the direct descendants of the Prophet of Islam, hereby condemn Mr Z.A. Ansari for his un-Islamic and anti-Muslim speeches in Parliament. The Quran no where says that a Muslim should have four wives.'[13]

For the moment I shall not go into such issues. All I shall add is that in India, we have always been slightly embarrassed about this modern classification or ordering in our political life, for we know that the Father of the Nation does not fare very well when the classification is applied to him.

[11] Mulk Raj Anand, 'New Light on Iqbal', *Indian Express*, 22 September 1985.

[12] Rahi Masoom Raja, 'How to Resolve the Babari Masjid-Ram Janmabhoomi Dispute', *Sunday Observer*, 18 January 1987.

[13] Rahi Masoom Raja, 'In Favour of Change' (letter to the editor), *The Illustrated Weekly of India*, 16 March 1986.

Fortunately for some modern Indians, the embarrassment has been resolved by the fact that this classification is not working well today. It is not working well because it has led neither to the elimination of religion and ethnicity from politics nor to greater religious and ethnic tolerance. This is not the case only with us; this is the case with every society which has been put before Indians, at one time or the other, as the ideal secular society.

Thus, problems of ethnicity and secularisation today haunt not merely some of the capitals of the world—Washington, Bonn, Paris and Moscow—they even haunt the country which older South Asians have been trained to view as remarkably free from the divisiveness of ethnicity and religion. For over a hundred and fifty years Indians have been told that one of the reasons Britain dominated India, one of the reasons why Indians were colonised, was that they were not secular whereas Britain was. That was why Indians did not know how to live together, whereas Britain was a world power, perfectly integrated and fired by the true spirit of secular nationalism. Now we find that, after nearly 300 years of secularism, the Irish, the Scots and the Welsh are together creating as many problems for Britain as some of the religions or regions are creating for Indians.

Why is the old ideology of secularism not working in India? There are many reasons: I shall mention only a few, confining myself specifically to the problem of religion as it has become intertwined with the political process in the country.

First, in the early years of Independence, when the national élite was small and a large section of it had face-to-face contact, we could screen people entering public life, specially the upper levels of the public services and high politics, for their commitment to secularism. Thanks to the growth of democratic participation in politics—India has gone through ten general elections and innumerable local and state elections—such screening is no longer possible. We can no longer make sure that those who reach the highest levels of the army, police, bureaucracy or politics believe in old-style secular politics.

To give one example, during the last two decades, there have been, consistently, ministers in the central cabinet in India and high-ups in major national parties like the Bharatiya Janata Party and the Indian National Congress who have been accused not only of fomenting, organising and participating in communal riots but also of protecting the guilty and publicly threatening civil rights workers engaged in relief work. One chief minister was accused of importing rioters from another state on payment of professional fees to precipitate a communal riot as an antidote to violent inter-caste conflicts. Another organised a riot some years ago so that he could impose a curfew in the state capital to stop his political opponents from demonstrating their strength in the legislature.

Such instances would have been unthinkable twenty years ago. They have become thinkable because India's ultra-élite can no longer informally screen decision-makers the way they once did. Political participation is growing and the country's political institutions, particularly the main parties that increasingly look like electoral machines, are under too much strain to allow such screening. Religion *has* entered public life, but through the back door.

Second, it has become more and more obvious to a large number of people that modernity is now no longer the ideology of a small minority; it is the organising principle of the dominant culture of politics. The idea that religions dominate India, that there is a handful of modern Indians fighting a rearguard action against that domination, is no longer convincing to many modernising Indians. These Indians see the society around them—and often their own children—leaving no scope for a compromise between the old and new, and opting for a way of life that fundamentally negates the traditional concepts of a good life and a desirable society. These Indians now sense the 'irreversibility' of secularisation and they know that, even in this subcontinent, religion-as-faith is being pushed to the corner. Much of the fanaticism and violence associated with religion comes today from a sense of defeat in the believers, from their feelings of impotence, and from their free-floating anger and self-hatred while facing a world which is increasingly secular and desacralised.

Also, when the state makes a plea to a minority community to secularise or confine itself to secular politics, it tells the community in effect to 'soften' its faith so that it can be more truly integrated in the nation-state. Usually it simultaneously offers the community a gesture, in the form of a tacit promise, that it will also force the majority to ultimately dilute its faith. What the state implicitly says to a religious community, the intelligentsia often explicitly tells the individual: 'give up your faith, at least in public; others will do so too and together everyone will live in freedom from religious intolerance.' As it happens, however reasonable the solution may look to the already secularised, it is hardly appealing to the faithful. For those with religious faith, religion is an overall theory of life, including public life, and life does not seem worth living without a theory, however imperfect—of transcendence.

Third, while appealing to believers to keep the public sphere free of religion, the modern nation-state has no means of ensuring that the ideologies of secularism, development and nationalism themselves do not begin to act as faiths intolerant of other faiths. That is, while the modern state builds up pressure on citizens to give up their faith in public, it guarantees no protection to them against sufferings inflicted by the state in the name of its ideology. On the contrary, with the help of modern communications and the secular coercive power at its command, the state frequently uses its ideology to silence non-conforming citizens. The role of such secular ideology in many societies today is no different from the crusading and inquisitorial role of religious ideologies. And in such societies, citizens often have less protection against the ideology of the state than they do against religious ideologies or theocratic forces. Certainly in India, the ideas of nation-building, scientific growth, security, modernisation and development have become parts of a left-handed, quasi-religious practice—a new demonology, a tantra with a built-in code of violence.

In other words, to many Indians today secularism comes as part of a larger package consisting of a set of standardised ideological products and social processes—development, mega-science and national security being some of the most prominent among these. This package often plays the same role *vis-à-vis* the people—sanctioning or justifying violence against the weak and the dissenting—that the church, the ulema, the sangha, and the Brahminic order played in earlier times.

Finally, the proposition that the values derived from the secular ideology of the state will be a better guide to political action, to a less violent and richer political life (as compared to the values derived from religious faiths) has become even more unconvincing to large parts of Indian society than it was a few decades ago. It has become increasingly clear that, as far as public morality goes, the culture of the Indian state has very little moral authority left; nor have ideologies that tend to conceptualise the state as the pivot of social and cultural change. The hope that a secular Indian state will provide a set of values to guide a devout Hindu, Muslim or Sikh in day-to-day public behaviour lies splintered. The deification of the state may go down well among those Indians who have access to the state or who thrive on its patronage, but it palls on most decent citizens outside the charmed circle of the state sector. Obviously, we are at a point of time when old-style secularism can no longer pretend to guide moral or political action. All that the ideology of secularism can do now is sanction the imposition of an imported language of politics on a traditional society that has an open polity. Let me spell this out.

In most postcolonial societies, when religion, politics or religion-and-politics is discussed, there is an invisible reference point. This reference point is Western Man. Not Western Man in reality or the

Western Man of history, but Western Man as the defeated civilisations of our times have construed him. This Western Man rules the world, it seems to the defeated, because of his superior understanding of the relationship between religion and politics. To cope with this success, every major religious community in the region has produced three responses—I should say two responses and one non-response. These responses have clear-cut relationships with the splitting of religions into ideologies and faiths, described at the beginning of this essay; actually, they derive from the split.

The first response—it is not easy to capture its spirit—is to model oneself on Western Man. Here, something more than mimicry or imitation is involved. The response consists in a desperate attempt to capture, within one's own self and culture, traits seen as the reasons for the West's success on the world stage. Seemingly, this is a liberal, synthesising response and it is often justified as a universal response. It has for long been part of the political and cultural repertoire of modern India. A neat example is mathematician-philosopher Raojibhai C. Patel's essay, in which the analysis is almost entirely in terms of the Western experience with religion and politics, and the conclusions are all about India.[14]

The second response to Western Man is that of the zealot. The zealot's one goal is to somehow defeat Western Man at his own game, the way Japan, for instance, has done in economic affairs. This is a crude way of describing a complex response, yet it does convey that what passes as fundamentalism, fanaticism or revivalism is often only another form of westernisation becoming popular among the psychologically uprooted middle classes in South Asia. (A newspaper interview of nuclear physicist A.Q. Khan of Pakistan is a copybook instance of the same response.)[15] In India the heart of the response is the faith that what Japan has done in relation to the economy, we can do in the case of religion and politics. One

[14] Raojibhai C. Patel, 'Building Secular State, Need to Subordinate Religion', *The Times of India*, 17 September 1986.

[15] 'Pak a Few Steps from Bomb', *The Times of India*, 29 January 1987.

can, for example, decontaminate Hinduism of its folk elements, turn it into a classical Vedantic faith, and then give it additional teeth with the help of Western technology and secular statecraft. Hindus can then take on and ultimately defeat all their external and internal enemies, if necessary by liquidating all forms of ethnic plurality within Hinduism and India, thereby equalling Western Man as a new *ubermenschen*. The zealot judges the success or failure of a religion only by this criterion.

Historian Giri Deshingkar gives the example of a book on Mant-rashastra written by one of the Shankaracharyas, known for his zealotry, which justifies the sacred book by claiming that its con-clusions are supported by modern science, as if that made the text more sacred. The title page of the book—a commentary on an ancient text by a guru of the world, a *jagadguru*—also says that its author is a B.A., Ll.B. If this is the state of the Indian élite's cultural self-confidence, it is not surprising that newspapers carry, every other month, full-page advertisements by Maharishi Mahesh Yogi suggesting that Vedanta is true because quantum physics says so.

Such responses of the zealot are the ultimate admission of defeat. They constitute the cultural bed on which grows the revivalism of the defeated, the so-called fundamentalist movements in South Asia, based on the zealot's instrumental concept of religion as an ideological principle for political mobilisation and state formation. Modern scholarship sees zealotry as a retrogression into primitiv-ism and as a pathology of traditions. On closer look it turns out to be a by-product and a pathology of modernity. For instance, what-ever the revivalist Hindu may seek to revive, it is not Hinduism. The pathetically comic, martial uniform of khaki shorts, which the RSS cadres have to wear, tells it all. Modelled on the uniform of the colonial police, these khaki shorts not merely identify the RSS as an illegitimate child of Western colonialism, but even as a direct progeny of the semiticising Hindu reform movements under colo-nialism. Like these movements, the RSS is sold to Orientalist con-cepts of 'proper' religion and modern Western concepts of the nation-state, nationality and nationalism. Once such concepts of religion and state are imported into Hinduism, the inevitable happens. One begins to judge the everyday lifestyle of Hindus, their diversity and heterogeneity, negatively, usually with a clear touch of hostility and contempt. Likewise, there is nothing fundamentally Islamic about fundamentalist Muslims who have to constantly try to disenfranchise ordinary Muslims as peripheral and delegitimise the religious practices of a huge majority of Muslims the world over as un-Islamic. The same forces are operating within Sikhism and Sri Lankan Buddhism too.

There is however a third response that comes usually from the non-modern majority of a society, though to globalised middle-class intellectuals it may look like the response of a minority. This response does not keep religion separate from politics, but it does say that the traditional ways of life have, over the centuries, developed internal principles of tolerance, and that these principles must have play in contemporary politics. This response affirms that religious communities in traditional societies *have* known how to live with each other. It is not modern India which has tolerated Judaism in India for nearly two thousand years, Christianity from before the time it went to Europe, and Zoroastrianism for more than twelve hundred years; it is traditional India which has shown such tolerance. That is why today, as India gets modernised, religious violence is increasing. In the earlier centuries, according to available records, inter-religious riots were rare and localised; even after Independence, we had only one episode of religious strife a week; now we have more than one a day. More than ninety per cent of these riots begin in urban India and, within urban India, in and around industrial areas. Even now, Indian villages and small towns can take credit for having mostly avoided communal riots. Thus we find that, during ten years of bitterness since the mid-1980s, Punjab's villages were still free of riots; they only saw assassinations by small gangs of terrorists and riot-like situations in the cities. Obviously, somewhere and somehow, religious violence has something to do with the urban-industrial vision of life and with the political processes that vision lets loose.

An awareness of this political process has convinced a small but growing number of Indian political analysts that it is from non-modern India—from the traditions and principles of religious tolerance encoded in the everyday life associated with the different faiths of India—that one will have to seek clues to the renewal of Indian political culture. This is a less difficult task than it first seems. Let us not forget that the great symbols of religious tolerance in India over the last 2000 years have not been modern, though modern Indians have managed to hijack some of these symbols.

For example, when modern Indians project the ideology of secularism into the past and assert that Ashoka was 'secular', they ignore that Ashoka was not exactly a secular ruler; he was a practising Buddhist even in his public life. He based his tolerance on Buddhism, not on secularism. Likewise, the other symbol of inter-religious amity in modern India, Akbar, derived his tolerance not from secularism but from Islam; he believed that tolerance was the message of Islam. And in this century Gandhi derived his religious tolerance from Hinduism, not from secular politics.

Modern India has much to answer for. So have cosmopolitan intellectuals in South Asia who have been insensitive to traditions of inter-religious understanding in their societies. These traditions may have become creaky but so is the ideology of secularism. As we are finding out the hard way, the new forms of religious violence in this part of the world are becoming, paradoxically, increasingly secular. The anti-Sikh riots which took place in Delhi in November 1984, the anti-Muslim riots in Ahmedabad in 1985 during the anti-reservation stir, and the 'anti-Hindu' riots in Bangalore in 1986—they were all associated not so much with religious hatred as with political cost-calculations and/or economic greed.[16] The same can be said about the riots at Moradabad, Bhiwandi and Hyderabad earlier. Zealotry has produced many riots, but secular politics too has now begun to produce its own version of 'religious riots'. As for the victims of a riot, the fact that the riot was organised and led by people motivated by political cost-calculations and not by religious bigotry is hardly a solace.

The moral of the story is simple. It is time to recognise that, instead of trying to build religious tolerance on the good faith or conscience of a small group of de-ethnicised, middle-class politicians, bureaucrats and intellectuals, a more serious venture would be to explore the philosophy, symbolism and theology of tolerance nascent in the faiths of citizens. Such a venture could be based on the hope that state systems in South Asia may learn something about religious tolerance from everyday Hinduism, Islam, Buddhism, and Sikhism, rather than wish that ordinary Hindus, Muslims, Buddhists and Sikhs will learn tolerance from various fashionable secular theories of statecraft.

III. The Heart of Darkness

The last point needs to be clarified, and I shall try to provide this clarification by putting my arguments in a larger psychological and cultural frame. The accompanying table gives an outline of the frame. It admits that the Western concept of secularism has played a crucial role in South Asian societies, it *has* worked as a check against some forms of ethnic intolerance and violence, it *has* contributed to humane governance at certain times and places.

By the same token, however, the table also suggests secularism cannot cope with many of the new fears and the intolerance of religions and ethnicities; nor can it provide protection against the new

[16] A comparable example from outside India will be the case study of the 1983 riots in Sri Lanka, in Veena Das (ed.), *Mirrors of Violence* (New Delhi: Oxford University Press, 1991).

Table 1. The Changing Nature of Ethnic/Religious Violence
and Counter-Ideologies

Sectors involved	Typical violence	Model of violence	Locus of ideology	Nature of motives	Effective counter-ideology
Non-modern, peripheralised believers	Religious wars	Traditional sacrifice of self or other	Faith	Passion	Critiques of faith/ agnosticism
Semi-modern zealots	Riots	Exorcism/ search for party	State	Passion and interest	Secularism
Modern rationalists	Manufa-tured riots, 'assembly-line' vio-lence	Experimen-tal science (vivisection), or industrial management	Bismarck-ian concept of state	Interest	Critiques of objecti-fication and decarlisation

forms of violence which have come to be associated with such intolerance; nor can secularism contain those who provide the major
justifications for calculated pogroms and ethnocides in terms of the
dominant ideology of the state.

These new forms of intolerance and violence are sustained by a
different configuration of social and psychological forces. The rub-
rics in the table allude both to these forces as well as to the growing
irrelevance of the broad models proposed by a number of important empirical social and psychological studies done in the fifties
and sixties—by those studying social distance in the manner of
Emory Bogardus, by Erich Fromm in his early writings, by Theodor Adorno and his associates working on the authoritarian personality, by Milton Rokeach and his followers exploring dogmatism,
and by Bruno Bettelheim.[17] The stereotyping, authoritarian submis-
sion, sadomasochism and heavy use of the ego defences of projection, displacement and rationalisation which went with

[17] Emory S. Bogardus, *Social Distance* (Yellow Springs, Ohio: Antioch
Press, 1959); Erich Fromm, *Escape from Freedom* (New York: Farrar and

authoritarianism and dogmatism, according to some of these studies, have not become irrelevant, as Sudhir Kakar shows.[18] There are resolute demonologies that divide religious communities and endorse ethnic violence. But these demonologies have begun to play a less and less central role in such violence. They have become, increasingly, one of the psychological markers of those participating in the mobs that are involved in rioting and pogroms, not of those planning, initiating or legitimising mob action.

This is another way of saying that planners, instigators and legitimisers of religious and ethnic violence can now be identified as secular users of non-secular forces and impulses in society. There is very little continuity between their motivational structures and that of the street mobs that act out the wishes of the organisers of a riot. Only, the mobs now represent—and that too partially—the violence produced by the predisposing factors described in the social-science literature of earlier decades. In place of these factors has come a new set of personality traits and defence mechanisms, the most important of which are the more 'primitive' defences such as isolation and denial. These defences ensure, paradoxically, the primacy of cognitive factors in violence over the affective and the conative.

The involvement of these ego defences in human violence was also first noticed in the 1950s and 1960s. But those who drew attention to these defences did so in passing (for instance Erich Fromm in one of his incarnations, and Bruno Bettelheim) or from outside the ambit of empirical social sciences (for instance Joseph Conrad and Hannah Arendt).[19] Moreover, these early analyses of

---

Rinehart, 1941); Bruno Bettelheim, *Surviving and Other Essays* (London: Thames and Hudson, 1979); T.W. Adorno *et al.*, *The Authoritarian Personality* (New York: Norton, 1950); Milton Rokeach, *The Open and Closed Mind* (New York: Basic Books, 1960).

[18] Sudhir Kakar, 'Some Unconscious Aspects of Ethnic Violence in India', in Das, *Mirrors of Violence*, pp. 135–45.

[19] Erich Fromm, *Anatomy of Human Destructiveness* (New York: Holt,

the 'new violence' were primarily concerned with 'extreme situations', to use Bettelheim's term, and not with the less technologised and less extreme violence of religious feuds or riots. Even when the violence these analyses dealt with did not directly involve genocide and mass murders, they involved memories of genocide and mass murders, as in the well-known book by Alexander and Margarete Mitscherlich.[20]

Only now have we become fully aware of the destructive potentials of the once-low-grade but now-persistent violence flowing from objectification, scientisation and bureaucratic rationality. The reasons for this heightened awareness are obvious enough. As the modern nation-state system and the modern thought machine enter the interstices of even the most traditional societies, those in power or those who hope to be in power in these societies begin to view statecraft in fully secular, scientific, amoral and dispassionate terms.[21] Modernist élites in such societies then begin to fear the divisiveness of minorities and the diversity which religious and ethnic plurality introduces into a nation-state. These élites then begin to see all religions and ethnic divisions as hurdles to nation-building and state-formation, and as dangers to the technology of statecraft and political management. New nation-states in many

---

Rinehart and Winston, 1973); Hannah Arendt, *Eichmann in Jerusalem* (New York: Viking, 1963); and *On Violence* (London: Allen and Unwin, 1969); Joseph Conrad, *Heart of Darkness* (Harmondsworth: Penguin, 1973).

[20] Alexander and Margarete Mitscherlich, *The Inability to Mourn: Principles of Collective Behaviour* (New York: Grove, 1984).

[21] That is, in terms of what Tariq Banuri calls the impersonality postulate in his 'Modernisation and its Discontents: A Cultural Perspective on the Theories of Development', in Frederique Apffel Marglin and Stephen Marglin (eds), *Dominating Knowledge: Development, Culture and Resistance* (Oxford: Clarendon Press, 1990), pp. 73–101. See also Ashis Nandy, 'Science, Authoritarianism and Culture: On the Scope and Limits of Isolation Outside the Clinic', in *Traditions, Tyranny and Utopias: Essays in the Politics of Awareness* (New Delhi: Oxford University Press, 1987), pp. 95–126.

societies tend to look at religion and ethnicity the way the nineteenth-century colonial powers looked at distant cultures that they came to dominate: at best as 'things' to be studied, engineered, ghettoised, museumised or preserved in reservations, at worst as inferior cultures opposed to the principles of modern living and inconsistent with the game of modern politics, science and development, and therefore deservedly facing extinction. No wonder the political cultures of South Asia have begun to produce a plethora of official social scientists who are perfect analogues of those colonial anthropologists who once studied the 'Hindoos' and the 'Mohammedans' on behalf of king and country.

This state of mind is the basic format of the internal colonialism at work today. The economic exploitation to which radical economists mechanically apply the epithet 'internal colonialism' is no more than a by-product of the internal colonialism I am speaking about. This colonialism validates the proposal, which can be teased out of the works of philosophers such as Hannah Arendt and Herbert Marcuse, that the most extreme forms of violence in our times come not from faulty passions or human irrationality but from faulty ideologies and unrestrained instrumental rationality. Demonology is now for the mobs; secular rationality is for those who organise, instigate or head the mobs: unless of course one conceptualises modern statecraft itself as a left-handed, magical technology and as a new demonology.[22]

As I have already said, this state-linked internal colonialism uses

[22]Thanks to a few photographs that a diplomat secretly shot, one image that persists in my mind of the anti-Sikh pogrom in Delhi in 1984 is of the scion of prominent family owning one of Delhi's most exclusive boutiques, directing with his golf club a gang of ill-clad arsonists. I suspect that the image has the potential to serve as the metaphor for the new forms of social violence in modern India. Also notice that, of the hundreds of published photographs of mobs destroying the Babri mosque, not one shows, to my knowledge, anyone wearing a dhoti—in a region where the dhoti is standard apparel among rural men.

legitimating core concepts like national security, development, modern science and technology. Any society—for that matter any aggregate—that gives unrestrained play or support to these concepts automatically gets linked to the colonial structure of the present-day world and is doomed to promote violence and expropriation, particularly of the kind that are directed against smaller minorities (such as tribals and indigenous peoples) which can neither hit back against the state nor avoid the modern market.

Secularism has become a handy adjunct to this set of legitimating core concepts. It helps those swarming around the nation-state, either as parts of the élite or of the counter-élite, to legitimise themselves as the sole arbiters among traditional communities, to claim for themselves a monopoly on religious and ethnic tolerance and political rationality. To accept the ideology of secularism is to accept the ideologies of progress and modernity as the new justifications of domination, and the use of violence to sustain these ideologies as the new opiates of the masses.

Gandhi, an arch anti-secularist—if we use the proper scientific meaning of the word 'secularist'—claimed that his religion was his politics and that his politics was his religion. He was not a cultural relativist and his rejection of the first principle of secularism—the separation of religion and politics—was not a political strategy meant to ensure his political survival in an uniquely multi-ethnic society like India. Indeed, sociologist Bhupinder Singh tells me that Gandhi may have borrowed this anti-secular formulation from William Blake. Whatever be its source, in some version or the other this formulation is becoming the common response of those who have sensed the new forms of human violence that have been unleashed by post-seventeenth-century Europe in the name of Enlightenment values. These forms of violence, which have already taken a toll of more than two hundred million human lives in the twentieth century, have come under closer critical scrutiny in recent decades mainly because they have come home to roost in the heart of Europe and North America, thanks to the Third Reich, the Gulag, the two World Wars, and the threat of nuclear annihilation.

Many modern Indians who try to sell Gandhi as a secularist find his attitude to the separation of religion and politics highly embarrassing, if not positively painful. They like to see him as a hidden modernist who merely used a traditional religious idiom to mobilise his unorganised society to fight colonialism. Nothing can be more disingenuous. Gandhi's religious tolerance came from his anti-secularism, which in turn came from his unconditional rejection of modernity. And he never wavered in his stand. Note the following exchange between him and a correspondent of the *Chicago Tribune* in 1931:

> 'Sir, twenty-three years ago you wrote a book *Hind Swaraj*, which stunned India and the rest of the world with its terrible onslaught on modern Western civilisation. Have you changed mind about any of the things you have said in it?'
>
> 'Not a bit. My ideas about the evils of Western civilisation still stand. If I republish the book tomorrow, I would scarcely change a word.'[23]

Religious tolerance outside the bounds of secularism is exactly what it says it is. It not only means tolerance of religions but also a tolerance that is religious. It therefore squarely locates itself in traditions, outside the ideological grid of modernity. Gandhi used to say that he was a *sanatani*, an orthodox Hindu. It was as a *sanatani* Hindu that he claimed to be simultaneously a Muslim, a Sikh and a Christian, and he granted the same plural identity to those belonging to other faiths. Traditional Hinduism, or rather *sanatan dharma*, was the source of his religious tolerance. It is instructive that the Hindu nationalists who killed him—after three unsuccessful attempts to kill him over twenty years—did so in the name of secular statecraft. That secular statecraft now seeks to dominate Indian political culture, sometimes in the name of Gandhi himself. Urban, Westernised, middle-class, Brahmanic, Hindu nationalists and Hindu modernists often flaunt Gandhi's tolerance as an

[23] Quoted in T.S. Ananthu, *Going Beyond the Intellect: A Gandhian Approach to Scientific Education* (New Delhi, Gandhi Peace Foundation, 1981), mimeo., p. 1.

indicator of Hindu catholicity but contemptuously reject that part of his ideology which insisted that religious tolerance, to be tolerance, must impute to other faiths the same spirit of tolerance. Whether a large enough proportion of those belonging to the other religious traditions show *in practice* and *at a particular point of time and place* the same tolerance or not is a secondary matter. Because it is the imputation or presumption of tolerance in others, not its existence, which defines one's own tolerance in the Gandhian worldview and praxis.

That presumption must become the major source of tolerance for those who want to fight the new violence of our times, whether they are believers or not.

CHAPTER 4

Coping with the Politics of Faiths and Cultures

Between Secular State and Ecumenical Traditions in India

By the 1980s India was at the threshold of a new phase in the politics of nationalities and religious violence. In the previous three decades, riots had increased six-fold (Figure 1) and casualties in such riots had increased nearly ten-fold. Given the nature of official data, both figures are probably under-estimates. This massive increase in violence brought home to the Indian literati and political activists what was already a platitude in some parts of the world: that modernisation in general, and economic development and the spread of the culture of modern science in particular, were no barriers against ethnic and religious violence. In fact, they sometimes stoked such violence. Since then, though in some years the toll has gone down, the country has not had a real respite.

This increase in violence is not distributed randomly. A large proportion of all violence takes place in six states—Andhra Pradesh, Bihar, Gujarat, Maharashtra, Rajasthan, and Uttar Pradesh. In four states, much violence is infrequent. In ten other states, virtually no riot ever takes place, not only showing the difficulty of formulating pan-Indian propositions, but also the difficulty of relating such propositions to the general content of faith. After all, many of the ten states that are almost entirely peaceful are inhabited by the

Figure 1. Decades-wise Rise in Rates of Communal Violence
in India (casualties per 1 million)

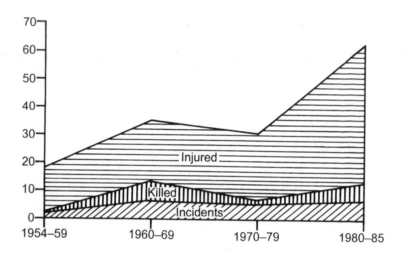

same religious communities. At least one of them, West Bengal,
underwent a communal holocaust in 1946–8. Also, in the two
states where separatist violence has broken out in recent years, there
has been no serious communal violence. In the Kashmir valley, few
Hindus are now left, though it was not so only a few years ago; so
the absence of riots there cannot be attributed to the absence of a
targeted minority. In Punjab, presumably fatigued by the massive
carnage during 1946–8, communal riots have not been a problem
at all during the last five decades, not even when Hindu–Sikh relations were at their nadir.

Within the ten states in which the bulk of riots take place, a vast
majority of the violence happens in cities. Of the deaths due to
communal violence in the last fifty years, only 3.6 per cent have

taken place in villages.[1] In addition, of all the deaths in cities, about half take place in eight riot-prone cities.[2] According to Gopal Krishna, of the 7964 incidents of communal violence between 1961 and 1970, only 32.55 per cent took place in rural India, though at the time roughly 80 per cent of Indians stayed in villages.[3] Data for recent years are not available, but Rajagopal says that 46 per cent of communal incidences in 1985 were rural.[4] That may have been an aberrant year; there are indications that rioting in villages is increasing at a much slower rate than in the cities, except probably in eastern India. However, it *is* growing, especially in villages close to cities; though if one goes by the place where riots originate, cities probably account for more than nine-tenth of all riots even today.[5]

Communal violence in India tends not merely to be concentrated in cities but, within cities, in industrial areas, where modern values are more conspicuous and dominant, and where secularisation and homogenisation of lifestyles have gone further. As Asghar Ali Engineer puts it in a moment of absent-mindedness, communalism is an urban phenomenon whose roots may be traced to the

[1] Ashutosh Varshney, 'Introduction', Civic Life and Ethnic Conflict, unpublished ms.

[2] Ibid.

[3] Gopal Krishna, 'Communal Violence in India: A Study of Communal Disturbance in Delhi', *Economic and Political Weekly*, 12 January 1985, 20, pp. 62–74; see p. 64.

[4] P.R. Rajagopal, *Communal Violence in India* (New Delhi: Uppal, 1987), p. 20.

[5] To be fair to the Indian experience, there is also the possibility that the Indian over-concern with religious and ethnic violence is partly a result of the over-concern with communal violence in the national media, particularly the publications that cater to the north Indian audience. Sukumar Muraliharan, 'Mandal, Mandir aur Masjid: "Hindu" Communalism and the Crisis of the State', in K.N. Panikkar, *Communalism in India: History, Politics and Culture* (New Delhi: Manohar, 1991), pp. 196–218, esp. pp. 206–18.

middle and lower classes; peasants, workers, and the upper-class élite are seldom affected by communalism.[6] Though recent experience has betrayed Engineer's winsome faith in workers, on the whole his formulation holds. Equally revealing are the causes of communal violence between 1961 and 1970 identified by the Home Ministry, Government of India. They show that a majority of riots during the period were triggered not by religious but secular conflicts (Table 1). If one excludes from consideration Bihar—a state chronically prone to rural violence, where 33.17 per cent of the riots over religious matters took place, almost all of them in villages—the trend becomes even clearer. Though a clear separation between the religious and the secular is not maintainable in any society, the data nonetheless hint at the growing ethnicisation of 'ordinary' social conflicts in India.

Table 1
Causes of Communal Violence in India, 1961–70 (N= 841)

Causes of violence	Per cent
Religious causes	
Festivity/celebrations	26.75
Cow slaughter	14.39
Desecration of religious places	4.04
Disputes over graveyards	2.14
Subtotal	47.32
Secular causes	
Private property disputes	19.26
Quarrels over women	16.89
Personal transactions, enmities, etc.	16.53
Subtotal	52.68
Total	100.00

Source. Adapted from Krishna, 'Communal Violence in India', p. 66.

[6] Asghar Ali Engineer, 'The Ideological Background of Communal Riots', quoted in Hussain Shaheen, 'Software and Hardware of Communalism', in Asghar Ali Engineer and Moin Shakir (eds), *Communalism in India* (Delhi: Ajanta, 1985), pp. 82–7, see p. 85.

These data are obviously not compatible with popular perceptions. Indeed, they seem to support the proposition that as the modernisation and secularisation of India have progressed, religious violence too has increased. It is a major paradox in contemporary India that religious passions now play a diminishing role in religious violence; money, politics and organised interests play a much more important part.[7] Could it be that communal violence in India, though wearing the garb of traditional hostilities, is a culturally distinctive expression of the same kind of free-floating 'anomic' violence that has been associated with industrial growth and urbanisation in other parts of the world? Can ethnic and religious strife in contemporary South Asia be seen as a part of the costs that must be paid for the modernisation and creation of a mass society in the region?

These questions contextualise the ways in which contemporary India has grappled with religious and ethnic violence, and adjusted its principles and practices of governance and civic life for the purpose. The main agency for such adjustments has been the Indian state, though in recent decades non-party political processes, represented by a whole range of political and social movements, have come to play an increasingly important role.

I

Broadly speaking, ethnic, cultural or religious differences and conflicts in politics have been handled in South Asia, particularly India, within three 'models', serving sometimes as implicit strategic frames for political and social intervention and sometimes as frames for popular interpretations of these differences and conflicts. These models constitute strands within the culture of Indian politics rather than well-formatted ideological streams. That is, while there

---

[7] See 'The Politics of Secularism and the Recovery of Religious Tolerance' in this volume.

may be some sophisticated academic statements associated with the three positions, they are basically meeting points between politics and its ideology, action and ideas, and theories of the state and self-aware statecraft.

Each of the models has its strengths. Each also has its distinctive pathologies and practical problems, both in terms of the political processes they endorse and the formulations they offer for public consumption. Also, while all three models have grown out of society's efforts to contain conflicts, they differ (a) in the extent to which they are respectful towards each other, (b) draw upon the long experiences of communities in coping with such conflicts, and (c) venture exclusive claims to social and political truths. They also differ in the way they are customised to meet local needs and local theories of violence.

The first of the three models can be called the centralised secular model. I deal with it first because it is the best known of the three and considered consistent with 'sane' and rational governance not only by important sections of the Indian middle class, but also by a majority of the country's social scientists. However, the model has rarely been tried out in its pristine form in Third World politics. The exceptions probably are a few aggressively modernising states (such as the Turkey of Kemal Ataturk, and for a while Gamal Abdel Nasser's Egypt) or self-righteous socialist states (such as the Soviet Union, Yugoslavia and China during the Cultural Revolution). Even in Latin America, the socialist states have usually had a complex relationship with the Catholic church; certainly their model of governance does not qualify as fully secular.[8] However, much of the

---

[8] Describing practices which have striking resemblance to some increasingly vestigial traditions in Indian politics, Richard Falk says in the context of a continent which may have more in common with South Asia:

> The revolutionary triumph in 1979 and subsequent twelve years of Sandinista government in Nicaragua involved the most significant fusion of Marxism and Christianity. . . . It was such a troublesome phenomenon for conventional Western thought that its reality was largely denied.

postcolonial world has borrowed its political categories not from living political realities in the West, but from Western texts and ideas that were exported to the tropics during the heyday of colonialism. The politics that contextualised the translation of texts and ideas into political practice and everyday culture of politics in the West, moderating the purism of formal political thought and scholarly convictions, never really fascinated the modern intelligentsia in the South. Naturally, the secular model is the one that the Third World intelligentsia and public figures in India have most aggressively propounded and, at every opportunity, demanded from their respective states.[9] Ideally, what they have in mind is some variation on the contemporary French model of secularism with the following near-canonical features:

At one stage in the mid-1980s Foreign Minister Miguel de'Escoto, one of four ordained priests among the nine top Sandinistas, requested a leave of absence so that he might fast in protest against the extension by Congress of further aid to the contras. Even if such an act is discounted as a gesture, it was a symbolically significant reflection by a supposedly radical, Marxist-oriented political movement of its renewed willingness to join arms with those who find religion at the centre of their personal and revolutionary being. Such a premodern form of political expression by a high government official alters the public understanding of political language, creatively implying the potency of nonviolent and religiously sanctified instruments of protest and resistance.

Richard Falk, *Explorations at the Edge of Time: The Prospects for World Order* (Philadelphia: Temple University Press, 1992), pp. 26–7. One only needs to add that not merely conventional Western thought but also imitative Western thought in the Southern world too have found such instances indigestible.

[9] An early and particularly usesful collection of essays on these lines is V.K. Sinha (ed.), *Secularism in India* (Bombay: Lalvani, 1968) which, despite sometimes excellent diagnoses of some of the central problems of secularism in India, is framed by the assumption that the concept or the ideology of secularism is not essentially a space- or time-bound concept. For a neat and typical exercise along these lines, see P.C. Chatterji, *Secular Values for a Secular India* (New Delhi: Lola Chatterji, 1984).

First, an area in society must be marked out and declared as secular (that is, outside the reach of religions and ethnicity). This area should include the state, politics in general, and large parts of civil society—especially the educational system, the sciences, and the economy. Religion and ethnicity may enter these sanitised areas, but they must do so stealthily—the stealth being subject to critical analysis by a whole range of people—from makers of public opinion such as newspaper columnists to political historians to deconstructionists. (From Vallabhbhai Patel to Sampoornanand, a large number of important public figures have been subject to such critical estimates, in life and in death.) This model expects that there will be a tacit, wide-ranging, political consensus on such sanitisation, and those flouting the consensus will be forced to either dishonestly explain away their behaviour as not deviating from a 'true' or 'genuine' secularism or hide their behaviour as a secret sin.

Second, the model presumes that, while there are many ways of being religious, there is only one way of being secular. So secularism in this model is identical with those secular trends which transcend social and cultural differences between communities, and which push towards a world where civil societies in different parts of the globe will eventually begin to look like one another. The presumption goes with the belief that as modern, secular institutions begin to impinge on the life of the non-secular citizenry in the Southern world, they destroy old communities but also build new ones. These new communities are called nationalities and sometimes, particularly when they create problems for the modern state, ethnicities. The modern state is expected to cope with the problem of nationalities, for it is believed to possess the necessary repertoire. It is expected cope with ethnicity less efficiently for, unlike nationality, ethnicity is seen as partly unmanageable within the modern state system. In both cases, the emphasis is on the citizen as an individual, and on an uncompromising denial of any idea of citizenship that links or locates the individual in a community with values adversarial to the modern state. Cultures are seen as basically unmanageable from the point of view of a modern state, unless one is talking of high culture—which is not seen as subversive of the state—and as something with which the élite, having access to the state, can establish some quid pro quo.[10] Consequently, cultures are often treated as nationalities and ethnicities by modern nation-states.

Third, the secular state, presiding over the secularised areas of society, is definitionally given the status of arbiter and ultimate court of appeal in inter-community disputes. Theoretically, until religious or ethnic conflicts persist in public life, but in practice in perpetuity. The state is also expected, in normal times, to take care of paranoic sentiments associated with fundamentalism and ethnic chauvinism. It is supposed to do this by ensuring transparent arbitration and management—better still, the transparent defiance of—nationalities and ethnicities in certain domains—especially law, national security, diplomacy, police and the military, and the professions.

In practice, this model of governance has met with a number of problems, some of them subversive of the long-term goals or concerns of the model. These problems can also be construed as costs that have to be paid by a polity that opts for the model. India, at this

[10] This, strangely enough, has often its obverse in the position taken by intellectuals that, though in a nation-state system the politics of nationalities is the most effective way of articulating demands and is something the nation-state system itself consistently and exclusively demands and promotes, practitioners of politics will somehow distance themselves from the political process, and articulate their demands, and organise their support-bases outside the framework of the politics of nationalities. Note the contradictory sentiments Syed Sahabuddin triggers in Indian politics.

These sentiments overlie another tacit consensus, among those playing the dangerous politics of nationalities, that politics in South Asia is a game of operating at the margins of society, and that people belonging to that liminal world, despite all the apparent clashes of interests, constitute a fraternity.

point of time, is paying this cost and that is probably why questions have arisen about the model at the peripheries of the culture of Indian politics.[11]

First, the secular state's efforts to transcend religious and ethnic differences is itself seen by sections of citizens in religious or ethnic terms. This is particularly true of communities which do not traditionally distinguish between the sacred and the profane in the public sphere, and are not modernised enough to have an adequate understanding/exposure to conventional statecraft. In some societies, absolute allegiance to modern political institutions and secular processes begin to look like absolute allegiance to Western culture, media, the global order of nation-states dominated by the West, and the Western knowledge industry (as happened in the Shah's Iran). The problem is aggravated in societies like India by the way in which the conceptualisation and organisation of the state ensures that a part of the discontent and anger against it rubs off on the ideology of the state and its various components, including secularism (as has happened in Algeria and Turkey). In India, too, there seems to be a certain tiredness with the ideology of the state; to many, it looks like a cover for an increasingly venal, crime-prone political class.

The consistent emphasis in post-World War II public culture, media and the social sciences on the Calvinist roots of Weberian modernity and capitalism, and on the Western philosophical roots of liberal democracy and human rights, further identifies the dominant culture of the state, including its version of ethnic tolerance, with Westernisation and deculturation. These connections have not been seriously challenged by the somewhat pathetic attempts

[11] In the peripheries because the space Hindu nationalism occupies in the mainstream culture of politics today is as an ideological movement that only challenges the misuse of secularism. In fact, Hindu nationalism has taken a lot of care to locate itself as the disowned 'genuine' self of secular nationalism and Indian modernism.

of Third World social scientists to distinguish between Western-isation and modernisation or by Third World despots talking of Confucian capitalism or Asian values.

The second major problem with the secular model is more serious. Once the secularisation of a society progresses beyond a certain threshold, its citizens begin to become uninterested in secularism as a sustaining political ideology. Often, this lack of interest turns into a fear of or active antipathy towards the ideology. The citizenry—as it begins to sense that their world is getting desacralised and being robbed of its older religious and cultural meanings—begins to fear the secularising thrust of modernity and begins to search, often desperately, for faiths, cultures and traditions to which they can be loyal. This reactive search often takes citizens to packaged forms of religiosity and ethnicity. Usually, and paradoxically, these forms derive strength from the modern—indeed secular—forms of religiosity and ethnicity, and are custom-made for those living in an urban-industrial world, and in situations of cultural flux or transition. It is remarkable how all the major ideological strains within Hindu nationalism have systematically derived core values from the standard ideology of the modern state, scientised history, and technocratic rationality. Equally remarkable is how almost all the pioneering thinkers, those whose enterprise made Hindu nationalism what it is today, had upper-caste, Westernised, professional backgrounds and scant concern with Hindu spirituality and faith.[12]

As these packaged ideologies look like and are sold as contemporary versions of ancient faiths, their appeal becomes irresistible

[12] Hence, probably, Gandhi's severe criticism and rejection of the Hindu reform movements in nineteenth-century India. As a serious counter-modernist, he identified and took seriously the modernist contents of these movements. See, on this theme, Ashis Nandy, Shikha Trivedy, Shail Mayaram and Achut Yagnik, *Creating a Nationality: The Ramjanmabhumi Movement and Fear of the Self* (Delhi: Oxford University Press, 1995).

to sections of the polity that are no longer deeply rooted in their culture or community. Attacks on some of these ideologies as extremist or fundamentalist versions of Hinduism or Islam further consolidate their stature as hard-core versions of religion.[13] Also, many forms of religious fundamentalism, being themselves progenies of the modern secular world, have a greater appeal for sections of citizens who suffer from doubts about their cultural and religious roots. Though they often elicit passionate allegiance, these forms of faith and piety are only a short step away from being political ideologies trying to pass off as faiths.[14]

Third, though the secular state is expected to remove the suspicions of the various ethnic and religious communities over which it rules, the paranoia of fundamentalists or religious and ethnic chauvinists often finds a new basis in the actions of the state, however secular.[15] Indian readers may remember the propaganda of the Sikh Brotherhood in the 1960s and the 1970s to the effect that the Indian state was anti-Sikh because the Indian army, which had been one-third Sikh, was by then only about one-fifth Sikh. This happened when the Sikh Brotherhood was trying to speak on behalf of a community that constituted roughly 1.5 per cent of the Indian population! But thanks to the Green Revolution, agriculture in

[13] Critiques of Hindutva, the reigning ideology of Hindu nationalism, are seen by important sections of Westernised or semi-Westernised Indians as attacks on Hinduism itself. The critics often see their target as a variant form of Hinduism, not as a political ideology. See for example, Nirmala Srinivasan, *Prisoners of Faith: A View From Within* (New Delhi: Sage, 1989).

[14] See on this theme, Nandy, 'The Politics of Secularism and the Recovery of Religious Tolerance'; and 'The Twilight of Certitudes: Secularism, Hindu Nationalism and Other Masks of Deculturation', in Ashis Nandy, *The Romance of the State and the Fate of Dissent in the Tropics* (Delhi: Oxford University Press, forthcoming).

[15] Tariq Banuri in fact doubts if ' plural society could exist without some perception of socio-economic discrimination among some of its members.' Tariq Banuri, 'Official Nationalism, Ethnic Conflict and Collective Violence', Sustainable Development Policy Institute, Islamabad, 1993, mimeo.

Punjab was getting industrialised during the period, leading to new forms of unemployment, dispossession, and cultural and territorial uprooting. The propaganda made sense to a lot of Sikhs.[16] Likewise, even though Muslims constitute less than 12 per cent of the Indian population and Hindus a little more than 82 per cent, many Hindu nationalists have felt provoked by what they see as the Indian state's consistent appeasement of minorities. Naturally, they have found the politics of the minorities unbearable and have even pleaded for their disenfranchisement. Others have come to believe that the birth rate of Muslims, combined with the leniency of the Indian state towards them, will turn Hindus into a minority in India within the next few decades.[17]

This suspicion is strengthened by the tendency of the state machinery, particularly at the lower levels, to turn blatantly partisan at times of communal or ethnic violence. This is so well known and widespread that it is almost an embarrassment to document it. To give only one instance, when nearly 4000 Sikhs were butchered or burnt on the streets of India's capital in 1984, the police filed only 359 instances of murder.[18]

Finally, the secular model, as usually propagated by crucial sections of the intelligentsia in South Asia, is simply unable to use the inner strengths of faiths and cultures that have for centuries co-survived in the subcontinent, by design or by default. In this experience of co-survival there have often been tensions, hostilities and violence, but also sophisticated adjustments and subtle reinterpretations of one's own faith and culture to accommodate the faiths and cultures of others. These adjustments and accommodations find no recognition in the ideology of secularism, its roots being in the European Enlightenment and in the mechanomorphic views of

[16] Vandana Shiva, *The Violence of Green Revolution: Ecological Degradation and Political Conflict in Punjab* (Dehradun: Vandana Shiva, 1989).

[17] Nandy, Trivedi, Mayaram and Yagnik, *Creating a Nationality.*

[18] N.S. Saksena, 'Brutalised India: Who Is to Blame?' *The Times of India,* 16 January 1991.

politics and society popularised by nineteenth-century Europe. Indeed, those allegiant to these models in contemporary times are prone to find such adjustments and accommodations either reactionary or retrogressive, or romantic and nonviable.

Understandably, most secular models heavily depend on the analysis of ideology to identify the sources of ethnic violence and fight them. Many influential explanations of communal riots in India stress communal ideology, believing that 'communalism as an ideology is the ultimate source of all communal riots.'[19] For some reason, the Indian state too has found such explanations congenial, and consistently tried to fight communal ideology, and the ethnic and religious stereotypes that go with it, as the final source of all religious and ethnic violence.

This fascination with ideology has many sources. Firstly, all political parties that have espoused the 'Hindu' or 'Islamic' cause have been heavily ideological. They have chosen to plead their case mainly on ideological grounds. Perhaps the stress on ideology makes organised violence against victim communities more palatable to the sections of the middle classes that have access to, or control over, the state machinery, the judiciary and the media. As a result, those who oppose such ideology have also come to look upon ideology as the prime mover of communal violence.

Second, communal ideology, though cast in the language of religion and tradition, is often crude, offensive and violent. When so, it makes excellent copy for the news media and creates a

---

[19] Rajagopal, 'Communal Violence', p. 20. See also Romila Thapar, Harbans Mukhia, and Bipan Chandra, *Communalism and the Writing of Indian History* (New Delhi: People's Publishing, 1969); and most of the papers included in Asghar Ali Engineer (ed.), *Communal Riots in Post-Independence India* (Hyderabad: Sangam Books, 2nd ed., 1991); and S. Gopal (ed.), *The Anatomy of a Confrontation: The Babri Masjid–Ram Janmabhumi Issue* (New Delhi: Viking, 1991). Neater examples are Akhilesh Kumar, *Communal Riots in India: Study of Social and Economic Aspects* (New Delhi: Commonwealth, 1991); and Srinivasan, *Prisoners of Faith*.

comfortable sense of distance between 'sane' modern citizens and 'irrational', bloodthirsty, atavistic fanatics who riot. When given massive publicity, communal ideology *can* be a triggering mechanism or organising principle in communal violence. Naturally, the spectators, the organisers and the perpetrators of such violence, all come to acquire a morbid fascination with ideology.

Thirdly, ideology is usually the most accessible part of a 'strange', unknown or distant collectivity, and most traditional communities are so from the point of view of the atomised, modern individual. An emphasis on ideology, therefore, gives outsiders a feeling that they have entered the mind of the ideologue and attained mastery over actions flowing from the ideology. In the case of communal ideologies, this accessibility and feelings of mastery come partly from the core concerns these ideologies share with modernity, even when the ideologies serve as internal critiques of modernity. Perhaps this is the reason why many interpretations of communal ideologies in India so easily become a play of liminalities and cross-projections, and an attempt by modernists to set up as an 'other' that which is an essential constituent of the self. It is painful to accept that the ideologue of communal hatred is basically a rejected part of the self and that most ideologues of communalism are, in that sense, not strange or unknown to the modern, secularised South Asian social scientist. For these social scientists, it becomes doubly necessary to first distance such an ideologue, and then, as a defensive strategy, bring him or her closer, safely ensconced in academic categories such as fundamentalism and fascism.

Strangely, this stress on ideology is often the forte of intellectuals who view human subjectivity as an artefact of more important political-economic factors, and communal divisions as a by-product of a history moving through evolutionary stages—from primordiality to modernity to postmodernity. The emphasis on ideology in such intellectuals sits uneasily upon the presumption that societies, like biological species, move from a more primitive stage encoded in traditions, towards a modern, secular humanism that de-ethnicises all communities. For such evolutionism, communalism defines an earlier stage of social development and is a throwback to such a stage, and the prognosis is that, with the forces of secular individualism gaining ground, communalism in South Asia will die a predictable death.[20] (Whether that death comes after one hundred years or five hundred is, of course, no one's concern!) For such a theory, communal ideology should be theoretically only a red herring.[21]

II

The second model, mainly a model of governance, is probably the most popular model in South Asian politics.[22] Certainly, it has been the dominant model in India throughout the last fifty years. Politicians pursue power and they are unlikely to pay heed to pure theories of politics ventured by academics and ideologues. So, irrespective of the ideological positions they often take for the consumption of their followers, when seriously in the business of power they

[20] This attitude is only an internalised version of the secular evolutionism that defines Western attitudes towards the non-West. 'Secularism once gave Western man and woman an assurance about their past that legitimated the extension of political and economic control over all traditional cultures and societies. The patterns of life of all traditional societies represented stages of human social development the West had transcended in its history. . . . All that the secular outlook admitted was a distinction in the form of domination: naked force as in chattel slavery or benign upliftment of the inferior according to the dictates of the master.' Ziauddin Sardar and Merryl Wyn Davies, *Distorted Imagination: Lessons from the Rushdie Affair* (London: Grey Seal and Kuala Lumpur: Berita, 1990), p. 243.

[21] For an example of such inner tension between communal ideology and political economy as the key explanatory variable, see Tapan Basu, Pradip Datta, Sumit Sakar, Tanika Sarkar and Sambuddha Sen, *Khaki Shorts Saffron Flags* (New Delhi: Orient Longman, 1993).

[22] On the medieval antecedents of the model, see Salim Kidwai, 'Precepts and Policy', *Seminar*, November 1995.

make compromises with cultures in some form or other. Sometimes, though proudly wedded to a pure theory of secularism,
ruling regimes in India have, as during the reign of Jawaharlal
Nehru at the Centre, or that of the Communist Parties in Kerala
and West Bengal, systematically flirted with the second model.
They have tried to 'manage' ethnic and religious sentiments, compromised with them, and occasionally even exploited them.[23]

This model tacitly admits that a modern state in a democratic
but predominantly non-modern society cannot afford to be purist.
An aggressively modern state can arouse immense antagonism and
rebelliousness, and compromise its own survival. However, this
model shares with the first a deep faith in the state, seen as representing the principles of rationality and progress. So these 'expe-
dient' compromises made with faiths and cultures are seen not as
failures of the state but as markers of its instrumental rationality in
negotiating an anachronistic culture of politics within a society as
yet unable to live with a fully secular public sphere. Because such
a state has to function in an open democratic society and because
the political parties running it have to function in a competitive
polity, the belief goes, they must adapt to the surviving primordial organisational principles: especially so, in the absence of self-
interest-based or contractual organisational principles that could
be politically mobilised.

Like the first model, though, this model expects that in the long
run such compromises will not be necessary. Firstly because the
state will have become more powerful and entrenched; secondly because citizens will get politically socialised to the idea of secular
statecraft; and thirdly because non-traditional divisions will have
become more legitimate and politically exploitable or viable. The
compromise, however, is usually ad hoc and arbitrary and guided
by political expediency, for it is not seen as part of an old heritage

---

[23] As, for instance, in carving out Muslim-majority districts and constituencies and in building a dedicated, sectarian support-base among specific
primordial communities.

which legitimises the mutual accommodation of state and society. On the contrary, all adjustments to the society, culture or religion are seen as deviations, however justified in the short run, from rational, informed statecraft.

Sometimes, however, under the influence of this model, such adjustments cross—by design or otherwise—the limits set by the ideology of secularism and even the ideology of the nation-state. Thus, in its early years the Indian state tolerated not only the burning of the Constitution and the Indian flag by the DK and DMK movements, but even floats taken out in Tamilnadu in which excited, almost hysterical, supporters of the movements symbolically beat the icons of Rama and Lakshmana with sandals. The assumption was that such hatred towards the religious beliefs of others would end with the passage of time and that people would learn not to bring it into public life. Likewise, at different times the Indian government has found it possible to make a deal with the likes of Farooq Abdullah in Kashmir (who for a while, it is said, was not even an Indian citizen) and Laldenga in Mizoram (when he was the self-declared general of a separatist, rebel army). Many found the deals compromising the dignity of the state and an encouragement to subnational ethnic identities. Others, however, saw in them a triumph of the political skills of the ruling party and Prime Minister Indira Gandhi, if not of Indian nationalism and secularism.

Such transgressions of the set ideals of the standardised nation-state are becoming rarer, though. One Pakistani ambassador to India was reportedly the first to have represented a country that he knew nothing about; he was recruited from India and joined duties in India. To crown such deviations from the standardised format of a nation-state, Rabindranath Tagore, author and composer of India's national anthem, is certainly the only person—and is likely to remain so—to have authored the national anthems of two countries and to have scored the music of a third.

Such instances are now viewed as markers of an immature nation and a not fully formed state. The expectation is that, as national selves get well-defined, they become more exclusive. The expectation has not been belied; national boundaries *are* hardening in South Asia. Indeed, today, even marriages taking place across national boundaries (say, between Muslims of India and Bangladesh or Tamils of India and Sri Lanka) can be seen as a betrayal of the nation or instances of extra-territorial loyalty.[24] Yet most ordinary citizens probably continue to see themselves as having a plural self. Many communities see themselves as simultaneously Hindu and Buddhist, Hindu and Muslim, and Hindu and Christian.[25] This is neither an instance of multiculturalism nor of, as properly educated Indians like to call it, syncretism. It seems to be the case of a society where identities are cross-cutting and the 'others' are telescoped into one's own self, and where none of the identities can be adequately depicted or defined without the presence of the others.

The second model too, then, is based on the assumption that both nationalism and the state have a universal sociology, if not politics. Like the first model, it also sees any deviation from this universality as a climb-down and a compromise with local atavistic forces. Certainly it does not see existing community traditions—or the religions around which they are organised or the idiom of cultural politics they use—as a heritage or baseline that could be used for building a more humane, open, culturally grounded polity. Only, unlike the first model, the second is sensitive regarding dangers to the survival of a modern state in a traditional society organised around religion. So, on political grounds, the second model accommodates the sentiments of the citizenry, feared and redefined as a less-than-mature electorate. That accommodation is seen as a part of clever, pragmatic, if amoral politics.

[24] The unacknowledged hero of such loyalists would be someone like the young Muslim cricket enthusiast in Bhopal who killed his own brother for supporting the Pakistani cricket team playing against the Indians during the 1996 World Cup in cricket.

[25] See for instance, K. Suresh Singh, *Peoples of India* (Calcutta: Anthropological Survey of India, 1994), vol. 1.

In practice, this is a broad model within which most important political decisions in India have been taken during the last fifty years. This, and not the first model—basically an ideological posture meant for political skirmishes in newspapers or in academe— has now begun to show signs of collapse. The first model faltered from the beginning. It is the collapse of the second model that has left a major void in the culture of Indian politics, which is now being sought to be filled by Hindu nationalism.

The collapse of the second model has been triggered by two main political forces. First, exactly as the rulers have tried to respect or at least compromise with religious or ethnic sentiments as part of impersonal, secular statecraft, those making demands on the state in the name of religion or ethnicity have also gradually begun to come from the secularised, modern citizenry. Religious and ethnic demands in India are increasingly being made by professional politicians trying to aggregate public sentiments that are non-secular. Often, these sentiments do not even exist; they are provoked or generated as part of electoral politics and support mobilisation. As a result, the model has ensured that the visible political domain is gradually occupied by fully secularised political actors speaking in the name of religious or ethnic communities. The conventional descriptive terms for such politics is the politics of nationality. As I said, up to a point a modern state is comfortable with such politics because it is played according to rules that are known to all shades of professional politicians.

Second, an accommodative gesture by the state or the ruling party towards those articulating religious or ethnic demands is sometimes seen as a compromise made by a weak state. It tends to escalate sectarian demands. It can be argued, for example, that the movement for the demolition of the Babri mosque was, towards the end, more a response to the perceived weakness of the Indian state than to popular sentiments.[26] This process is further strengthened

---

[26] Nandy, Trivedi, Mayaram and Yagnik, *Creating a Nationality.*

by the tendency of the model to presume that fundamentalists and ethnic chauvinists are the 'natural' if extremist leaders of a religious or ethnic community. Because this model operates with a limited understanding of religion and culture, the breach between a traditional faith and a modern religion-based ideology is not obvious to it.[27] This presumption of a natural leadership further legitimises those expressing sectarian demands and their ideologies, and gives them priority over less politicised but more respected religious leaders and even the preferences of the ordinary, believing citizenry.

A sub-category of this model tries to bypass all political expressions of religious and ethnic sentiments in politics in the belief that

[27] Perhaps a clarification is in order here. Some Marxist friends, reared ⌐
a staple diet of Marx's and Mannheim's concept of ideology, have bee·
comfortable with this distinction between faith and ideology, especi⌐ ´
context of the Left Hegelian view of religion as the ultimate ℯ·
ideology. I am here distinguishing, following standard social ·
age, between two structures of consciousness organised ⌐
dynamic principles. To get a rough idea of this stanᵈ
under 'Ideology' in *The Encyclopaedia of Social Sc·*
1968), vol. 7, pp. 66–85. This definition of ·
tical theory. For instance, the followinℊ·
cally-charged beliefs and expressior
world in a way designed to shapℯ
modes or courses of action ᵃ⌐
logy', in David Miller (ℯ ´
(Oxford: Basil Blacᵏ
language, the sᵃ⌐
drawn in A. Γ
and Politics: St.
at the Indo-Frenᴄ
Sense of Belonging',
2 November 1995, miɳ

democratic politics and the game of numbers should more or less automatically take care of the problem of religious and ethnic violence. This is not as cynical as it seems at first. Certainly, in India the model has often performed famously in the face of very dedicated attempts to exploit religious sentiments and ethnic wrath in politics. One of the best recent examples of this is that, within a few months of the demolition of the Babri mosque, in the March 1993 elections, Hindu zealots lost eight of the nine assembly constituencies comprising Faizabad district, where the mosque was located. All the constituencies had a heavy preponderance of Hindus. Electoral politics has a logic of its own, which sometimes converges with—and at other times negates—the politics of passion that temporarily dominates a polity. The 1993 elections were no exception. In Tamilnadu, once the Dravidian movement had established its political dominance, separatism was voluntarily given up, presumably because it had already done its job in the matter of mass mobilisation, electoral empowerment, and democratisation. It will not be surprising if the Hindu chauvinist parties also begin to sing a different tune once they have a stake in the system. This has already happened in the case of the Islamicist parties in Pakistan and Bangladesh, whose vote share has dropped dramatically in recent years.

There is also the logic of enumerative politics that allows a [mino]rity, if it is moderately inspired by community consider[ations] to exercise a certain political clout. Twelve per cent Muslims in the Indian polity and eleven per cent Hindus in the Bangladesh [...] in many ways, an analogous role. In both cases, they [...] capacity to crucially tilt the electoral scales in favour of [...] the other. And in both cases, zealots have campaigned

— [...]pt into my use of the term 'ideology'. Ideology, I now tend [...]s associated with a certain ambivalence or even contempt [tow]ards the supposed beneficiaries of the ideology. Funda[...]alent towards the ordinary believer; feminists towards [...]ds the proletariat.

e of an
ological us-
ng to different
e, see the entrie
New York: Macmilla
gy is not unknown to F
ogies are patterns of sym
esent, interpret and evalu
ase, direct, organise and justif
athematise others.' David Kett
e Blackwell Encyclopaedia of Politi
987). In a different context and us
nction between ideology and faith h
ustine, V.D. Savarkar, and Mahatma G
amaraju, 'Perspectives on the Relation
Colloquium on 'The Representatio
tre for the Study of Developin
I must however admit that

from the platform that there has been an appeasement of minorities by the party or parties in power. While this charge of appeasement often becomes an electoral issue in both countries, by itself it rarely reduces the clout of the minority. Usually, that clout can be used to moderate and tame zealots when they come to power. For in enumerative politics, even zealots show an uncanny attachment to power and the accoutrements of the modern state, however strong their declared belief in the transience, immorality or irrelevance of modern state and its secular power.[28]

As a technique of governance, this model does not have well-defined borders. It casts its shadow on, and is sometimes influenced by, other models. For practising politicians, it also serves as a fall-back position if they know, or at least sense, the power and psychological pull of the model. Like zealots, once they come to power they rarely rethink the modern concept of the nation-state or abjure modern technology while fighting for their cause. Enumerative politics—competitive politics based on the game of numbers—has the seductive power of dissolving ancient and contemporary animosities, alliances and ideologies.

It is against the backdrop of this model that structural factors, such as the geography of Hindu-Muslim violence, become part of the political landscape of the country. Witness how the spatial concentration of Muslims, for instance, has got intertwined with ethnic violence in India. This intertwining is not merely a direct product of the model but can even be read as one of the major problems it throws up.

Muslims are the largest religious minority in India. They probably constitute the world's second largest Muslim community.

[28] One remembers in this connection Gandhi's notorious advice to minorities, during the partition of British India into India and Pakistan, to stay put in their native land despite the pogroms and the discriminations. The politically creative possibilities of culturally plural polities were sensed by one whom his first serious antagonist, General J.C. Smuts (1870–1950), would have described as the most wily saint of our times.

Only Indonesia, with 153 million Muslims, boasts a larger settlement of Muslims. However, they are not distributed randomly; their proportion varies from state to state and seems to bear no relationship with the level of communal violence in a state (Figure 2). But the relationship changes when one shifts to cities, where more than 90 per cent of riots still reportedly originate. While Muslims are roughly 11.4 per cent of the Indian population, they are about 16.3 per cent of urban India. Also, the cities which have a higher rate of communal violence do tend to have larger proportions of Muslims (Figure 3).

It is possible that the places where Muslims are numerically

Figure 2. Proportion of Muslims in Riot-prone States

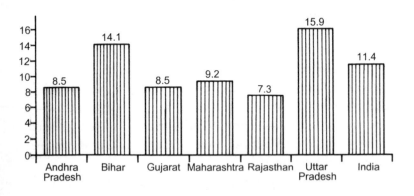

Source: Census of India: Household Population by Religion of Head of Household (New Delhi: Registrar General and Census Commissioner, India, 1984), pp. 2–25.

Figure 3. Hindus and Muslims in
Chronically Riot-prone Cities (per cent)

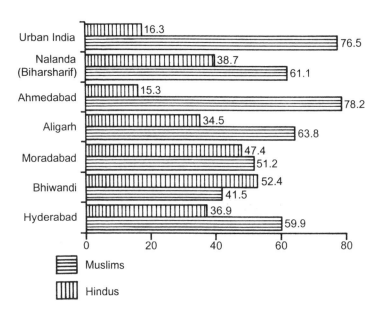

Source: Adapted from Rajagopal, *Communal Violence*, p. 19.

strong, and can take advantage of competitive democratic politics
to assert their rights, are more prone to communal violence. In such
places it is possible to mobilise larger sections of the majority community against the 'uppity' minorities and exploit the stereotype of
socio-economically aggressive ethnic groups exploited, taking advantage of their political clout to pose a threat to the social order 'naturally' dominated by the majority. There is scattered support for such
a formulation in the reports on riots in places like Moradabad,
Aligarh, Ahmedabad, Etawah and now Bombay. Often, riots in
such cities are not confined to random acts of violence; they end up

heavily damaging the socio-economic life-support systems of Muslims. The victims of riots, too, now seem to be aware of this. [29]

This linkage does not explain away the role of stereotypes, folk sociologies, and subjective 'justifications' for communal violence at the community level; indeed, it feeds upon them. Thus, in some metropolitan cities where Muslims are a sizeable proportion of the population, large sections of Muslim youth are unemployed or under-employed. Either due to poor access to modern skills, including modern education (borne out by the available data) or social discrimination (more difficult to document for the unorganised sector and the self-employed). They become easy recruits for criminal gangs and for vocations that are free from discrimination, such as smuggling, illicit distillation, and drug-pushing. This allows the negative stereotypes of minorities fuller play in such cities, and fear and anger against urban crime feed into communal hostilities. In many instances, such criminal elements precipitate riots by the very nature of their activities, as also by their attempts to redeem themselves in the eyes of their community by aggressively taking up the community's cause. There is some indirect support for the proposition in Krishna's data, which show that as much as 35.79 per cent of cases of communal riots are directly triggered by personal conflicts of various kinds (Table 1).[30] The existence of similar

[29] See for instance Ajay Singh, 'Mafia Politics led to Etah Violence', *The Times of India*, 9 December 1990; and Asghar Ali Engineer, *Delhi-Meerut Riots* (Delhi: Ajanta, 1987). Also Radhika Ramaseshan, 'A Date with Destiny', *The Pioneer*, 23 March 1992. In 1986 in Ahmedabad, for the first time, the Akhil Hindu Sanatan Samaj publicly gave a call to boycott Muslim shops; some pamphlets openly suggested that the Muslims should be 'killed' economically. See Nandy, Trivedi, Mayaram and Yagnik, *Creating a Nationality*, ch. 4. On the victims' perception, see Banu, *The Politics of Communalism* (London: Sangam Books, 1992), summarised in Table 4.

[30] Cf. Veena Das's proposition regarding the transient status enjoyed by those marginal to, or placed low in the social hierarchy, as heroic defenders of faith during communal violence. Veena Das, 'Introduction: Communities, Riots, Survivors—The South Asian Experience', in *Mirrors of Violence:*

marginal sections within the majority community not merely ensures a proper riot, it can also sometimes trigger one of the most feared forms of riot—the ones in which the slums explode.

While such formulations are politically incorrect and have not been explored by scholars and human rights activists fearful of compromising their secular credentials, they have been systematically used by grassroots workers of Hindu nationalist parties and organisations. The stereotype of Muslim aggressiveness, the perceived tendency in fanatic lumpen proletariat elements among the Muslims to precipitate communal clashes, and their disproportionate involvement in urban crime (either on account of their poorer access to the usual channels of employment, or marginalisation) are all popular themes in the mobilisations that precede a communal riot. These themes are also systematically used in *post facto* justifications of riots: they are offered for the consumption of the newspaper-reading public. As a result, Indian society has not been prepared for the vague consensus towards which American society has moved—namely that blacks, though they usually start race riots and other forms of racial violence, are pushed to do so by an oppressive social situation.

The mobilisation preceding communal violence is important also because it is now a part of 'normal' politics. Few social processes have contributed as handsomely to communal violence as the demands of competitive mass politics. These demands have turned communal violence into another form of organised politics. After all, communal attitudes by themselves do not lead to violence in a politically ill-organised society. The violence has to be specifically organised by groups keen to politically encash the fall-out of such violence. Those who organise the violence or encash it politically are not necessarily communal. They can even be fully secular in

Communities, Riots, Survivors in South Asia (New Delhi: Oxford University Press, 1990), pp. 1–36. Also see Sudhir Kakar, *The Colours of Violence* (New Delhi: Viking, 1997).

personal life and in political planning and be in league with politicians of even the victim communities. Engineer neatly sums up this part of the story when he says, 'the politicians are the principal and anti-social elements, at their beck and call, the subsidiary agents in promoting and inciting communal violence.'[31] He only ignores the impersonality and professionalism that have come to characterise such violence. Many key figures in communal riots should be willing to claim that there is nothing personal about the vocational responsibilities they have to bear. Communal riots *have* become over the years one of the most secularised aspects of Indian public life.

There is an elaboration of this part of the story in Zenab Banu's informative, if ponderous, book based on a study of riots in Udaipur and Ahmedabad.[32] She suggests that the nexus between political parties, urban crime and riots is viewed differently by different sections of the people, by the spectators and victims of riots, the Hindus and the Muslims. Crudely, while politicians and the intelligentsia seem to stress the involvement of criminals in riots, the victims seem to lay more stress on the involvement of politicians. Likewise, the Hindus perceive much greater participation by 'anti-social elements' in riots; the Muslims see a bigger role of political parties (see Table 2).

III

I now come to the third model. It is written up skeletally, as a political preface to a possible programme of research.

In this third model the 'patrimony' in the matter of interreligious or inter-ethnic understanding is acknowledged, selfconsciously or unwittingly. It is assumed that in a participatory

[31] Asghar Ali Engineer, 'Bombay-Bhiwandi Riots—A National Perspective', in Engineer and Shakir, *Communalism in India*, pp. 205–14, see p. 205. Also Dilip Simeon, 'Power at any Price is Communalism's Worst Legacy', *The Times of India*, 26 March 1990; and A.D. Bhogle, 'Communal Violence as a Political Weapon', *The Independent*, 14 December 1990.

[32] Banu, *Politics of Communalism*.

Table 2. Perceived Role of Political Parties and
Criminals in Riots in Two Cities (per cent)

Category	N	Ahmedabad Party volunteers	Ahmedabad Anti-social elements	N	Udaipur Party volunteers	Udaipur Anti-social elements
Riot victims	30	40.0	73.3	30	80.0	83.3
Intellectuals	25	56.0	80.0	25	60.0	80.0
Student	25	64.0	84.0	25	40.0	72.0
Politicians	25	36.0	84.0	25	40.0	80.0
Religious leaders/ Social workers	15	53.3	86.6	15	86.6	66.6

Source: Zenab Banu, *Politics of Communalism*, Table 7, pp. 105–6.

Table 3. Hindu and Muslim Perceptions of Main Activists
in Udaipur and Ahmedabad Riots (per cent)

Category	N	Party volunteers	Anti-social elements	Poor, beggars	Lower classes
Hindu	159	44.16	91.19	61.10	59.12
Muslims	121	70.24	58.68	41.32	40.50
Total	280	53.21	77.14	52.50	51.10

Source: Adapted from Zenab Banu, *Politics of Communalism*, Table 7a, p. 107.

democracy, however imperfect, citizens will employ categories and interpretative frames in the public sphere known to them through their heritage, in turn transmitted through religious, community and family traditions. The deployment of such categories and frames is not usually a well-thought-out cognitive choice; most people using them live in a world defined by these categories. Even more important, the model recognises that the right to use such categories and frames cannot be snatched away from those who use them by law, clever sloganeering, or the use of the coercive apparatus of the state. Indeed, others in a minority, even when convinced that they have a better set of categories, are compelled by the logic of the political process to learn either to hitch their own categories to the popular ones, or to use the language of which these popular categories are a part.

These odd formulations subsume the awareness that large parts of Indian society still do not use the language of the Indian state and have no access to the idiom of secular politics. They also cannot imagine separating their religious and political lives, and do not feel morally obliged to do so. They are serious believers, and yet they do resist communal violence on the basis of their religious sensitivities, everyday morality, and plain commonsense. Evidently, the paradoxical consequences of building an 'ethnically blind system of constitutional representation', as Darini Rajasingham describes it in another context, have not dramatically altered their consciousness as yet.[33] ·

The model, never tried out at the national level in South Asia in this century, was a crucial component in the Gandhian freedom struggle and informed much of pre-independence and post-independence politics at the grassroots levels. Even the much maligned Khilafat movement, usually seen as misguided encouragement given to mullahs by Gandhi, can be read as his attempt to recognise the role of communities, community leadership and traditions in the public life of a deeply religious society. Perhaps it can be proposed that the relative absence of religious and ethnic strife in India's countryside is primarily the gift of this model, functioning as an important component of a surviving worldview.[34] The model,

---

[33] Darini Rajasingham, 'Proposal for the Study of State Manangement of Ethnicity and Local Models of Multiculturalism and Co-Existence in Sri Lanka', paper presented at the meeting of the Culture and Identity Project at the International Centre for Ethnic Studies, Colombo, 8–9 July 1995.

[34] It is one of the paradoxes of South Asian political experience that Gandhi, who was dismissive towards anyone who sought to keep apart religion and politics, is the patron-saint of a country that has sustained the ideology of secularism as a state policy much better than Pakistan, a country which has as its patron-saint Mohammed Ali Jinnah, who was primarily a classical liberal willing to concede much less public space to religions theoretically.

Table 4. Perceived Targets of Attack during Riots in
Udaipur and Ahmedabad (per cent)

Category	N	Residen-tial places	Residen-tial colonies	Commercial establish-ments	Markets	Women, children
Udaipur						
Riot Victim	30	20.0	100.0	66.0	10.0	13.3
Politicians	25	20.0	80.0	28.0	24.0	32.0
Intellectuals	25	12.0	96.0	32.0	16.0	56.0
Students	25	36.0	80.0	36.0	24.0	40.0
Labourers	20	30.0	90.0	40.0	25.0	30.0
Religious leaders/ social workers	15	46.6	100	13.3	26.6	40.0
All respondents	140	25.7	90.7	28.5	20.0	34.2
Ahmedabad						
Riot Victim	30	63.0	83.0	30.0	96.0	81.0
Politicians	25	52.0	60.0	36.0	84.0	76.0
Intellectuals	25	56.0	64.0	24.0	96.0	60.0
Students	25	60.0	48.0	52.0	96.0	72.0
Labourers	20	70.0	65.0	45.0	15.0	47.0
Religious leaders/ social workers	15	60.0	73.3	20.0	93.3	66.7
All respondents	140	58.5	65.0	35	93.5	68.5

Source: Adapted from Zenab Banu, *Politics of Communalism*, Table 9.

on its part, probably derives political strength from the tacit awareness in many sections of South Asian society that it has not only
often worked in the past but has also helped restore inter-communal relations after violent upheavals. It did so even after the holocaust of 1946–8. In different times that worldview has been
represented by larger-than-life individuals such as Khan Abdul
Ghaffar Khan in Pakistan and populist leaders like Maulana Bhasani in Bangladesh.

Today, even in urban India this model seems to provide a touch
of restraint in cases of religious and ethnic violence. Banu's data
on the perceptions of the main targets of communal violence in
Udaipur (a relatively less industrialised city, less susceptible to

communal violence in a riot-prone state) and Ahmedabad (an industrial city infamous for its chronic susceptibility to communal violence since the riots there in 1969) hint at this. Though the intelligentsia, which includes the press in this case, and the politicians in her sample do not seem to differ noticeably in their perceptions of how far women and children are targeted in their cities, the riot victims in the two cities differ dramatically in this respect (Table 3). Udaipur, they seem to hint, has still not been as brutalised by the experience of violence as Ahmedabad.

Though rarely brought into national politics successfully, as happened during the 1920s and 1930s, the model either redefines secularism or underplays or drops the idea of secularism altogether, so as to self-consciously accommodate non-secular modes/codes of tolerance in faiths and cultures and then empowers these categories through political movements that do not feel obliged to make full sense or be transparent to the modern world. As it happens, a political movement, to survive politically and be accessible to the citizenry, cannot afford to be choosy; it has to establish some *quid pro quo* with the available cultural strains within a polity. The third model makes a virtue of this constraint. Often practised by the large state systems in pre-colonial India, the model was also used intermittently by the British colonial state during the first seventy-five years of the Raj, when it was trying to survive intuitively in what it saw as alien cultural terrain (before the Utilitarians convinced the British-Indian state that such alien cultures were in reality perfectly familiar as Asian versions of Europe's dark ages). The colonial state was in its first phase willing to learn, from the experience of its predecessors in empire-building, that this model empowered—and itself derive power from—the codes of mutual understanding or tolerance that had come to characterise the major religious traditions in the subcontinent.

Such accommodations can be politically creative in any society; they are not unique to South Asia. Ali Mazrui gives the example of Leopold Senghor who, though belonging to a small Christian minority in a predominantly Muslim society, happily ruled Senegal for more than two decades without arousing anxiety in the majority.[35] However, something that does not arouse anxiety in Africa may be a source of much distress to the South Asian élite—particularly if one reads Senghor's instance not as a cute example of pre-modern proto-secularism but as an indicator of alternatives to the ideology of secularism that exist in many cultural traditions. When read as an instance of primitive secularism, from within the framework of standard anthropological or cultural-historical studies of communities, such proto-secularism appears politically safe and is encouraged by the Indian state and the academic establishment. A large number of such studies are in fact being done all over India. However, as an important factor in the culture of Indian politics or as a principle of governance, the third model no longer remains a politically correct instance of so-called incipient or proto-secular formations, but becomes a direct threat to the established wisdom in modern governance. It seems to snatch all political initiative from the state (seen as a predominantly rational agency, providing justifiably greater access to the social classes wedded to the state's version of rationality) and hands it over to society (seen as fundamentally flawed by its accommodation of and openness to more atavistic political strains).

Politics does not yield perfect solutions; it is the art of the possible, as the old cliché goes. This model, too, has two identifiable problems. First, when wedded to competitive democratic politics, it sometimes arouses deep anxieties in ethnic minorities. As majority values and symbols get increasingly encoded into mainstream

[35] Ali A. Mazrui, 'The Impact of Modernisation on Political Development: How Power Structures Respond to Change', Lecture at the Symposium on Transitions of Power: Perspectives from the Post-Colonial World, Asia Society and Centre of Asian Studies, Hong Kong, 20 May 1994.

political culture, they begin to look to the vocal middle class and the media, not as aspects of the culture of the majority but as national values and symbols. This threatens the minorities, who become more defensive about their cultures, including those parts of culture they themselves were previously careless about or which they themselves would probably have jettisoned. The ambivalence in some sections of intellectuals in India and Pakistan towards Vivekananda and Gandhi, as leaders who successfully introduced religious symbols in pre-Independent Indian politics, is a good instance of this political process. One wonders if a similar ambivalence towards the dalit movement would have developed if its ultimate symbol had become not B.R. Ambedkar but Jyotiba Phule or Narayan Guru.

On the other hand, any threat to majority values also, after a while, begins to look like an anti-national act. Even social reforms once possible become politically untenable as 'intolerable interference' in community life and matters of faith, especially when they are supported by outsiders who are known as hostile to the community. In the process, even political attempts to balance one kind of ethnicity and another is often forgotten. For instance, the special tax privileges of the Hindus under the name of the Hindu undivided family are often forgotten by Hindu-nationalist zealots when they criticise the state's attempts to mollycoddle Muslims in the matter of Muslim Personal Law.

Secondly, as the proportion of urban, media-exposed, partly decultured, middle classes grow in a polity, the appeal of a model such as this declines. Given its heavy dependence on surviving community ties and cultural roots, not only does it seem to bypass the state sector and the instrumentality of the nation-state, it also looks like an effort to politically marginalise the modernised sectors of society. It naturally arouses deep anxieties in that part of the bourgeoisie that processes such ideologies for the tertiary sector.

However, as the model has never been tried out seriously at the national level in independent India, it is probably premature to identify the specific problems it might pose if used as a principle of governance. In fact, it may be more useful to discuss its roots in Indian society and how its possible cultural location can be examined.

The frame or model—I use these expressions reluctantly and in the absence of better words—has to depend heavily on existing codes of inter-community relations and the sanctions for such relations in local traditions, customary laws, religious heterodoxy, existing cosmological visions and alternative traditions of cosmopolitanism that have shaped India's encounter with the European Enlightenment and modernity.

First, the *jajmani* system in India itself, however flawed it might otherwise be, has traditionally provided a powerful countervailing force to the forces of communalism.[36] The caste system does frame—some would say infect—not only Hinduism but all major faiths in India. Castes often cut across religions; they have porous and fuzzy borders, complex relationships with each other, and spill over ethnic boundaries. For instance, castes such as Jats and Rajputs, two of the most politically important and powerful castes in northern India, come in three varieties: Hindus, Muslims and Sikhs. They do not inter-marry and inter-dining is limited, but they do retain highly nuanced, complex relationships among themselves which simultaneously preserve their separate religious identities while consolidating their Jat or Rajput identity. Other castes divided by religion may go further. Not only is inter-religious marriage

[36] M.N. Srinivas, presentation on '*Grambharat*', at *Samskritishivira* (workshop on cultural studies) organised by Ninasam, Heggodu, Karnataka, 10–20 October 1994.

possible among them, till recently it was preferred.[37] Similar examples are available in practically every part of India.

Some castes and communities, on the other hand, have developed bicultural identities which involve a 'hierarchically ordered' religious selfhood. Thanks to scholarly work, such as that of Shail Mayaram, we now know how rich and resilient this tradition is in certain communities.[38] Tracing their ancestry from the Mahabharata clans, the Meos, the community that Mayaram has studied, have continued to live a rich Islamic life within a cultural frame which would today be called 'Hindu' by modern South Asians—a fact which is simultaneously a source of deep anguish to fundamentalist Muslims and movements like Tabligh, and to Hindu nationalist formations like the Rashtriya Swayam Sevak Sangh and the Vishwa Hindu Parishad. In recent decades a series of dramatic events, such as Partition, and the political emergence of movements trying to sharply define the cultural boundaries of religions have put Meo identity, myths and cosmological codes under severe stress. But traditional Meo religious and cultural life is not yet dead, even though younger sections of the community are now trying to redefine Meo identity to make it conform to the conventional, increasingly standardised, dominant, modern, global concept of religion and of the Muslim.[39] Perhaps the most dramatic instance of such bicultural traditions are those of the More Salam Rajputs, who continue

[37] Shail Mayaram, 'On Being a Muslim', presented at the Indo-French Colloquium on The Representations and Uses of the Sense of Belonging, Centre for the Study of Developing Societies, Delhi, 1–2 November 1995, mimeo.

[38] Shail Mayaram, *Resisting Regimes: Myth and Memory in a Muslim Community* (New Delhi: Oxford University Press, 1997).

[39] This identity of the Muslim is dominant but it is certainly not global. It is not even a feature of a majority of Muslims. Its dominance and centrality is a direct outcome of nineteenth-century colonialism and European scholarship. As a by-product of the process, at a rough guess more than 80 per cent of the Muslims of the world today have been redefined as peripheral.

at birth to give their children two names, one Hindu and one Muslim. These traditions are only the more dramatic articulation of a more pervasive religious and public consciousness in South Asia which has remained, to use the expression of D.R. Nagaraj, playfully incommunicado—to modern Indians. These are the kinds of tradition to which Gandhi sought to link his personal fate when he made his famous claim that he was a Hindu, Muslim, Sikh, Christian and a Jew, and so were others.

These communities are not exceptions. According to one estimate, there are about 400 communities in India with more than one religious identity. Going back to K. Suresh Singh's mammoth survey of communities in India, completed as late as 1994, roughly 15 per cent of all Indian communities fall in the same category. Singh estimates this figure to have been much higher in earlier times.[40]

Corresponding to these two forms of traditional social order that sustained communal and ethnic coexistence, there are two other levels at which inter-religious and inter-ethnic relationships are negotiated by society. Note that we are at the moment mostly outside the ambit of the state sector, for the state has little access to these forms or patterns of social organisation. At best, the state can protect such forms and indirectly use them as potential political and social forces through the available representational systems.

The first level can be crudely called the alternative traditions of cosmopolitanism. India may live in its villages, as many of its great social reformers and scholars have repeatedly affirmed, but it also has one of the world's oldest continuous traditions of urban living, centring around some of the world's oldest cities. These urban centres were always the site of encounters, interactions and cultural

[40] K. Suresh Singh, personal communication.

confrontations among not only known communities and races that could be called distant neighbours, but among strangers or alien communities from outside India—from West Asia, Europe, South East Asia, the Far East and Africa. This cosmopolitanism did not conform to the Enlightenment view of humankind, nor did it cater to the needs of a contemporary concept of global political economy, as we understand these needs today. But they did cater to inter-community, inter-cultural and inter-continental exchanges of a wide variety. Many of these cosmopolitan centres of learning—Varanasi is an obvious example—attracted mainly Hindu and Buddhist scholars; others like Ajmer attracted mainly Islamic scholars. Other cities were centres of commerce. Surat, Mangalore and Cochin immediately come to mind. They were simultaneously gateways to India—often to the entire Orient—for West Asia, North Africa and Europe.

Does anything of this pre-modern or non-modern cosmopolitanism survive? Can they open up new possibilities now, when the world is moving out of its uncritical commitment to the provincial universalism of nineteenth-century Europe? Amitav Ghosh's deeply insightful anthropological novel, *In an Antique Land*, seems to suggest that while the tradition may be moribund, it is not entirely dead.[41] Can this tradition be rediscovered, re-tooled or renegotiated? Can something be built on it? Can we find out the nature of inter-community relations that were once built on this now-moribund tradition? If revived, can these traditions make more sense to contemporary urban India than the impersonal, contractual, highly individuated set of relationships that characterise contemporary urban living? Empirically, these are still open questions; one will have to find out the possible answers.

At the second level, overarching and informing each of these different ways of negotiating religion and ethnicity, self and others, insiders and outsiders, is a cultural and psychological process which I can only call multiplicity of self. The subcontinent—or at least

[41] Amitav Ghosh, *In an Antique Land* (London: Granta, 1992).

the major traditions within it—has never conceptualised the self in culturally 'pure' terms. It has seen the self as essentially plural, necessarily located in more than one culture. South Asians have tended to define others not only as a set of distinct not-selves threatening the self but as parts of a hierarchised and prioritised self. It can even be argued that the social and cultural landscape of *homo hierarchicus* is basically a projection of this hierarchised self, and the harsher aspects of the landscape were sometimes mitigated by this plural concept of the self.[42] 'Self' in India is not only a process, as McKim Mariott and his followers insist; it is also a configuration of self and aspects or 'attenuated' forms of not-selves or others. The other is not only an other who defines the self by being a not-self; the other is simultaneously the definer of the self by being a part of the self.

This does not obviate or eliminate ethnic, religious or cultural strife. One can sometimes turn against a part of one's rejected self with more venom than on the other-who-is-only-a-stranger. The recent conflicts between Hutus and Tutsis, and Bosnian Muslims and Serbs (35 per cent of Bosnian Muslim families reportedly have Serb relatives by marriage), are easy but striking examples of people turning against parts of themselves with unimaginable viciousness and rage. However, such plural or multiple selves do constitute a different kind of social bedrock than does the individuated self in other societies or, for that matter, in modern India.

That this plural self has on occasion become a source of violence—Mayaram has documented how the cultural embeddedness of Meos has at times made them particularly vulnerable because

---

[42] It is the tacit acceptance of the concept of plural self that makes works such as that of Gananath Obeysekere and Stanley J. Tambiah on the Sri Lankan society often more relevant to the communal situation in India today than many Indian works on India. See Gananath Obesekeyre, *The Cult of the Goddess Pattini* (Chicago: University of Chicago Press, 1984); and Stanley Tambiah, *Buddhism Betrayed? Religion, Politics and Violence in Sri Lanka* (Chicago: University of Chicago, 1992).

they tend to get marked as a battleground between two sets of fanatics[43]—means certain psychological and cultural barriers in India
have either collapsed or are facing enormous strains on account of
social and political change. But neither the collapse nor the strains
can be an argument against the proposition that any study of ethnic
and communal violence in the subcontinent must start from a
vantage ground that takes into account the distinctive traditions of
cosmopolitanism and plurality of self in the region.

[43] Mayaram, *Resisting Regimes.*

CHAPTER 5

A Report on the Present State of Health of the Gods and Goddesses in South Asia

Great Pan is not dead;
he simply emigrated
   to India.
Here, the gods roam freely,
disguised as snakes or monkeys. . . .
It is a sin to shove a book aside
   with your foot,
A sin to slam books down
   hard on a table, . . .
You must learn how to turn the pages gently
Without disturbing Sarasvati,
Without offending the tree
From whose wood the paper was made.

—Sujata Bhatt, 'A Different History' (1993)

Some years ago, in the city of Bombay, a young Muslim playwright wrote and staged a play that had gods—Hindu gods and goddesses—as major characters. Such plays are not uncommon in India; some would say they are all too common. This one included gods and goddesses who were heroic, grand, scheming and comical. This provoked not the audience but a formation of Hindu nationalists, particularly the Hindu Mahasabha, which had been for long a spent political force in Bombay, the city being

dominated by another more powerful Hindu nationalist formation, the Shiv Sena.

It is doubtful if those who claimed they had been provoked were
actually provoked. It is more likely that a pretence of being offended was deployed to precipitate an incident which made their political presence felt. Vikram Savarkar of the Hindu Mahasabha—a
grandson of Vinayak Damodar Savarkar (1883–1966), the non-
believing father of Hindu nationalism who thoughtfully gifted
South Asia the concept of Hindutva—organised a demonstration
in front of the theatre where the play was being staged. The de-
monstrators caught hold of the playwright and threatened to lynch
him. Ultimately, they forced the writer to bow down and touch
Savarkar's feet, to apologise for writing the play. The humiliation
of the young playwright was complete; it was duly photographed
and published in newspapers and newsmagazines.

Though Savarkar later claimed that Hinduism had won, for he
had not allowed a Muslim to do what Muslims had not allowed
Hindus to do with Islam's symbols of the sacred, at least some Hindus felt that, on this occasion Hindutva may have won, but Hinduism had lost. It had lost because a tradition at least fifteen hundred
years old was sought to be dismantled. During these fifteen hundred years, a crucial identifier of Hinduism—as a religion, a culture
and a way of life—has been the particular style of interaction
humans have had with gods and goddesses. Deities in everyday
Hinduism, from the heavily Brahminic to the aggressively non-
Brahminic, are not entities outside everyday life, nor do they preside over life from the outside; they constitute a significant part of
it. Their presence is telescoped not only into one's transcendental
self but, to use Alan Roland's tripartite division, also into one's
familial and individualised selves and even into one's most flippant,
comic, naughty moments.[1] Gods are beyond and above humans

[1] Alan Roland, *In Search of Self in India and Japan: Toward a Cross-Cultural
Psychology* (Princeton, NJ: Princeton University Press, 1988).

but they are, paradoxically, not outside the human fraternity.[2] You can adore or love them, you can disown or attack them, you can make them butts of wit and sarcasm. Savarkar, not being literate in matters of faith and pitiably picking up ideas from the culture of Anglo-India to turn Hinduism into a 'proper' religion from an inchoate pagan faith, was only ensuring the humiliating defeat of Hinduism as it is known to most Hindus.

Since about the middle of the nineteenth century, perhaps beginning from the 1820s, there has been a deep embarrassment and discontent with the lived experience of Hinduism, the experience that, paradoxically, the young Muslim playwright, Savarkar's victim, represented. Vikram Savarkar is only the last within a galaxy of people—Hindus, non-Hindus, Indians, non-Indians—who have felt uncomfortable with the overpopulated Indian pantheon, its richly textured, pagan personalities, its unpredictability, variety and all too human foibles. For nearly a hundred and fifty years, we have seen a concerted, systematic effort to either eliminate these gods and goddesses from Indian life or tame them and make them behave. I am saying 'Indian' and not 'Hindu' self-consciously, for these gods and goddesses not only populate the Hindu world but regularly visit, and occasionally poach on, territories outside it. They are not strangers outside India either.[3] By indirectly

[2] As a distinguished, expatriate ethnomusicologist, oblivious of the new, city-sleek 'defenders of Hinduism' has recently put it, '. . . the Gods and Goddesses are neither remote nor really frightening or incomprehensible, as in many other religions. Their adventures are real enough for us to empathise with them, and what makes for this feeling of reality is that they not only maintain lofty principles but also have some of our own weaknesses and feelings.' Nazir Ali Jairazbhoy, *Hi-Tech Shiva and Other Apocryphal Stories: An Academic Allegory* (Van Nuys, CA: Apsara Media, 1990), pp. viii–ix. See also Surabhi Sheth, 'Self and Reality', in D.L. Sheth and Ashis Nandy (eds), *The Future of Hinduism*, forthcoming.

[3] In Malaysia and Indonesia, for instance, they critically influence the mythic life of a majority of the people. Under the influence of Islamic revivalism, there are in Malaysia now stray attempts to purify Malaysian Islam and

participating in the effort to re-tool or gentrify them, Savarkar was only following the tradition of Baptist evangelists like William Carey and Joshua Marshman and rationalist religious and social reformers such as Rammohun Roy and Dayanand Saraswati in nineteenth-century India. They all felt that the country's main problem was its idolatry, and the rather poor personal quality of its gods and goddesses. These reformers wanted Indians to get rid of their superfluous deities and either live in a fully secularised, sanitised world in which rationality and scientific truth would prevail or, alternatively, set up a regular monotheistic God, as 'proper' Christians and Muslims had done. Vikram Savarkar was attacking in the playwright a part of his self that was no longer acceptable, but not easy to disown either.

Early attacks on the gods and goddesses by the various Hindu reform movements, from the Brahmo Samaj to the Arya Samaj, have been dutifully picked up by formations that were till recently at the periphery of Indian politics, such as those that centre around Hindutva. Today, overwhelmed by the experience of the Ramjanmabhumi movement and the destruction of the Babri mosque at Ayodhya in 1992, we no longer care to read the entire Hindutva literature produced over the last seventy-five years. We think we know what they have to say. If all nationalist thought is the same,

---

demands that the Malaysian sultans, who constitute a ruling council, drop the parts of their titles that are 'Hindu' or obvious remnants of pre-Islamic traditions. However, the sultans seem reluctant to do so, for a part of their legitimacy in a predominantly Muslim community is linked to their ritual status. Gods and goddesses can survive in odd places. See for instance Dilip Padgaonkar, 'Kuch Kuch Hota Hai in Indonesia', *The Times of India*, 30 January 2000.

as Ernest Gellner believed, Hindu nationalist thought cannot be any different, we are sure.[4] However if you read the literature of Hindutva, you will find in it a systematic, consistent and often direct attack on Hindu gods and goddesses. Most stalwarts of Hindutva have not been interested in Hindu religion and have said so openly. Their tolerance towards the rituals and myths of their faith have been even lower. Many of them have come to Hindutva as a reaction to everyday, vernacular Hinduism.

This rejection is a direct product of nineteenth-century Indian modernity and its models of the ideal Hindu as a Vedantic European or, for that matter, Vedantic Muslim. That is why till recently, in no *shakha* or branch of the Rashtriya Swayam Sevak Sangh (RSS) could there be any icon of any deity except Bharatmata, Mother India. The Ramjanmabhumi temple is the first temple for which the RSS has shed a tear, or shown any concern. And that concern, to judge by their participation in worship or rituals at the temple, seems skin-deep.

In 1990–1, I interviewed at great length the chief priest of the Ramjanmabhumi temple, a remarkably courageous, ecumenical man of religion who was murdered soon after the mosque was demolished. He said that, during the previous seven years of the movement in support of the temple, no major political leader of the movement had cared to worship at the temple, except one who had had a *puja* done without herself visiting the temple. At this point I should tell my favourite, probably apocryphal, story about the devotion to Ram of Hindu nationalists. Once, in course of his only visit to a RSS shakha, Mohandas Karamchand Gandhi reportedly looked around and found, on the walls of the shakha, portraits of some of the famous martial heroes of Hindutva, such as Shivaji and Rana Pratap. Being a devotee of Ram, Gandhi naturally asked, 'Why have you not put up a portrait of Ram as well?' Those were

[4] Ernest Gellner, *Nations and Nationalism* (Ithaca: Cornell University Press, 1983), p. 124.

not the days of the Ramjanmabhumi movement and the RSS leader showing him around said, 'No, that we cannot do. Ram is too effeminate to serve our purpose.'

I am not going to speak about a style of relating to gods and goddesses which invites one to fight their causes while caring nothing for them. I am going to speak about gods and goddesses who inhabit the world we live in, sometimes as house guests, sometimes as our neighbour's headache, sometimes even as private ghosts without whom we think we can live in greater peace. The literary theorist D.R. Nagaraj accused me of writing on these things as an outsider. 'You come to the gods and goddesses as an intellectual, academically,' he said. I often felt like telling him that though I did not want to come to them, they forced me. There is an inevitable logic through which these obstreperous deities infect our lives, pervade it, even invade and take it over, independently of our likes and dislikes. Like most other South Asians, belonging to a whole range of faiths, I have no choice in the matter.

For even within persons, communities, cults, sects and religions that deny gods and goddesses, there persist relationships more typical of religions with a surfeit of gods and goddesses. Gods and goddesses may survive as potentialities even in the most austerely monotheistic, anti-idolatrous faiths. They are not permitted into the main hall, but they are there, just outside the door, constantly threatening to enter the main hall uninvited—as in some of the best-known Indonesian mosques, where the entrance doors and boundary walls are guarded or manned by Hindu or Buddhist gods and goddesses. The reverse also holds true. Some gods and goddesses do have a special symbolic place for anti-polytheism. Lord Thirupathi, nowadays the presiding deity of India's high politics and entertainment industry, reportedly has a Muslim son-in-law whose temple is right within the Lord's campus. And Sabarimala, one of the more potent deities in South India, is also known for his Muslim friend.

Even in starkly monotheistic religions gods and goddesses are waiting just outside the doors of consciousness. Most of the anger against *The Satanic Verses* was inspired by the gratuitous insults that Rushdie heaped on some of Islam's revered figures, but part of it might also have been a response to the latent fear that the banished might return. The non-Islamic or pre-Islamic forms of consciousness that the book unwittingly invokes may or may not threaten 'mainstream' Islam, but they perhaps haunt many Islamic communities in those parts of the world where such forms are, as I remarked, no longer one's distant, superseded past. Thanks to colonial constructions of 'true' Islam in the nineteenth century, this past often seems an immediate, destabilising temptation in the neighbourhood. It is probably no accident that the main agitation against the *The Satanic Verses* took place in countries like Iran, Pakistan, and India, and among expatriate Indians and Pakistanis in Britain.

Shamoon Lokhandwala mentions a medieval religious composition of Western Indian Muslims that depicts Prophet Muhammad as the last of the ten avataras and which served as a sacred text of these Muslims.[5] But even in the more austerely monotheistic versions of Islam, gods and goddesses may survive as aspects or qualities of God, as in the ninety-nine names of Allah. Even in Judaism, despite the faith's hard monotheistic core, the dialogical relationship between God and humans in everyday life has many of the features of pantheistic faiths. In this relationship, much sarcasm, wit, accusations of partiality and injustice, light-hearted banter and sharp criticisms of divine dispensation—of the kind that Vikram Savarkar did not relish—are all common. These are neither seen as blasphemous nor as detracting from the majesty of the divine. Such

[5] Shamoon T. Lokhandwala, 'Indian Islam: Composite Culture and Integration', *New Quest*, March–April 1985 (50), pp. 87–101.

dialogues can be found in old Judaic folk tales, in the work of con-temporary Jewish writers, and even in extreme conditions such as the recorded reactions of Jewish victims in Nazi concentration camps. Theological monotheism is not foolproof protection against theophily or attempts to fraternise with the sacred.

In South Asia, such dialogical relationships with divinity some-times acquire oracular grandeur. I must repeat here a story that philosopher Ramchandra Gandhi has made famous.[6] As he tells it, the famous religious leader and social reformer Vivekananda (1863–1902), while on a visit to Kashmir, went to a temple of the goddess Kali and asked her what many self-conscious Westernised Hindus must have begun asking since the nineteenth century— why had she tolerated so much vandalism and the destruction of temples. Vivekananda heard in his heart the reply of the great mother goddess: 'Do you protect me or do I protect you?' Even the most fearsome deities in South Asia have, I like to believe, a double responsibility which they must balance—they have to protect both their devotees and the humanity of their devotees. The human responses that gods and goddesses give to human predicaments may also be responses to the limited human ability to give or accept human answers grounded in secular reasons and secular morality. These responses may be another kind of self-excavation represented by visions within the devotee, where questions and answers are both latent in his inner self. In a cosmology dependent on gods and god-desses, this is a moral self-affirmation that can be simultaneously a rational argument.

A this-worldly articulation of the same process can be found in the Indian politician's perpetual fascination with astrology, palm-istry, *yajnas* or sacrificial rituals, and *tantra*. Prime Minister Indira Gandhi, for instance, undertook a series of pilgrimages during her last years. (She overdid it, some spitefully say, because her arith-metic was poor.) I have never heard of a politician, either in her

[6] Ramchandra Gandhi, *Sita's Kitchen: A Testimony of Faith and Enquiry* (New Delhi: Wiley Eastern, 1994), p. 10.

party or in the opposition, who underestimated her rational, cost-calculating, political self. Nobody believed she would passively manage fate by such pilgrimages. She went to the pilgrimages but retained her sharp, wily, ruthless political self. The issue of 'agency' in such matters is important but not simple. The heavens, though continuous with everyday life on earth, expect nobody to be passively dependent on them. They refuse to deliver results or confirm the belief that 'agency' has been transferred to the right quarters. This compact is fully understood by all the parties involved.[7]

Nothing shows this better than the art and science of astrology. Astrology is most popular in four sectors of South Asia: business (especially if it involves speculative ventures), spectator sports; the film world; and politics. However, I have never heard anyone claiming that successful business people of the region depend on astrology to solve their problems in the stock market. They do business to the best of their knowledge and understanding, *and* then take the help of astrologers, *tantriks* and temple priests to negotiate terms with gods and goddesses. As if there was a vague awareness that astrology could be another way of asking questions, the answers to which might be known but needed to be endorsed by superhuman specialists.[8] Thus, when despite elaborate rituals and consultations with astrologers, roughly 80 per cent of the nearly 500 commercial films annually produced in India bomb at the box office, film producers and directors do not gives up their belief in astrology. They blame failure on their own imperfect reading of the future, and on flawed ritual performance (which is another way of acknowledging one's faulty reasoning). Presumably, modernity will now make sure that psychotherapists occupy the

[7] For a more detailed discussion, see Ashis Nandy, *The Tao of Cricket: On Games of Destiny and the Destiny of Games* (New Delhi: Penguin, 1989), ch. 1.

[8] This part of the story is entirely missed by those who read all recourse to astrology as the denial of free will. For a recent example, see Peter R. deSouza, 'Astrology and the Indian State', *The Times of India*, 19 July 1996.

space astrologers and priests, backed by gods and goddesses, now occupy. It will be in many ways a less colourful cultural life, but that is a different story.

When gods and goddesses enter human life in South Asia, they contaminate it not in the way the modern, sophisticated, urbane believer fears they will. Nor do they do so the way the rationalist thinks the idea of God contaminates the lives of devotees. They enter human life to provide a quasi-human, sacral presence, to balance the powerful forces of desacralisation in human relationships, vocations and perceptions of nature. This familiarity has bred not contempt, as the Vikram Savarkars of the world suspect, but a certain self-confidence *vis-à-vis* deities. Gods and humans are not distant from each other; human beings can, if they try hard enough, approximate gods. They can even aspire to be more powerful and venerable than gods. *Tapas,* penance of various kinds, and sometimes even the benediction of one god, wisely or foolishly given, can give one superhuman, godly powers. First, spirituality is partly a gift of mortality; it is associated more with mortals than with gods, who are usually seen to possess a streak of hedonism. The persistent asceticism of Shiva is an exception rather than the rule. Second, defying Vivekananda, some gods can also be vulnerable and require the help of humans to fight demons or other gods.

That is, the human inferiority to gods is not absolute; no wide chasm separates the goals and motivations of gods and humans. Indeed, the difference between immortal humans and gods occasionally becomes notional. For the classicists, this proposition is not difficult to swallow because, of the seven immortals mentioned in the *puranas* (Ashvathama, Bali, Vyasa, Hanumana, Kripa, Vibhishana and Parashurama), none, except perhaps Hanumana, can claim divine status.[9] There *is* continuity between the divine and the

[9] Though I have recently found out that, in Sri Lanka, there is at least one temple where Vibhishana is worshipped. Of the seven immortals (*Ashvathama*

earthly; the chasm between gods and humans in South Asia is narrow or shifting. At times, some gods might even be less effective, potent or pious than humans.

Maybe that is the reason why allegiance to a deity is often personalised and looks like a bilateral contract or a secret intimacy between two unequal but sovereign individuals. This allegiance may often have little to do with one's faith—manifestly. Anybody who knows something about the great sarod players, Alauddin Khan and Ali Akbar Khan, will also know that both have been great devotees of goddess Saraswati. Yet, they have simultaneously been devout Muslims, and proudly so. That devotion to Islam and Islamic piety does not require them to reject their personal goddess or *isthadevi* who presides over the most important area of their life, musical creativity. Alauddin Khan once composed a new *raga* called Madanmanjari. As its name indicates, the *raga* immediately invokes Krishna and Vaishnava culture. When someone took the courage to ask the Ustad why he had used such a blatantly Hindu name, the Ustad, I am told, was surprised. 'Is it Hindu? I composed it in honour of my wife Madina Begum,' he is supposed to have said. What looked blatantly Hindu to some can look to others a marker of Islamic devotion. The piety of neither is disturbed.

While studying the Ramjanmabhumi movement, we found a hillock at Ayodhya, venerated both by local Hindus and Muslims. The Hindus considered it to be the discarded part of the sacred *Gandhamadan* of Ramayana, which Hanumana had foolishly

---

BalirVyaso Hanumanascha Vibhishanah Kripah Parashuramascha saptaite chiranjivinah), Ashvathama is the best known, and, until some decades ago, one could hear claims once in a while that he had been seen still moving around with a wound on his forehead, usually at the foothills of the Himalaya. I have never been able to decipher the fondness for the hills in this tragic *puranic* character.

Despite the unenviable state of *puranic* immortals, immortality has been a major fantasy in Indian cultural life. Indian alchemy has been more concerned with the search for an elixir of life, less with the transmutation of base metal into gold.

carried, unable to locate the magical drug Vishalyakarani that he was told to find on the hill for the treatment of Lakshmana's war wounds. The Muslims associated the same hillock with Hazrat Shish and considered it a remnant of Noah's ark, discarded of all places at Ayodhya after the great deluge.

When gods and goddesses invade our personal life or enter it as our guests, when we give them our personal allegiance, they may or may not have much to do apparently, with the generic faiths we profess. The theologian and painter Jyoti Shahi once reported a survey carried out in Madras where, according to official census, one per cent of the people are Christian. This survey found that about 10 per cent of the population identified Jesus Christ as their personal god or *isthadevata*. Such data warn us not to be taken in by what some politicians, acting as vendors of piety, and some experts on ethnic violence, tell us about the geography of faiths. The Indic civilisation has been there slightly longer than the Hindutva-peddlers and the Indologists have been, and it may well survive its well-wishers. The more continuous traditions of this civilisation may reassert themselves in our public life. A majority of people in South Asia know how to handle the gods and goddesses, their own and that of others. The gods and goddesses, on the other hand, not only live with each other, they also invite us to live with their plural world.

Years ago, while studying the psychological landscape of Western colonialism in South Asia, I checked some nineteenth-century documents on Calcutta, because Calcutta is where it all began. Not being a historian, many of the documents surprised me. For instance, certain scrappy details of British households showed that they had a large retinue of servants and retainers, including often a Brahmin priest who did *puja* in the house. Many British houses also had small temples which the Brahmin retainers took care of. Apparently, these householders went to Church on Sundays but found nothing inconsistent in the *puja* at home.[10] The standard reading, I guess, would be that the Indian wives or concubines of such Britishers—the Suez Canal was not yet dug and most had Indian spouses—required this facility. However, something else might also have been involved. For the East India Company itself owned 'shares' in at least two temples. During important religious festivals, the army band went and played at these temples and the musketeers of the Company fired volleys in the air to celebrate the occasion. In return, the Company was given a share of donations made to the temples. It also seems that many individual British residents in India, while proclaiming disbelief in the special spiritual skills of Brahmins and attacking them as charlatans, were at the same time scared stiff by their possible magical abilities. At least some British householders maintained temples at their homes not because they were lapsed Christians or crypto-Hindus, but because they were afraid of local gods and Brahmins and did not want to antagonise them. This was their idea of buying an insurance policy in matters of the sacred. The apparently sharp theological distinctions between some religions may, in specific cultural contexts, observe the logic of complementary self-organisation.

I have come to suspect that theistic worlds in South Asia observe a series of principles of mediation in their relationships with each

---

[10] What arouses anxiety in modern Indians does not apparently do so in societies where the élite has not lost its cultural self confidence. I am told that it has become fashionable in recent years for young Japanese couples to get married in picturesque European churches. They get married there according to Christian rites and the marriages are perfectly acceptable in Japan, legally and socially. Has this openness something to do with the 8 million gods in Shinto cosmology?

other. These mediations ensure continuity and compatibility, but also a degree of anxiety, hostility and violence, though not perhaps distance or incomprehension. Whether the protagonists are Bosnian Muslims and Serbs in East Europe, or Hutus and Tutsis in Africa, or Hindus and Muslims in South Asia, fractured familiarity can breed contempt and venomous, genocidal passions: more so in a context of imminent massification, threatening cultural identities.

A respected Pakistani political analyst and journalist once claimed that the ultimate fear in many Pakistanis was that, if they come too close to India, they would be fitted in the Hindu social order, mostly in the lower orders of the caste hierarchy. India and Pakistan have separated fifty years ago; there is hardly any Hindu left in Pakistan. Most Pakistanis have not even seen a single Hindu in their life; they have seen Hindus only in films and on television. Why then this anxiety? My Pakistani friend himself seemed perplexed, but insisted that there *was* this lurking fear in Pakistan that Hinduism was not something outside, but a vector within. Probably, living in two complementary worlds—of legends, folk tales, rituals, marriage rites, music, craft, traditions and, even, some of the same superstitious, fears, gods and demons—also has its costs. Perhaps many of the anti-idolatrous faiths in South Asia—they include many Hindu sects—are not merely negations of the sphere of gods and goddesses, but also constitute a system of internal checks and balances. Perhaps our gods and goddesses also need such checks.

When another faith provides such a counterpoint or balancing principle, it no longer remains an alien faith or someone else's faith. You do not have to open an inter-faith or inter-cultural dialogue with such a faith, to conform to contemporary sensitivities. The dialogue already exists, waiting to be joined. Islam, for instance, by the very fact that it denies gods and goddesses, provides in South Asia a different kind of meaning-system that becomes accessible to people who want to defy the world of gods and goddesses while living within it. So, even a threat of becoming a part of the Islamic order and disowning the Hindu pantheon, by, say, an oppressed

Dalit, becomes a particular way of interacting with the pantheon. Islam in South Asia may mean going outside the sphere of gods and goddesses, but it may also mean renegotiating terms and conditions with one's traditional gods and goddesses.

It can even mean renegotiating the social status of communities sharing an overlapping structure of sacredness. Many of the most famous temples of Ayodhya, the pilgrimage centre that has become a symbol of religious intolerance in South Asia today, were built with the help of land grants and tax exemptions given by the Shia Nawabs of Avadh in pre-colonial days. By being patrons of Ram temples, they were making a statement both on their position *vis-à-vis* the Ramanandis who dominated the sacred city, and the Sunnis, who constituted an important component of the Muslim community there. Likewise, B.R. Ambedkar, the Dalit leader and the author of India's Constitution, when he decided to convert to Buddhism along with a sizeable section of his followers, did so after much deliberation. It was not standard Therawada Buddhism, with its abundance of deities, that Ambedkar chose, but a more austere Buddhism that, by being close to Islam and Christianity would represent a sharper disjunction with Hinduism. By his conversion he was making a statement to the Hindu world.[11]

A more intense form of such interrelationship is the South Asian version of multiculturalism which does not remain a cultural artefact, but gets telescoped into the self of the individual. Kumar Suresh Singh's survey of Indian communities shows that hundreds of communities in India can be classified as having more than one 'religion'. (It is doubtful if these believers see themselves as having multiple religious identities; they define their Hinduism or Islam or Christianity in such a way that the symbols of sacredness of another faith acquire specific theological, cultural and familial status.) Thus, there are 116 communities that are both Hindu and

[11] That ultimately things did not go the way Ambedkar thought they would go, and that he himself had to end up as a part of the Buddhist-Hindu pantheon of the Dalits, is, of course, a different story.

Christian; at least 35 communities that are both Hindu and Muslim. Sant Fateh Singh, who fought for the cause of Khalistan, was said to be a convert from Islam and a part of his family, I am told, remains Muslim, exactly as a part of the family of Guru Nanak, the founder of Sikhism, remains Hindu. L.K. Advani, a leader of what is reputed to be one of the world's largest fundamentalist formations, is probably the only one of his ilk to have publicly proclaimed that, in his personal religious sensitivities, he is closer to Sikhism than to the religion he fights for, Hinduism. M.A. Jinnah, the founder of Pakistan, which separated from India on grounds of religion, belonged to a Muslim community that, to many 'thoroughbred' Muslims, still looks more Hindu than many Hindu communities. When he spoke of the Hindus and Muslims of South Asia being two nations by virtue of their faith and lifestyle, one wonders if he was not compensating for being part of a community that many Gujarati Hindus and Jains did not even include among the Muslims till a few decades ago. In all these instances, I am not talking of recent converts retaining traces of their older faiths; I am speaking of identities that appear to encompass more than one faith, culturally *and* theologically.

Such pluralism has its cost. The Meos, too, while being devout Muslims, trace their ancestry from the Mahabharatic clans and also often have Mahabharatic names.[12] Only in recent years, after being victims in a series of communal riots that have taken place since the days of Partition, have they begun to feel that they can no longer live in two houses, that they will have to choose. And some of them have chosen to be Muslim in the sense in which the Tabligh and the Jamaat-e-Islami define Islam. Apart from their own tradition of Islam, that is the only other Islam available to them in contemporary India. Similarly, in the re-conversion programmes being run

[12] Shail Mayaram, *Resisting Regimes: Myth, Memory and the Shaping of a Muslim Identity* (New Delhi: Oxford University Press, 1997); and 'Representing the Hindu-Muslim Civilisational Encounter: The Mahabharata of Community of Muslims' (Jaipur: Institute of Development Studies, 1996), unpublished ms.

by the Vishwa Hindu Parishad clandestinely, the aim is to introduce non-Hindus into the Hindu fold as so many low-status mimics of a shallow, neo-Brahminic Hinduism, because that is the only Hinduism the evangelists themselves know. This is a modern tragedy that we have not yet sensed and it affects hundreds of communities all over the region today: Muslims, Hindus, Christians, Sikhs, Buddhists. I think South Asia will be poorer if its rich, intricate tapestry of faiths gets destroyed through neglect or shrinks into six or seven standard, mutually exclusive faiths because, in the contemporary world, only such standard faiths enjoy respectability and political clout. It will simultaneously impoverish Hinduism, Islam and the other South Asian faiths.

I have said at the beginning that South Asian gods and goddesses, like their Hellenic counterparts, can sometimes be found on the wrong side of morality or law. The *puranas* and the *upakathas* are full of instances of how loyalty to and the instrumental use of certain gods and goddesses can destroy a person or a community. The *vamachari* tradition is old in South Asia, and there are deities that have a special relationship with deviant social groups. Years ago, while studying the nineteenth-century epidemic of sati in Bengal, I found out that the popular public worship of Kali (*sarvajanin puja*) became an important socio-religious festival in Eastern India only towards the end of the eighteenth century. Previously Kali— the fierce, violent, dark goddess of popular imagination—had been primarily the goddess of marginal groups such as robbers and thieves, and some incarnations of her were associated with certain dangerous diseases.[13] These gave her an ambivalent status. Now,

[13] Some folk tales presume Olaichandi, who presided over cholera for instance, to be a thinly disguised incarnation of Kali. Her Islamic edition was Olaibibi. Often, in a village or town, if Olaibibi was seen as more potent, the Hindus also went to her and vice versa. Exactly as many Muslims in Dhaka

along with Durga, she emerged as one of Bengal's two presiding deities from the great traditional mother goddess of the region, Chandi. After the great famine of 1772 killed off a of Bengal and the colonial political economy caused massive cultural dislocations, Kali continued as the goddess of marginal groups, becoming for instance the presiding goddess of the Thugs ravaging the countryside and pilgrimage routes. But she also acquired a new connection. She gradually became the chosen deity of the anomic, culturally uprooted, urban, upwardly mobile, upper castes in greater Calcutta and areas heavily influenced by the British presence, where a new political economy and urban culture were ensuring the collapse of traditional social norms. Durga became a more benevolent incarnation of Chandi and gradually emerged as the most important deity in Bengal. This changing cartography of gods and goddesses, who can be benevolent but are also associated with the extra-social, the amoral and the criminal, gives an altogether different set of insights into cultural changes. It profiles the anxieties, fears and hopes of a society that neither a desiccated, formal study of theology and high culture yield, nor any ethnography of the better-known deities.

To give another example, in 1994, during the last episode of plague in India, I discovered that, while there were goddesses for cholera and smallpox in large parts of India there was probably no popular goddess for plague except in Karnataka. I wondered why the goddess, Pilague-amma, found her congenial abode only in that state, and why she had that Anglicised name, as if she was a newcomer to India. Could it be that plague was a pestilence that did not arouse crippling anxieties in most parts of India? Could it be a

---

go to the Dhakeshwari temple for specific forms of protection or blessings. Dhakeshwari, some believe, still protects people from serious accidents and few among them want to take the risk of testing the truth of this—not even in an Islamic society.

pestilence with which most Indians did not have to wrestle psycho-logically, except perhaps in western coastal towns in contact with merchant ships coming from West Asia, Africa and Europe? I do not know. Perhaps there *are* goddesses corresponding to Pilague-amma in southern Gujarat and in Konkan; only I have not had the privilege of their *darshan* yet. Once again, the geography of popular religion gives one a clue to the reasons why plague in India has not triggered the imageries and passions it has in Europe since medieval times and why Indians have never fathomed the anxieties that incidents of plague in India arouse in other parts of the world.

This brings us to a central feature of South Asian concepts of divinity: the intimate relationship between gods and goddesses on the one hand, and demons, *rakshasas* and ogres on the other. The *suras* and the *asuras*, the *adityas* and the *daityas*, the *devas* and the *danavas,* are all dialectically interrelated; gods and goddesses can-not survive or be imagined—they are not even complete—without their counterparts among the demons.

The divine pantheon—populated by the good and the bad, the targets of right-handed worship and those associated with left-handedness, *vamachara*—is part of a larger cosmic order. The gods and goddesses are integrally related to the anti-gods or demons. No theory of violence, no metaphysics of evil in this part of the world, is complete unless it takes into account this relationship. The fuzzy boundaries of South Asian concepts of evil, the temporal and spatial limitations of the concept of *papa* (that distinguish it from the more 'intense' Judaeo-Christian concept of sin, which is more sharply defined but, paradoxically, expected to transcend space and time more easily), and the tolerance of diverse moral universes can be read as reflecting the inextricability of the ideas of the good, the divine and the godly from those of the evil, the desacralised and the ungodly. Appropriately, the mother of the gods and goddesses in mythic India, Aditi, is a sister of the mother of the demons, Diti, and in story after story there is an intricate, personalised, ambivalent relationship between gods and demons. Even Ravana, the fearsome Brahmarakshasa, the worst kind of rakshasa, is intertwined with Rama in the cosmic order as two approaches to the same divinity. Circumstances and accidents separate the approaches and only in death is the contradiction resolved. By dying at the hands of Rama, an incarnation of Vishnu, Ravana reaches his personal god, Vishnu.[14] Even the gift of the great Indian thinkers, writers, and painters to sometimes turn gods into villains and demons into heroes, and the ability of the less Sanskritised sectors to erect temples to persons as ungodly as Duryodhana or as demonic as Hidimba, carry a message. Devotees at such temples do not see them as temples of evil. Nor are such devotees parts of any cabal, eager to fulfill secret ambitions through ritualised Satanism (though that can happen on occasions). Rather, the worshippers seem to have an alternative idea of divinity in which Duryodhana has a place that in more respectable versions of the Mahabharata, his popular cousins monopolise.

These permeable borders between gods and demons, between the definitions of what is sacred in everyday life and what is not, are a major source of social tolerance and of the tacit awareness that the evil excluded from the self cannot be entirely projected outwards. For such projected evil remains only apparently outside, at a safe distance from the self. Indeed, the godliness one acknowledges and the ungodliness one is forced to acknowledge are ordered as two sets

---

[14] So the great act of rebellion of Michael Madhusudan Dutt (1824–73), his epic *Meghnadbadh Kavya*, which makes a hero out of Ravana and a villain out of Rama, as in some of the earlier dissenting premodern Ramayanas, was after all not as disjunctive with the original as Dutt might have thought. I think I now know why, despite being taught like all Bengalis to hero worship Dutt, I could still enjoy my grandmother's conventional version of the Ramayana.

of potentialities. They supply the culture's distinctive theories of violence and oppression. The politics of confrontation does not go far in India because, as an aging radical activist told me some years ago, 'the people are like that!'

But people are like that because there is a cosmology to back them up. That cosmology textures and configures the good and the evil differently. These configurations—and the moral ambiguity that can go with it—deeply offended even a compassionate observer like Albert Schweitzer. Schweitzer believed that such a cosmology was morally flawed because it did not clearly separate good and evil. He felt that some forms of social intervention and altruism were just not possible in such a frame of morality.[15] Maybe he was right. But that limitation also ensures that some forms of violence, based on the absolutisation of differences, are not easy to precipitate in South Asia. In the long run, all attempts to draw conclusive, non-equivocal lines between the insiders and the outsiders, between the godly and the ungodly, seem eventually doomed in the region. Even during the fearsome communal violence during the partitioning of British India, the killings were often interspersed by resistance and mutual help that crossed religious borders, for these borders were never frozen.

Can this interpretation be read as an instance of camouflaged cultural nationalism? 'Why have all the avataras been born in India, nowhere else?', an academic once asked me aggressively. Answers to such questions can only be as clear—or vague—as a culture insists on giving. According to many versions of popular Hinduism there are roughly 330 million gods and some of their avataras might have been born elsewhere in the world. At least one important one, I

[15] Albert Schweitzer, *Indian Thought and its Development* (New York: Beacon, 1959).

know, was born in Nepal, at Lumbini. A proper census of these 330 million gods and goddesses and their countless incarnations is still awaited.

Such questions are also partly answered every day by some of the apparent accidents of history, such as the existence of a city called Ayodhya in Thailand. Thai Ayodhya is not only sacred, it is rather unlikely that the Thais will concede it to be a copy of the Indian Ayodhya. Exactly as Tamilians are unlikely to concede that Madurai is only a derivative of Mathura. However, once you historicise Rama, once you locate his birthplace at a particular Ayodhya at a particular point of time, either to territorialise his claim to a temple or to oppose it, you automatically deny or diminish the sacredness of the other Ayodhya and, while you may establish Rama as a historical figure or national hero, you cannot sustain his status as a god who, as a god, has to exist *today*. If Rama *was*, he is no Rama. If Rama *is*, only then is he Rama. That is the paradox in which one gets caught when one accepts the language of the Hindutva-hawkers and the secular fundamentalists.

There is also the question D.R. Nagaraj raised about the status relations between the Brahminic and the non-Brahminic deities. Nirmal Kumar Bose wrote years ago about the South Asian stratarchy of gods, based on the caste system.[16] And M.N. Srinivas grappled with the same issue more than thirty years ago, though as a problem of ethnographic *versus* textual reality. Srinivas, had found during his field work that it was not unusual for the learned to attribute qualities to a deity that others did not; that even in the case of Sanskritic deities, the qualities associated with them in the Vedas and the Puranas were not often relevant in the field.[17] This sanctions a distinctive politics of cultures, perhaps even some play in

[16] Nirmal Kumar Bose, *Culture and Society in India* (New Delhi: Asia, 1967).

[17] M.N. Srinivas, 'A Brief Note on Ayyappa, the South Indian Deity', in K. M. Kapadia (ed.), *Professor Ghurye Felicitation Volume* (Bombay: Popular Book Depot, 1954), pp. 238–43.

matters of spirituality. First, the higher the status of a deity, the less directly helpful and relevant in everyday life he or she usually is.[18] Thus, Indra, the king of gods, has a high status in the pantheon but his potency as a god relevant to our day-to-day existence is not particularly high, at least not in our times; likewise with Brahma, creator of the universe and senior-most in the pantheon. Hindu temples within the precincts of most Buddhist temples in Sri Lanka tell the same story. Devotees see the Buddhist divinity as too austere and otherworldly; for everyday purposes they prefer to deal with more amenable, lower-ranked Hindu deities. The stratarchy balances the Brahminic and the non-Brahminic, the greater Sanskritic and the local, the Buddhist and the Hindu.[19]

One's manifest loyalty to a deity, too, may not say much about the powers one imputes to the deity. Thirty-five years ago, when I joined a psychoanalytic research centre and clinic at Ahmedabad, most of the patients who came to the clinic were upper-caste Gujarati Vaishnavas. Ahmedabad itself was then an identifiably Vaishnava city, a sharp contrast to my native Calcutta. My teacher, the psychoanalyst Shiv Kumar Mitra, however, pointed out to me that the Vaishnava style overlay a clear Shakto substratum, with its usual bevy of powerful mother goddesses. When confronted with serious illness or a financial crisis, many residents of Ahmedabad rushed to these goddesses. Popular temples, in normal times, were not necessarily the same as temples popular at times of crisis. It was as if Ahmedabad recognised that goddesses could not only be more

[18] This also seems to indirectly emerge from Veena Das, 'The Mythological Film and its Framework of Meaning: An Analysis of Jai Santoshi Ma', *India International Centre Quarterly*, 1981, 9(1), pp. 43–56. There is a glimpse into the politics of the language the gods speak in 'Lingua Franca of Tamil Gods: Sanskrit or Tamil', *The Statesman*, 11 November 1990. Predictably, the Hindu nationalists have taken up the cause of Sanskrit.

[19] Appropriately enough, Simhala chauvinists have begun to interpret this expression of mutuality as an instance of contamination of Buddhism by Hinduism.

powerful than gods, but also a corrective to the secular status of women.

There can also be a hierarchy of godliness patterned by lifecycle. Some gods are more divine as children than as adults. Krishna, the king in the Mahabharata, is a god all right, but not a god of the same stature as he is as the child-god Balakrishna of the Bhagavata. Exactly as the status of the temple of Bhadrakali at Ahmedabad tells us something about the status of women in Gujarati society, the status of Balakrishna is a statement on childhood in India.[20] Likewise, Rama as a raja may have one set of devotees; Rama as an avatara of Vishnu has another. While working at Ayodhya in 1990–2, I was surprised to find a section of the priests there convinced that the Ramjanmabhumi movement was a Shaivite plot to take over the pilgrimage centre. With the whole of India on fire on the Ramjanmabhumi issue, some priests insisted that the movement was a political ploy to defeat not the Muslims, but the Vaishnavas. A few openly expressed their displeasure that the leaders of the movement, especially the firebrand Shaivite *sannyasins* like Uma Bharati and Ritambhara, talked of Rama primarily as a king.

If there are checks and balances within the pantheon in terms of power, interpersonal relations, status, morality and their following, there are human checks, too, against gods and goddesses. This is so, not only in the form of pious men, women and children with unblemished records of penance whose spiritual powers make gods tremble, but also in the form of heroic, epical, if flawed figures and ordinary folk who take up a position against mighty gods on moral grounds. Karna's defiance of fate and his disarming by Indra, Chand Saudagar's defiance of the goddess Chandi and her jealous revenge against him and his family, are instances. Parents in Mithila

[20] Interested readers may look up Ashis Nandy, *The Intimate Enemy: Loss and Recovery of Self Under Colonialism* (New Delhi: Oxford University Press, 1983); 'Politics of Childhood', in *Traditions, Tyranny and Utopia: Essays in the Politics of Awareness* (New Delhi: Oxford University Press, 1987), pp. 56–76.

even today reportedly refuse to allow their daughters to marry someone from Ayodhya, however eligible the prospective bridegroom (because of the ill treatment of Sita by Rama and the residents of Ayodhya). The practice has lasted for centuries and may outlast the Hindu nationalist politicians shouting themselves hoarse about Ram being a national hero or affirming the unity and homogeneity of the Hindu nation. I am sure there are devotees of Rama who support the Ramjanmabhumi movement and vote for Hindu nationalists, yet would not like their daughters to marry someone from Ayodhya. Is this refusal only comic folk superstition, or is there in this obstinacy an embedded comment on the limits of the spiritual and moral status of Rama—or, for that matter, gods and goddesses in general? Do we have access to the complexity of such discriminations and loyalties?

Finally, the matter of birth and death of gods and goddesses. New gods and goddesses are regularly born in South Asia.[21] Despite their theoretical immortality they also die frequently. They die not of illness or accidents but out of forgetfulness or deliberate erasure. These diseases are not uniquely South Asian; they are becoming epidemic the world over. Iconoclasm has killed fewer gods than have erasure or reconfigurations of memory. Certainly, evangelical Christianity between the sixteenth and the nineteenth century could not, despite its best efforts, manage to finish off gods and goddesses—coming from a Christian family, I know how much my family lived with them while aggressively denying that they did. And mine was not an atypical Christian family.[22] My father's

[21] Veena Das gives a fascinating account of the birth of a god sired by commercial cinema; see Das, 'Jai Santoshi Ma'. Such entry into the pantheon can even be quite enduring. Only a few weeks ago, writing this essay, I chanced upon a temple at Madangir, New Delhi, which, to spite Das, claimed to be an ancient Santoshi Ma temple, *Prachin Santoshi Mata Mandir*.

[22] Probably, gods have another kind of incarnation, not captured in any *avatara* theory. As we know, many of the European Christian saints, in their Latin American incarnations, bear clear imprints of pre-Christian Aztec

Christ, in retrospect, was remarkably Vaishnava. Official Christianity need not be the last word on Christianity, which Gandhi recognised in his wry comment that Christianity was a good religion before it went to Europe. There are Christian sects and denominations that have made systematic *theological* deals with vernacular concepts of divinity. At a pinch, most religions probably know how to live with each other; it is probably the turn of some religions to re-learn how to live with each other.

While gods and goddesses *are* mainly responsible to their devotees, not to outsiders scrutinising them 'scientifically', even for such outsiders they often faithfully hold in trust, on behalf of future generations, parts of their selves that devotees disown and would like to jettison. Gods and goddesses do get born, they live and die; their birth, life and death record not only what they are but also what we are. The historian of popular religion Michio Araki claims that the premodern Japan we know is not the Japan that encountered the West in Meiji times, for Japan only theoretically escaped colonisation. With two great civilisations, India and China, succumbing to European powers in the neighbourhood, Japan has always lived with the fear of being colonised. This has forced Japan to redefine even its traditions and its past. Araki adds that clues to what Japan was before the Western encounter and before it retooled its self-definition cannot be found in available histories of Japan but in its popular religion.

Not being a believer, I have come to gods and goddesses through politics, mainly through the politics of knowledge and democratic participation. I am all too aware that the world of gods and goddesses with which we are acquainted will not die soon. For our gods and goddesses, like Vivekananda's Kali, can take care of themselves. However, there are other worlds of gods and goddesses that

---

deities. Even the figure of Christ has been transformed into a Meso-American one, far removed from the standardised figure of Christ in European Christendom.

are facing extinction. These gods and goddesses are exiting the world stage silently, without any fanfare, lament or scholarly obituary.

Some years ago I studied India's first environmental activist, Kapil Bhattacharjea (1904–89), who opposed the Damodar Valley Corporation (DVC), the multi-purpose project of dams, hydel plants and irrigation systems modelled on the Tennessee Valley Authority (TVA). I arrived at the usual story—that when the DVC was built in the 1950s and 1960s, hundreds of thousands of people were uprooted, a majority of them tribals. They were given paltry compensation and told to settle elsewhere. And as usually happened during those tumultuous times in a newly born nation-state pathetically trying to catch up with the West, these displaced people went and quietly settled elsewhere, lost touch with their past, their inherited skills and environmental sensitivities (the ecology of resettlement area being usually different). Mostly belonging to the non-monetised section of the Indian economy, they also quickly spent the money they received as compensation on alcohol and fictitious land deals. Soon they became like any other uprooted community, migrant labourers working in small industrial units or landless agricultural labourers.[23] They were some of the earliest members of that growing community—an estimated sixty-odd million Indians whom development has uprooted during the last fifty years. This is more than three times the number of people displaced during the Partition riots in 1946–8. People have not forgotten the sixteen million displaced by Partition but they have forgotten these sixty million. A large proportion of the displaced are tribals and Dalits; one-third of India's entire tribal population has been uprooted in the last fifty years and 15 per cent of our tribes

[23] Ashis Nandy, 'The Range and Limits of Dissent: Kapil Bhattacharjea's Critique of the DVC', Presented at the Conference on the Greening of Economics, Bellagio, 2–6 August 1993. To be published in Frédérique Apffel Marglin (ed.), *People Count*, forthcoming.

have been fully uprooted.[24] The gods and goddesses of these vanishing communities who face, silently and invisibly, threats of extinction, are those that have made me aware of a divine species which, unlike Vivekananda's Kali, requires something in addition to devotion. There are also communities that, after centuries of oppression, have begun to undervalue or forget their gods and goddesses, so that they can redefine themselves as only a group of oppressed poor, operating from a clean cultural slate.[25] I believe that all these gods and goddesses—as 'living' biographies of threatened cultures, as symbols of their resilience and resistance against the juggernaut of mega-development—deserve something more than standard, rationalist, dismissive ethnographies or archeologies. We owe something not only to them and their humble devotees, but also to our own moral selves. For no intervention in society, politics and culture becomes moral because we cannot at the moment think of an alternative to it.

[24] Smitu Kothari estimates that of the 60 million aboriginal tribals in India belonging to some 212 tribes, 15 per cent have been displaced by development projects. Smitu Kothari, 'Theorising Culture, Nature and Democracy in India' (Delhi: Lokayan, 1993), ms. Other estimates are as high as 33 per cent.

[25] Many Dalit communities in contemporary India are good examples of such deculturation. In response, some sensitive Dalit writers have made a conscious effort to rediscover and defend Dalit cultural traditions. See for instance, D.R. Nagaraj, 'From Political Rage to Cultural Affirmation: Notes on the Kannada Dalit Poet-Activist Siddalingaiah', *India International Centre Quarterly*, Winter 1994, 21(4), pp. 15–26.

CHAPTER 6

Time Travel to a Possible Self

Searching for the Alternative Cosmopolitanism of Cochin

> For over a quarter of a century the Indic world confirmed
> what since my birth was only a blurred feeling: the self-iden-
> tity of Man is transcultural, and thus cannot have any single
> point of reference. . . . Pluralism is not synonymous with
> tolerance of a variety of opinions. Pluralism amounts to the
> recognition of the unthinkable, the absurd, and up to a limit,
> intolerable. . . . Reality does not need to be in itself trans-
> parent, intelligible.
>
> —Raimundo Panikkar, 'Personal Statement'

Cochin (or Kochi) is one of the few cities in India where pre-
colonial traditions of cultural pluralism refuse to die. It is
one of the largest natural harbours in India and has also become, during the last fifty years, a major centre of the Indian navy.
With the growing security consciousness of official India, it has
recently become less accessible to non-Indians, particularly if they
happen to be from one of the countries with which India's relationship is tense. Few mind that; the city no longer means much to
the outside world. For Indians, too, except probably for the more
historically conscious Malayalis, Cochin is no longer the 'epitome
of adventure' it was to Mohandas Karamchand Gandhi; nor a cru-
cible of cultures, as it is to its former mayor, K.J. Sohan.[1] For most,

[1] 'Celebrating Diversity in Cochin', *Culture and Identity Newsletter*, October 1997, 1(3), p. 1.

it is now one of those many regional cities that are not quite up to the standard of India's major metropolitan centres.

Yet Cochin is, for its residents, the ultimate symbol of cultural diversity and religious and ethnic tolerance or, to use the expression recommended by Madhu Prakash and Gustavo Esteva in place of secularism, hospitality.[2] The city still bears the imprint of its record, stretching across at least six centuries, as a place where China, Africa, South East Asia, West Asia, and Europe met. At least fourteen communities still live in the city—ranging from Jews and Eurasian Parangis to Tamilians and Saraswats. Some ethnic communities have blended with the locals and are no longer clearly identifiable, such as the Yemeni Arabs; some have moved away entirely, such as the Chinese; still others are about to, such as the Jews. Most of these communities are not even listed in the Indian census because they are identified with castes, and official India has been given up caste enumeration after 1935 lest the data are misused politically.[3]

Cochin has seen adventurers, invaders, and pirates. It has seen people seeking refuge from oppression and discrimination in other parts of the world. It has also seen occasional communal skirmishes among different communities, but for centuries it has not seen a bloodbath, not even a proper riot. This does not mean there is no hostility among communities. Nor does it mean that communities do not have their own distinctive written and unwritten memories of past injustice and violence against them. Syrian Christians remember the destruction of sacred books and documents by Catholics, Jews the harassment of their forefathers by the Portuguese. The Chinese are said to have been driven away by the Arabs; Tipu

[2] Madhu S. Prakash and Gustavo Esteva, *Grassroots Postmodernism: Remaking the Soil of Cultures* (London: Zed, 1998).

[3] That does not prevent political parties of all hues from maintaining their own secret data bases on castes for electoral purposes. However, these are not accessible to outsiders.

Sultan, some believe, attacked the Jews at Cranganore; and Konkanis talk about how they fled to Cochin from the Inquisition at Goa.

Virtually every community has its 'history' of struggle and believes it to be the best, if not in the world, certainly in Cochin. Every community also has its own hierarchy of communities, in which it places the others according to a remembered or mythic past. Each community sees some communities as good, others as bad. There are also, in many cases, apparently historicised memories of how other communities and one's own have fought in the past. Even these memories do not lead to impassioned hatred. The Jews and the Syrian Christians talk disdainfully about the Portuguese and their fanatic Catholicism, not about the Catholic communities that trace their origins to the Portuguese. The Konkanis talk of an attack on their temple by a king of Cochin, not of the hostility of any community. One comes to suspect that most memories of communal strife are props to a community's self-esteem and self-definition rather than stereotypes with murderous implications. Whether they can be used at some point to mobilise communities against each other remains an open question.[4]

[4] Perhaps this is not unique to Cochin; it has only been patterned and institutionalised in a somewhat unique fashion there. Compare, for instance the autobiographical account of the well-known New York designer, Anita Lobel, *No Pretty Pictures—A Child of War* (New York: Greenwillow, 1998). Lobel is a Polish Jew who, along with her brother, was protected during the war years by her Polish Christian nanny who, at the same time, was anti-Semitic. In the Sri Lankan context, Michael Roberts has argued against the 'simplistic argument' that cosmopolitanism or cultural diversity cannot coexist within chauvinism and xenophobia. See Michael Roberts, 'Prejudice and Hate in Pluralist Settings: The Kingdom of Kandy', paper presented at the Neelan Tiruchelvam Commemoration Programme, Colombo, 30 January-1 February, 2000. But it may be as simplistic to believe that cultural likes and dislikes and ethnocentrism automatically lead to xenophobic or rabid nationalist violence.

Zigmunt Bauman draws a distinction that may be tangentially pertinent to

There is little defensive search for purity in the communities of Cochin either. Probably because they have not sensed threats to their lifestyles and are culturally self-confident, they can borrow from each other with fewer inhibitions. Fort Cochin has mosques that are hundreds of years old and share the region's distinctive ancient style of Hindu temple architecture and sacred decorative designs; there are synagogues so unique that at least one has been dismantled and rebuilt by a Malabari Jewish community near Jerusalem: it has become a tourist attraction there.

During the last few centuries Cochin seems to have thrived on the checks and counter-checks provided by its low-key communal loves and hates. Having stereotypes and disliking other communities, yet granting them a place in the sun and even the right to dislike and keep a distance from one's own community, is obviously one of the building blocks of Cochin's version of cultural plurality.

---

our story: 'as a conception of the world, and even more importantly as an effective instrument of political practice, racism is unthinkable without the advancement of modern science, modern technology and modern forms of state power. As such, racism is strictly a modern product. . . . Racism differs from both heterophobia and contestant enmity. The difference lies neither in the intensity of sentiments nor in the type of argument used to rationalise it. *Racism stands apart by a practice of which it is a part and which it rationalises: a practice that combines strategies of architecture and gardening with that of medicine—in the service of the construction of an artificial social order, through cutting out the elements of the present reality that neither fit the visualized perfect reality, nor can be changed so that they do. . . .* In the modern world distinguished by its ambition to self-control and self-administration racism declares a certain category of people endemically and hopelessly resistant to control and immune to all efforts at amelioration. To use the medical metaphor, one can train and shape "healthy" parts of the body, but not cancerous growth. The latter can be "improved" only by being destroyed. . . . However abominable they are, and however spacious the reservoir of potential violence they contain, heterophobia and boundary-contest anxieties do not result—directly or indirectly—in genocide.' See Bauman's *Modernity and the Holocaust* (Ithaca, NY: Cornell University Press, 1989), pp. 61, 65, 81.

Hardboiled social scientists claim that three factors have contributed to Cochin's historic communal harmony. First, there has been trade, especially in spice, fishing, coir, and shipbuilding. Trade has made communities interdependent; none can do without the others. Second, there has been a common language. Almost everyone speaks Malayalam at Cochin—from the European-looking white Jew to the language-conscious Tamilian. Even the smattering of white, former colonial bureaucrats or businesspersons who have stayed back in Cochin know the language. Third, Cochin is located in a part of India that is highly literate, urbanised and secular. Many like to see its communal peace as a triumph of modernity over an atavistic past.

While these factors might have played an important role in Cochin's civic culture, none seems an adequate interpretation. For economic interdependence means that each community has specialised in certain enterprises or professions. They are, therefore, badly represented in other kinds of jobs and professions. As we know from the experiences of other parts of India, this, by contemporary standards, is not 'real' equality. Ideally, in a modern and fully individualised society, each community must be well represented in all sectors; or else dedicated ethnic chauvinists will exploit the under-representation of a community in some sectors of the economy. Similar situations have led to much bitterness and demands for affirmative action elsewhere. Likewise, instances of communal violence between two groups that speak the same language but are divided by caste or religion abound in India. India's worst communal riots took place in Punjab and Bengal, at the time of Partition, between communities that were parts of the same culture and linguistic group. And education, industrialisation and urbanisation, combined with secularisation, have often stoked communal strife, instead of containing it.[5] A huge majority of communal riots have

[5] See Ashis Nandy, 'Coping with the Politics of Faiths and Cultures: Between Secular State and Ecumenical Traditions in India', in Joanna Pfaff-Czarnecka, Darini Rajasingham-Senanayake, Ashis Nandy and Edmond

in India taken place in large cities, despite three-fourths of Indians living in villages. The fear of losing one's faith can be a destructive force in a secularising world; it can hand over entire communities to venomous identity politics.

One will have to search elsewhere for the sources of Cochin's tradition of alternative cosmopolitanism and cultural pluralism. This essay represents such a search and should be read more as the diary of a personal, cultural-psychological journey rather than as professional ethnography. The search is not grounded in history. It rejects history as a guide to the 'living past' of Cochin. The only kind of history considered relevant here is the clinician's idea of case history, where the past is configured as an immediate, felt reality— indeed as a part of the psychodynamics of health and ill-health. In this instance I have focussed mainly on the perceived sources of health in the remembered or fantasised past. There must be other pasts within Cochin, but I leave it to others to excavate them. For me, an exhaustive, fully objective pathological report usually comes in the form of a post-mortem, not a diagnosis or prognosis.

I

Cochin is one of three cities on the Malabar Coast—the other two being Calicut and Mangalore—traditionally known as places where West Asia, Europe, Africa, South East Asia and China met. In the self-definition of its citizens, Cochin's territoriality has two dimensions, one land-based, the other determined by traditional sea routes converging at the city. As we were to find out, to many Cochinis, the city is only apparently located in one corner of India, in the small state of Kerala. To them it is at the centre of the Indian Ocean, presiding over memories of these sea routes, and of

---

Terence Gomez, *Ethnic Futures: The State and Identity Politics in Asia* (New Delhi: Sage, in press); and 'The Twilight of Certitudes', *Postcolonial Studies*, November 1998, 1(3), pp. 283–98.

a once-flourishing spice trade. To these Cochinis, West Asia, parts of East Africa and South East Asia often seem, defying their own nationalist sentiments, psychologically closer than Delhi.[6] Cochin is not a large city by Indian standards, though it is the largest in Kerala. The population, according to the 1991 census, is a little over 1.14 million. The District Gazetteer says nearly 95 per cent of the residents are literate. Literacy is higher among women than among men.[7] Cochin City is in Ernakulam district, one of the smallest in India (with a population of roughly 30 million). This leads to some confusion, for Ernakulam city is now, for all practical purposes, a part of Cochin city, which itself was, until fifty years ago, part of a princely state, also called Cochin.[8]

Though the traditional spice trade survives, Cochin's economy now depends heavily on the coir industry and the shipyard. But, as will gradually become evident from this story, the spice trade—and the myths and fantasies surrounding it—define the city. Cochin without the spice trade is no Cochin. One of the characters in a Salman Rushdie novel, progeny of a family of spice traders, turns the link into a grander if comic vision:

> the pepper, if you please; for if it had not been for peppercorns, then what is ending now in East and West might never have begun . . . we were 'not so much sub-continent as sub-condiment', as my distinguished mother had it. 'From the beginning, what the world wanted

[6] This is probably true not only of Cochin but of a number of cities of the region. At this point, I should also put on record my debt to Amitav Ghosh, whose brilliant ethnographic novel, *In an Antique Land* (London: Granta Books, 1992), has been a source of my insights into the civic culture of the cities on the Malabar Coast.

[7] S.C. Bhat (ed.), *The Encyclopaedia District Gazetteer of India: Southern Zone* (New Delhi: Gyan Publishing House, 1997), 2, pp. 727–41. Recent reports say that the entire district is now 100 per cent literate.

[8] Actually, each informant seems to have his or her own view of geographical Cochin, perhaps because the Cochin of the imagination transcends cartography and official boundaries.

from bloody mother India was daylight-clear,' she'd say. 'They came for the hot stuff, just like any man calling on a tart.'[9]

Cochin lies in a particularly green part of India, though industries and urban growth have begun to take their toll. Despite its high population density, most visitors to the city are struck not so much by its civic structures and narrow, crowded streets as by the omnipresence of water and greenery. Quiet waterways and rich tropical lushness temper the sudden ferocity of heat and humidity that one faces when emerging from a plane. The small, humble airport, unable to cope with the new international stature given to it by the Malayali propensity to globetrot, complements that impression. It is built on the sparsely populated, thickly green Willington Island, which the British artificially created during the high noon of the raj. The island strengthens the image of a large city that magically retains the touch of a tropical village.

There are various explanations of the name Cochin. Some say it is a derivative of 'Kochi', the name of a river nearby. Others claim Chinese settlers gave the city its name. There are other theories. It is possible that the name has meant different things at different points of time; it certainly means different things to different communities in the city. Even the geography of Cochin seems to change, depending on the person one is talking with. Some mean Cochin State when they talk of Cochin; others mean the present city, including Ernakulam; still others mean mainly Mattancherry or the area around Fort Cochin.

The official past of Cochin is well known and does not need repetition. It is part of the history of the Malabar coast that, in the pre-colonial and early colonial period, Cochin played a central role in the world of the Indian Ocean, with its crisscrossing sea routes connecting cultures, histories and geographies.[10] The erstwhile

[9] Salman Rushdie, *The Moor's Last Sigh* (London: Jonathan Cape, 1995), pp. 4–5.

[10] For a proper history of that part of the story, see Sanjay Subrahmanyam,

princely state of Cochin was a small state of about 1400 square miles, with a population of around 25 million. Cochin's royal house, Perampadappu Swarupam, had its original capital at Vanneri. It moved to Mahodayapur in Cranganore in the late thirteenth century after an attack by the Zamorin—the ruler of Calicut. Cochin became the capital of Cochin State in 1405. Others say Cochin became important only after the Portuguese came to India; the Portuguese saga in Cochin began when Vasco da Gama landed near Calicut in 1498. Cochin's kings were friendly towards the new immigrants, who gradually turned Cochin from a fishing town to an important commercial centre. The Portuguese were also enthusiastic builders. They built forts, churches and European-style houses in the city. When the Dutch won control of Cochin from the Portuguese in 1663, they also turned out to be eager builders. Fort Cochin still has a large number of houses that are Dutch in style and distinguishable from other buildings. Despite the proliferation of standardised, tasteless structures, often built by newly rich Malayalis with a West Asian connection, these parts of Cochin still remain distinctive and identifiable. In 1795 the British wrested control of the city from the Dutch but did not interfere much either with the indigenous lifestyle or the Dutch political order.

Though historical Cochin is remembered mainly as a centre of spice trade by many, it was also known for its shipbuilding facilities, which the Portuguese turned into an important trade. Some say that shipbuilding around Cochin began as early as in the Sangham period, at Cranganore. The Dutch further developed these facilities. In independent India, too, Cochin continues to be a major shipyard:[11] only, the Indian navy now dominates the facilities. The

---

The Career and Legend of Vasco da Gama (New Delhi: Cambridge University Press, 1997).

[11] K.L. Bernard, 'Ship Building in Ancient Cochin: A Historical Study', C.K. Kareem (ed.), *The Kerala History Association Golden Jubilee Souvenir*, 1995, pp. 39–57.

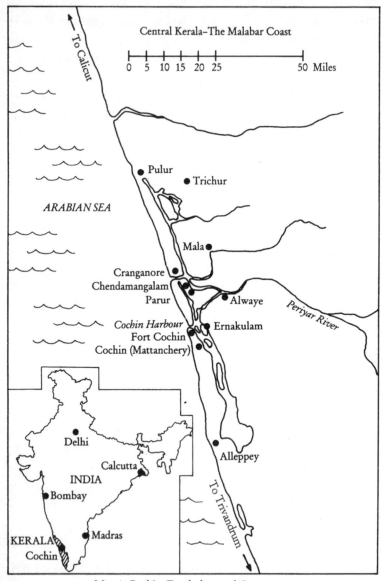

Map 1: Cochin, Ernakulam and Cranganore

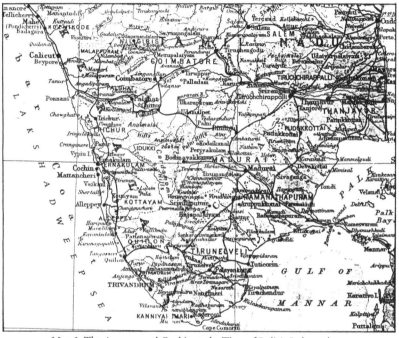

Map 2: The Area around Cochin at the Time of India's Independence

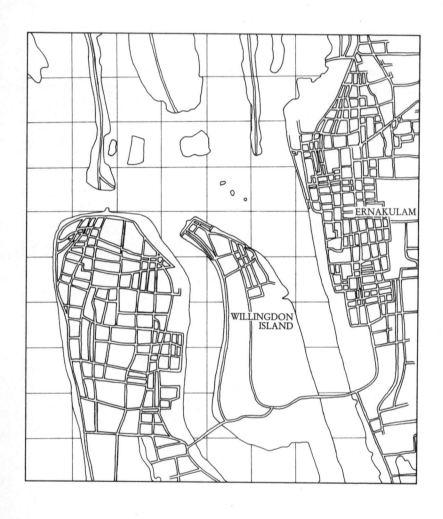

Jews of Cochin played an important role in shipbuilding during the Dutch period (1663–1795).

Official history, however, is not the last word on Cochin. There are shared memories, partly mythical, of Chinese fishermen and seafarers who inhabited Cochin till the fourteenth century. The Arabs reportedly defeated the Chinese and settled down in the city. These memories also claim that Cochin was cosmopolitan and international even before the Portuguese came. Many residents know that early European accounts talk of Cochin being a small fishing village next to the river Kochi (in Malayalam 'small place'), but many also know that the Sanskrit *Kerala Mahatmyam* already called it Balapuri, 'a small town'. While admitting that early travellers did not mention Cochin in their chronicles, some Cochinis point out that Ma-Huan, a Chinese Muslim, was the first to mention the city in AD 1409. That was before Cochin became a 'proper' port. These memories are kept alive by popular 'histories' of Cochin, which sometimes confirm the memories, sometimes not, but always stoke a reactive return to unofficial memories.[12]

[12] We met at the office of historian C.K. Kareem (Secretary of the Kerala History Association) two local Christians, both highly educated professionals: Dr A. Noble, a retired government scientist, and Colonel K.I. Thomas, formerly of the Indian army. They were researching the historical roots of their family. They claimed that they had learnt from their elders that, when Tipu Sultan attacked the Jewish Kingdom at Cranganore and began a massacre, 10,000 Jews ran away and converted to Christianity. Our newly found acquaintances claimed they were the descendants of two such converted families. Kareem, a polite leftist, patiently explained to them that historical records showed that no such incident had taken place. The visitors did not look particularly happy but appeared convinced by these words of reason. Later, when we interviewed them at their homes, they were back to their original version of the story. One of them hinted that Kareem might have denied the story because he was a closet fundamentalist.

Particularly important in this context is Cochin's remembered historical geography, which includes elements crucial to its psycho-geography. For instance, we are told that 'oceanic convulsions' in the fourteenth century turned Cochin into a safe natural harbour and threw up the Vypin Island. Previously, a small river near Cochin opened into the sea; the floods of AD 1341 created Cochin as we know it today. The geography of that creation shapes Cochin's self-definition even today.

. Public memory does not look at Cochin as an eternal city, the way it looks at Varanasi, Ujjain and Delhi. However, such memories do push the beginning of the history of Cochin as far back as possible, almost into a prehistoric, mythic past. In that past a series of immigrant communities plays an important part—as refugees fleeing oppression, natural calamities and war. They brought to Cochin their distinctive skills in business, craft or art. These refugees—or *abhayarthis*, as the Konkani-speaking Cochinis call them—have played an important role in Cochin's well being and there are memories of local kings even quarrelling amongst themselves for the privilege of having them as subjects. Perhaps these memories give a certain strength, resilience and legitimacy to Cochin's pre-modern culture, increasingly under threat from the quick urban growth taking place in the city. Its residents like to see Cochin as a place where the new has never defeated the old and is, in fact, parasitic on the old.

The Two Wings of Mythic Cochin

However, shareable public memories are not the whole story. There are also tacit memories, constituting an identifiable, communicable 'unconscious'.[13] It took me many months to find out

[13] Elsewhere, I have called this a secret self, to distinguish it from the standard, Freudian unconscious. The presumption is that the secrecy is imposed, in this instance by categories associated with dominance, but is also partly internalised. As a result, the socialised self learns to keep double ledgers, one

that beneath the social reality called Cochin there was also a mythic entity that went by the same name. That other Cochin is not openly recognised in Cochin's public life or its public self-reflection. Thanks to the long exposure to mechanical, state-centric, positivist cultures of Leninism and Nehruvian socialism, to many sectors of Kerala's society the mythic Cochin means only a false, unreal Cochin—a collection of superstitions, stereotypes, and surviving symbols of a lost 'golden' age. The mythic Cochin is the opposite of the historical Cochin; it is what Cochin is not.

Only gradually does one realise that the mythic Cochin is at least as important as the historic Cochin if one wants to grasp the city's culture today. In many respects, the former is the heart of Cochin, for Cochin's traditional cosmopolitanism lives to the extent the mythic Cochin lives. The city's political culture is organised around that city of the mind. The day that phantom city dies, Cochin will die and become like any other small South Asian city trying desperately to become a standard metropolis.

It is, however, not easy to identify the components of mythic Cochin. Many of them are probably inaccessible to outsiders, particularly if they do not speak Malayalam. Nor is it always possible to separate the private or tacit from the mythic or the unconscious. I have already mentioned how the co-ordinates of geographical Cochin are not merely land-based but, perhaps in more important ways, also defined by the traditional sea routes to Cochin. One suspects that such historical geography is mainly tacit knowledge, part

---

for public or official consumption, the other for private moments or for transmission as unofficial memories or the creation of contraband histories. This paper suggests that not merely individuals but even communities sometimes have their secret selves. See Ashis Nandy, 'The Savage Freud: The First Nonwestern Psychoanalyst and the Politics of Secret Selves in Colonial India', in *The Savage Freud and Other Essays on Possible and Retrievable Selves* (New Delhi: Oxford University Press, 1995), pp. 81–144; and 'The Other Within: The Strange Case of Radhabinod Pal's Judgment on Culpability', ibid., pp. 53–80.

of the everyday wisdom within Cochinis, though never entirely acknowledged as such in school texts. But that does not make it part of any disowned aspects of the self. The first component of the disowned Cochin of the mind, though, is easy to identify. Cochin is a direct progeny and heir to the mythic epicentre of Kerala society—Cranganore. Cranganore had to die—as a harbour, a habitat and as the cultural capital of Kerala and Malabar—for Cochin to be born in 1341. People talk about the 'oceanic convulsions' that silted up and made Cranganore port unusable and created the Vypin Island and the natural harbour at Cochin as if the convulsions were the birth pangs of a unique city. The disaster that killed the former was the one that created Cochin. The city not only has two histories, one realistic and the other fantastic, it also lives with two geographies; even physically, the city's past is part of a larger map of the mind.

Cranganore seems to have many names. It is also known as Kodungalloor. In earlier times it was also known as Muziris and in Tamil as Muchiri. It is not merely a sleepy city to the north of Cochin that has a once-glorious past; Cranganore is the mythic capital of mythic Kerala and mythic Malabar. In the minds of many, it is still the first city of Kerala. The Malayali public consciousness and self-definition inextricably centre on that lost city. Unless you are talking to historians, everything began at Cranganore. Even the famous spice trade—mainly involving cardamom, cinnamon, ginger and the black gold, pepper—began at Cranganore. Some Cochinis make it a point to remember that, as early as in the first century, Pliny the Elder (AD 23–79) had grumbled about the drain on the Roman empire by purchases of an 'useless' commodity, pepper, from Muziris. Others point out that in AD 403 Alaric the Goth lifted his siege of Rome reportedly in exchange for 3000 pounds of pepper—purchased from, where else, but Muziris.

Most communities link their remembered pasts to Cranganore. The Jews trace their Indian origin to the city; so do some communities of Muslims, who talk of the city as one of the early bastions of Islam. Some of the most sacred texts of Tamilian Hinduism, especially Shaiva Siddhanta, are supposed to have been written at Cranganore. Christians too seem eager to point out that St Thomas landed at Cranganore in AD 52. No popular history is complete unless you have somehow related it to something that has happened at some time in Cranganore. Though some members of Cochin's erstwhile royal family speak of the consolidation of the Cochin kingdom as a slow and laborious process that lasted decades, in popular genealogy the dynasty emerged in a fully formed fashion at Mahodayapur at Cranganore.

So, we are told, did the city's religious and ethnic tolerance. Cranganore remains the ultimate symbol of Cochin's ecumenism. Balagopalakrishna Menon, a successful lawyer who has been close to Cochin royalty for more than five decades, only endorses the widely shared image of the mythic capital of Kerala and Malabar when he talks of the Cheraman Masjid at Cranganore. He claims that it is the world's only mosque that faces east because it was a temple that was allowed to be converted into a mosque by Cheraman Peruman, the legendary king of Kerala, a contemporary of Adi Shankara in the eighth century.

Why do all journeys begin from Cranganore? What is the magic of the city? One part of the answer is that Cranganore was a thriving port until 'natural calamities'—in some stories a flood, in others an earthquake—destroyed it. Others talk of 'the mysterious Malabar mud-banks' that moved inshore to clog the mouth of the river Periyar to end the long career of Muziris as a port that the Phoenicians, Egyptians, Persians, Chinese, the Romans and Arabs frequented. In Cochini imagination, Cochin is the rebirth of that dead, ancient, cultural 'capital' of Kerala and, unless one knows about Cranganore, one cannot be expected to fathom its reincarnated version. Cranganore is the clue to Cochin's *karmic* past.

The Jewish synagogue at Fort Cochin, for instance, has a panel of paintings that depicts the Jewish journey through time at Cochin. This too begins at Cranganore. Only, for some unknown reason, the Jews call the city Shingly. It tells how the Jews not only saved themselves from a flood and an invasion, but also how its Jewish king escaped to safety in Cochin, according to one respondent by swimming with his Torah and wife on his back and his people on his side. It is impossible to tell the Jewish story of Cochin without the Jewish construction of Cranganore and the small Jewish principality that once existed there.

The 'memories' of Cranganore are often bitter-sweet. Even among the Jews, the story of a unique Jewish kingdom is bordered by the myth of how Cranganore's first eight hundred Jewish settlers, under the leadership of a rather formidable widow called Kadambath-Achi, were doing well till the king's son fell in love with her daughter. As Ruby Daniel tells the story, she refused to marry her to a gentile prince who, pining for the daughter, fell ill. The angry king ordered the Jews out of his kingdom and they ran away. The widow and her daughter stayed back to ground their jewellery and precious stones into powder, throw them into a pool, and commit suicide by swallowing diamonds. The pool is still called Jutha Kulam (Jewish pool) and the hill nearby Jutha Kunna (Jewish hill). 'People living there still say they sometimes find tiny pieces of gold in the sand of that pool.[14] The memories of Jews at Cranganore also survive in Malayali songs and stories. More 'realistic' are the stories about being expelled from Cranganore by the Portuguese and the Moors, which scattered the Jewish communities to places such as Mala, Chendamangalam and Parur.[15]

The story of the dead city of Cranganore, now surviving as an inconsequential district town with a magical past and serving as the

[14] Ruby Daniel and Barbara C. Johnson, *Ruby of Cochin: An Indian Jewish Woman Remembers* (Philadelphia and Jerusalem: The Jewish Publication Society, 1995), pp. 8–9.
[15] Ibid.

underside of the story of the living city of Cochin, is incomplete without the story of the Cochin kings. The memories of its kings constitute the other pivot of mythic Cochin. After long lectures on feudalism, caste domination and the oppressive contents of the religious way of life, informants begin to speak, diffidently and defensively, about the Cochin kings as the source of most things that are adorable in Cochin's culture. These kings helped communities to settle down in Cochin, ensured their security, and gave them a sense of participation in civic life. Though the dynastic rule of the family ended fifty years ago and its royal privileges were abolished, the maharajas of Cochin continue to preside over the minds of Cochinis. This is a different kind of rule; most people do not even know the names of members of the erstwhile royal family. But their constructions of the city have to come back to princely rule, the same way they always come back to Cranganore.

A recently published encyclopaedia blandly states that the pre-Portuguese history of Cochin and the origins of Cochin's royal family are unknown.[16] Well, that is not the impression one gets in the city. Residents seem to believe that the full history of the city and the royal dynasty is known. For the spaces left by gaps in data and memory have been occupied over the years by collective fantasies and mythography. One member of the royal family, Rameshan Thampuran, is working on a genealogy. According to this the Cochin dynasty owes its origins to the last king of the Chera empire, Rama Varma Kulasekhara, who divided his empire among his own and his sister's children, and among other relatives. He then embraced Islam and, reportedly, went away to Mecca. (Family lawyer Menon, while admitting that the story of conversion to Islam is by far the most popular, points out that it has to contend with another story about Rama Varma's conversion to Buddhism. Indeed, there is a third version of the story in which Rama Varma dies a Hindu by taking *samadhi* at Trikaryuor.) The Cochin dynasty began with

[16] M.J. Koshy, *The Encyclopaedia of India* (New Delhi: Rima Publishing House, 1994), vol. 20: Kerala, pp. 42–4.

the grandson of Rama Varma's sister. While the Travancore kings, descendants of Rama Varma's sons, enjoyed more political salience, the Cochin kings were always more significant spiritually. This was mainly because they, though Kshatriyas, managed to represent both temporal and spiritual authority, captured in the expression *koviladhikarikal* (temple authorities). Thus, when they gave rights and privileges to various trading and professional communities or treated certain communities—such as the Syrian Christians—as their favourites, it had a special meaning. Their promises carried weight.

All this does not mean that there is no ambivalence towards the dynasty outside modern, ideologically tinged Cochinis. Even those who speak highly of the dynasty sometimes have their favourite villains. The Konkanis speak of the 'notorious' Sakthan Thampuran, a king who killed many Konkanis and attacked and plundered the community's main temple, Thirumala Deva at Cochin. The priests, along with a large part of the community, fled to Aleppy, then under the Raja of Travancore, and stayed there sixty years despite Sakthan Thampuran's efforts to get them back through an agreement with the raja. However, there are often built-in checks in shared memories against such painful pasts. The Konkanis themselves speak of how, after sixty years, another Cochin king suffered from rheumatism and astrologers told him his suffering was due to the displeasure of Thirumala Deva, whose devotees had been ill-treated by his ancestor. The king had to spend much energy and effort to bring back the icon of the temple to Cochin along with the community.[17]

II

I now try to tell the same story in a roundabout way, based on our conversations with a few persons belonging to different communi-

---

[17] S. Sreekala, interview with Purushothama Mallayya on the Kokanis in Cochin, 1999.

ties. These conversations are not the full story, but I hope they give a flavour of the attitudes, beliefs and passions that animate Cochin's public culture. Two caveats, at this point: First, the contradictions or inconsistencies in dates, figures and events in the following pages have been deliberately retained as parts of the narratives with which the people of Cochin live. Second, for the moment I have chosen the witnesses arbitrarily, to flesh out the arguments already made and to hint at a few of the cultural-psychological principles of Cochin's ecumenism.

It is not easy to construct the story of Cochin by talking to its inhabitants; for, the past of Cochin has been aggressively historicised during the last fifty years. Like Gujarat and West Bengal, Kerala has undergone a middle-class revolution in recent years. Not only do cities now dominate the landscape of the state, differences between the village and the city are no longer sharp. Both have been heavily infiltrated by school-texts-based, politically correct stereotypes inspired by some rather crude, tropicalised versions of left-Hegelian European thought of the 1930s. It has become difficult to get private narratives reflecting much privacy or personal feelings.

At first, all witnesses seem brainwashed to believe in the right values and Cochin's cosmopolitanism seems to be a triumph of secularism, rationalism, high literacy, the rudiments of a welfare state, Indian nationalism, urbanity and egalitarianism. If one is to trust these witnesses, these values seem to have entered Cochini society in the early medieval period, if not earlier, uncannily before they were formally launched as parts of the Enlightenment project in South Asia under the auspices of a series of colonial regimes. All Cochinis, in the beginning, seem to speak the same language, cite the same examples, and seem equally proud of Cochin's multi-culturalism and 'perfect' communal harmony. As the ideological strands associated with the culture of the Indian state exercise less control over the life stories and memories of the interviewees, a slightly different set of categories takes over. Then one finds, with some surprise, that most Cochinis have a partly shared, quasi-private theory of what makes Cochin tick. Only gradually do they come out with personal experiences and family histories that are no ordinary histories but emotionally-laden constructions of the city's past, transmitted over generations. They are first offered hesitantly, almost as skeletons in the family cupboard. Only after a while do some interviewees own them up as unofficial narratives, with which they 'partially agree'. In these narratives other communities, and even parts of one's own community, emerge as scheming villains, conquerors, victims, traitors, friends, enemies and protectors. There are moving stories of how one's own community survived and grew through its ingenuity, courage, cunning, and sometimes with the help of other communities. Cutting across ideological lines, however, the city itself always emerges as the hero.

The First Family of Cochin

The concept of 'feudalism', when mechanically imported and indiscriminately applied to pre-colonial structures and experiences in South Asia, often hides more than it reveals. In its decontextualised forms it can even sometimes begin to underscore self-serving, blinkered analyses of structures of authority that are unfamiliar and outside the range of one's own culture. Examined closely, these 'feudal' authorities often turn out to have enjoyed fewer privileges and standards of living than those enjoyed by their fire-eating critics adorning academe, the press, and policy-making bodies, and passing casual summary judgements on entire ways of life and eras of history.

Thus, the Dutch Palace at Mattanchery in Cochin, the former residence of the Cochin kings and a favourite of tourists, looks more like the enormous, pretentious home of a village landlord. A successful businessperson in contemporary India will not want to be caught dead in it. It exudes considerably less opulence and comfort than the homes of many who write fiery prose on the evils of feudalism. The royal temple adjacent to the palace, too, is a modest affair. Cochinis, however, are proud of both, for the Cochin kings are remembered with much reverence and fondness by their now-liberated subjects.[18]

The royal dynasty of Perumpadappu Swarupam is predictably Kshatriya. But they brought to their style of governance a touch of Brahminic austerity and self-denial. (As we shall see, some of their former subjects believe them to be Brahmins.) Indeed, almost all the members of the family I contacted referred to themselves as 'poor kings', known for their piety and scholarship.

There are, it is said, 800 to 900 members of the royal family in Cochin itself; 716 members share the family estate. Though traditionally matrilineal, the family has acquired a touch of primogeniture in recent decades. Its religious identity, too, has undergone subtle changes. Like most ruling Kshatriya families, it is technically Shaivaite; the family deity at Pazhayannur, Trichur, is an incarnation of the goddess Bhagawati. The temple, said to be an *Arjuna pratisthan* (that is, established by Arjuna, the hero of the Mahabharata), is at some distance from Cochin. Previously, blood sacrifices were offered at the temple. Now, as a symbol of those days, cocks are flown from the temple. Somewhere along the line, however, the Cochin kings have acquired the looks of a Vaishnava

[18] Years ago, freedom fighter and alternative historian Dharampal told me of a letter from a viceroy he discovered in the India Office Library at London. In it, the viceroy complained that the Maharana of Udaipur, the doyen of Rajput principalities, did not know how to live in kingly dignity; nor did the British in India know how to treat their friends and allies. The viceroy grumbled that the maharana received a monthly stipend of only Rs 3000 from his own treasury. Of this, about half was spent on commensal lunches; every day hundreds of ordinary peasants came and ate with the maharana. The viceroy recommended that the stipend be increased to Rs 3000 per day. This was duly done. At first nothing changed; only the number of peasants at lunch increased. However, in another generation and a half, inter-dining stopped and the dynasty began to show many of the 'classical' signs of feudal decadence, including flamboyant, mindless consumption and wastage.

family. The deity in the family temple at Tripunithura, Sri Purnath-rayeesa, is Vishnu.

Kerala Varma Thampuran, one of the four members of the family with whom we talked, is a cousin of the last king of Cochin, Pareek-shit Varma.[19] The king was a scholar in Sanskrit and English; his cousin is an unassuming journalist and a former captain of the first batch of Cochin State Forces. Raised in the 1940s as the Nair Brigade, it was later integrated in the Indian army. The brigade's name was changed in 1945 when the maharaja, Aikya Kerala Varma—so named because of his willingness to relinquish his throne to help the cause of India's unity or *aikya*—allowed other castes to join it. Kerala Varma has seen action in World War II. He also was on garrison duty at Mhow, Madhya Pradesh, where he looked after Italian prisoners of war. Afterwards, he managed for a while his brother-in-law's large rubber plantation. He could not manage it well, he admits, and it had to be sold.

Kerala Varma is now seventy-eight, but does not look it. He is slim, erect and projects self-assurance. With his white moustache, a touch of army manners, his *vesti* and plastic sandals, he looks more like a retired petty army officer than an erstwhile prince. Actually, he identifies himself as a journalist. He is friendly and helpful and, after talking with me at some length, took me to meet some other members of his family nearby. He seems for some reason to be the obvious choice as a spokesperson of the family. A number of persons suggested that we meet him.

[19] In the Cochin dynasty, the first three sons usually have the following names: Rama Varma, Kerala Varma and Ravi Varma, though there are odd exceptions. The king who gave up his kingdom to join the Indian Union was named Aikya Kerala Varma because of his commitment to Indian unity; another king came to be known posthumously as Madras Thampuran; he had died in Madras.

Presently, Kerala Varma stays at a house that belongs to his daughter; she and her husband are in West Asia, working on an oil-rig. It is a modest house at the fringe of the family estate in Tripunithura, which might have been a separate town once but is now a suburb of Cochin. The estate, studded by a large number of independent houses belonging to different members of the family, constitutes an updated, ancestral, dynastic township. The Sri Purnathrayeesa temple dominates it. Kerala Varma himself has married into the Travancore royal family; his wife, an impressive, self-confident woman, prepared and served us tea. I also met a couple of other members of the family. The house, the dress of the householders, the furniture and the crockery, indeed everything about the family, looked terribly middle class to me.

Our interviewee's colourful past, though, belies his appearance. A leftist and a modernist, Kerala Varma has fought elections with the support of the Communist Party of India. He was also the architect of the late V.K. Krishna Menon's victory in an election to parliament in the 1950s. Menon, Nehru's controversial friend and confidant, contested from Trivandrum; at the time, Menon presided over India's foreign office. 'I am a communist,' Kerala Varma blandly declares. He hastens to correct the 'general impression' that his entire family is communist. There are other shades of political opinion in the family; some are supporters of the Indian National Congress. Others supported the Gandhian freedom movement before Independence.

It soon becomes obvious that Kerala Varma tries hard to see the world through his ideology. The strain shows. Like some others in his family, he is obviously ambivalent about his origins and one can detect a touch of defensiveness towards his family. To him, time is basically an evolutionary unfolding of hierarchical and more liberal social practices. He remembers his childhood mainly as days of unmitigated conservatism, when he and his brothers went to school on horseback, sat separately from other children, and were often surrounded by bodyguards. In sum, he almost grudges the fact that he was brought up as a prince. (In practice this meant that, after the fourth grade, he was in a special school. That school was evidently special in more than one sense: it even had a Hebrew teacher, though there were only three or four Jewish boys in the school.) The Cochin royalty, he adds, was more conservative than the Travancore one. At first the family opposed the entry of lower castes into the palace temple. Only in 1950 did the Sri Purnathrayeesa temple allow entry to low castes. This was despite the fact that, in the family, males customarily married Shudras or low castes and women married Namboodiri Brahmins. The family never marries within itself, because it traces its origins to two sisters.

Gradually, as we continue talking, Kerala Varma becomes less self-conscious and begins to take liberties with his ideological posture. He is unhappy that E.M.S. Namboodiripad, the communist politician and former chief minister of Kerala, has called Aikya Kerala Varma a counterfeit coin and a hypocrite. He feels vindicated by the admiration that another communist chief minister, C. Achyuta Menon, had for the king. Kerala Varma now warms to the subject and begins to talk about his family's ecumenism with a touch of pride. He points out that though people usually notice the synagogue close to the Dutch palace, there is also a mosque close by. He claims that ecumenism has coloured the personal lives of some of his ancestors and relatives. The first Hindu–Christian marriage in the family took place around 1990. One member of the family married a lowly Puleya at around the same time. He mentions the case of a relative, Gopalika, who got trained as an Arabic teacher. When she, a Brahmin, was appointed to a Muslim school in Malapuram, there was strong opposition; she was made to resign. However, there was even greater opposition to this injustice and she got her job back in 1987, during the Left Front rule. Islam comes back to the royal family in insidious ways.

In political matters, Kerala Varma says, the Cochin kings were liberal. Responsible government was introduced in Cochin State in 1932, before such reforms were introduced in any other princely state of Kerala. A minister for harijan and rural welfare was appointed at around this time. In 1946, a year before Independence, King Aikya Kerala Varma signed the instrument of accession to the Indian Union. He did so at a time when some states, including Travancore, were toying with the idea of declaring Independence. Indeed, he was the first ruler to join the union and one of only three to do so voluntarily. (The other two were the maharajas of Mysore and Baroda.) All he wanted in exchange was an almanac. The king was 'the author of a cultural revolution in India,' Kerala Varma grandly declares, now more confident of himself. He forgets what he has told me earlier about his family's conservatism about temple entry and claims the family ensured temple entry among low castes in 1936.

The Cochin kings might have looked reasonably autonomous during their 600 years of reign, but in practice their lifestyles and choices were framed by a cultural and psychological triad that included the kings of Travancore and the Zamorins, the kings of Calicut. As we have seen, according to popular belief they all came from the same family and there was much social interaction as well as inter-marriage among them. But there was also competition, jealousy, and attempts to be distinctive. These attempts shaped politics and social policies, and ensured the emergence of three different styles of governance in the region. To judge by the comments of some members of the royal family whom we met, the Cochin maharajas were the simplest and, perhaps, the most naïve of the three. According to these informants, the Travancore kings were rich, powerful and shrewd—some of them were warrior-kings—and the Zamorins were aggressive, overly ambitious, and perhaps slightly inferior socially. (We were told more than once that the Zamorins, though Kshatriyas, did not wear the sacred thread and were not allowed to marry women of the Cochin family.) One suspects that while the Cochin kings did not dare to take on the Travancore family and felt inferior to them in the princely pecking order, they considered themselves superior to the Zamorins. This was not acceptable to the Zamorins. To put it another way, the Cochin family considers the Travancore family to be its real counterplayer, not the Zamorins. Yet, in practice, while the Zamorins and the Cochin kings competed and fought for generations, the Travancore kings were too powerful to be bothered with either.

There are, however, dissenting voices. According to one family friend of the Cochin kings, the Zamorins were the ones who courageously resisted the Portuguese, the Dutch and the British. The Travancore and Cochin kings compromised at every step. The self-image of the Cochin dynasty is that of humble, folksy people given to piety, simplicity and poverty. Even while granting their right to that self-image, it is obvious that this friend would have liked them to have shown more aggressive resistance to the colonial powers.

Though Kerala Varma has married into the Travancore royalty, his loyalties are clear. He claims that the people were made to respect the Travancore kings, whereas the Cochin kings were respected spontaneously. One suspects that, like most members of his family, Kerala Varma, too, carries a certain ambivalence towards the Travancore family—a family which, according to him, was sometimes tyrannical.

Venkitangu Jairaman supplies some of the missing footnotes to Kerala Varma's story. Jairaman is an art critic, writer and journalist. He is fifty-four and has been writing in the *Indian Express* for years. Slim, bespectacled, with closely cropped greying hair, white shirt, a sandalwood mark on forehead, a *vesti*, he look likes any other upper-caste Malayali. 'My father belonged to the royal family; I do not,' he said, probably hinting at the matrilineal traditions in his family. He has mostly been an independent writer but has worked in a press for a while. He writes mainly on classical Carnatic music, theatre and paintings. He chose to meet me at my hotel, perhaps to spare me the problem of locating his house in the crowded city centre.

Like many others, Jairaman starts by saying that Cochin is a loveable city. It has retained a touch of its 'semi-urban', 'semi-pastoral' past and can be habit-forming; 'those who come to the city do not go back.' As a result, the older residents of Cochin are becoming a minority. Other cities are not like this, Jairaman insists. Trichur, another cultural centre of Kerala nearby, is meant for Trichuris; Cochin is for everyone. Jairaman traces this openness to Cochin's erstwhile monarchs. They were 'pious and Spartan'. They 'never amassed wealth' and were 'perfectly secular'. For these qualities they were 'considered foolish by others'. Yet these qualities explain why they have survived the demise of the princely order. They can live within their means because their needs are few. Their emphasis on education has also helped. The entire family, including the women, is well educated. Today, all the royal women are employed and almost all are college graduates. No royal family in India enjoys this advantage.

The family, because it was born from two sisters, was previously strictly exogamous. Now, endogamy is not unknown to it. 'The texture of the family' has changed. There is much more intimacy within the family, Jairaman believes. In this respect, too, the family is different from the Travancore royalty. According to Jairaman, the looser family ties of the Travancore dynasty are a legacy of Martanda Varma, the warrior-king of Travancore.

Jairaman moves on to an aspect of Cochin rarely talked about: its contribution to the arts, especially music. He points out that T.N. Krishnan, N. Rajan and L. Subrahmanyam are all from Cochin. The city has produced a large number of musicians and artists, less due to royal patronage than to royal openness to the new and the strange. Unlike other Indian princes, the Cochin kings never directly patronised music. Nor did they produce anyone like Swathi Thirunnal, the king of Travancore who renounced everything to write devotional lyrics and compose music. But the Cochin kings had that crucial ecumenical attitude—'anything that came up, they allowed'. Cochin flourished culturally as a result. The family can even take credit for innovating the game of one-day cricket, some fifty years before it was formally launched in world cricket.

Because the kings were liberal, Jairaman says, the people were also liberal. Cochin's 'soil has not been fertile for fundamentalism or communal riots.' This liberalism of the kings came from their piety. Foreigners were often 'at first taken aback by the simplicity and piety of the kings.' It is said that once, on the occasion of an eight-day ritual feast at the family temple, someone discovered a systematic theft of foodstuff and complained to the maharaja. The maharaja took it calmly; he said it was a good way for the conse-crated food, *prasadam*, to reach a larger circle of people. Sadly, oth-ers interpreted such piety and tolerance as weakness. V.P. Menon swooned when the Cochin maharaja only asked for an almanac and a hand-fan in return for joining the Indian Union and giving up his royal privileges and rights.[20]

The same attitude of openness informed other areas of political action. When some members of the family turned anti-British in colonial days, no one interfered; it was seen as part of their personal ethics. Once, during World War I, a king even had to abdicate be-cause of his differences with the British. 'They were not supine or invertebrate, despite their piety,' Jairaman says. Perhaps this is his reaction to a feeling which exists even in those close to the family—that while the Zamorins courageously fought the Portuguese, the Dutch and the English, Cochin's kings, like their counterparts in Travancore, 'adjusted' to changing realities.

[20] The belief is widespread that invaders often took advantage of the naïve tolerance of the Cochin kings. According to Nobel, the scientist researching the Jewish roots of his family, the Portuguese took full advantage of the reli-gious tolerance of the ruling family to introduce religious chauvinism in Cochin. They destroyed the churches and sacred objects of Syrian Christians and harassed the Jews.

The Jewish Diaspora

There are two main Jewish communities in Cochin: the White Jews and the Black or Malabari Jews. The latter are also known as Myuchasims. 'Black' and 'white' are terms the Cochinis and the communities themselves use; there is no defensiveness associated with them. In recent decades, however, subtle changes have crept into these self-definitions. As the Jews themselves have become a major symbol of Cochin's multiculturalism, the two main Jewish communities have simultaneously come closer and moved further away. Of the two communities, the Black Jews claim to have a hoarier past, but the White Jews are the more conspicuous presence. That too is a source of a minor tension now; some Black Jews feel the White Jews are separating themselves from others; this they never did in the past.[21]

Even before the founding of a proper Jewish settlement and, later, a Jewish kingdom in Cranganore, Jewish oral traditions claim that Jews were in Malabar, in and around Cochin. Since the time of King Solomon, some of them say, they traded in gold, ivory, sandalwood, peacock feathers and, of course, spice. This old connection is said to have encouraged the settlement of Jews after the destruction of the second temple and, in another wave, around AD 1000. This was when full rights were given to them to settle in the area.

There might have been a third community once, the Meshuhrarim, literally 'freed slaves'. Much less is known about this, though a charming autobiography gives clues to their lifestyle.[22] We have not met anyone who admits being a Mushuhrarim; all of them might by now have migrated to Israel. In any case, it is a controversial category; some deny that such a community existed at all.

[21] Some accounts suggest that the tension between the two Jewish communities was a gift of colonialism and the politics of colour. See, for example, Daniel and Johnson, *Ruby of Cochin*, pp. 132–3. See also below.

[22] Ibid.

We also heard of a few Baghdadi Jews who were at Cochin once, but they were individuals and families brought to the city mainly by work. Most of them migrated to Britain soon after Independence. However, the most famous Baghdadi Jewish family in India, the Sassoons, established a more enduring connection with the city; one of the Sassoons married into Fort Cochin's most illustrious Jewish family, the Koders.

According to Samuel Halegua, the acknowledged leader of the community, at the moment there are about twenty families of White Jews left in Fort Cochin and thirty-four families of Black Jews in Ernakulam. He says that in the Cochin region there are eight synagogues, two of them in Ernakulam. The Paradesi synagogue at Fort Cochin is the most famous of them. It is the oldest synagogue in the British Commonwealth.

We first met Samuel Halegua when he made a presentation at a meeting of community leaders at Cochin. He was introduced there as a leader of the city's Jewish community. He made an excellent and, in many ways, moving presentation on the history, experiences and concerns of Cochin Jews.

Later we met him, his wife Queenie, and a few others from his community, including Joseph Halegua, the sexton of the synagogue. Samuel Halegua is sixty-six but looks much younger. He is self-confident and articulate. Like some others in his community he has the looks of a Southern European, but unlike some others cannot pass off as a North Indian. Though he does not say so, he began as mainly a leader of the White Jews of Cochin who, according to some, came into India as late as the thirteenth century. With the dwindling population of Jews, he has almost automatically become the main spokesperson of the city's Jews. While talking to us, he shifts between the White Jews, all Cochin Jews (including the Malabari Jews), and Indian Jews; and the dates he mentions do not often sound right. However, as far as Jewish history in India is concerned, he talks on behalf of all Jews and traces the origin of Judaism in India through its quasi-mythical history stretching two thousand years.

Samuel Halegua and Queenie stay in a large, modest but enchanting, two-storied house on the Jew Street, Fort Cochin. They are cousins, and when they fell in love and married their marriage was seen as a continuation of the long tradition of intermarriage between the Haleguas and the Koders, two of the most important families of Fort Cochin. The Halegua family has never had much to do with Cochin's famous spice trade; they have mainly been gentlemen-farmers. They still own some agricultural land where they grow rice and coconut. Some of their ancestors could be called merchant-princes. Samuel Halegua's grandfather brought electricity to Cochin and pioneered a highly profitable ferry service in the city. This gave employment to a number of Jews, and the Jews usually travelled free on the ferries. The Cochin royalty valued the Haleguas; one in the family was given the title of Mudaliar (though the Levys produced the first Mudaliar among the Jews of Cochin). Evidently, the community did not put much emphasis on formal education; the women in particular did not go in for higher education. Samuel's grandfather was the first matriculate in the community, his aunt the first woman matriculate and graduate. Jewish society tends to be patriarchal, he adds almost apologetically.

Samuel and Queenie might have been brought up in an extended-family-like environment, but now they have to live by themselves in a large house. Their children have migrated to Israel. But they continue to come back to Cochin every year, not merely to meet their parents but also to participate in various community festivals. The house the Haleguas live in is roughly 250 to 300 years old. It is on a narrow street, with a few well-stocked antique shops and a couple of small, attractive bookstores. The houses on the street are joined together by common walls. They all once belonged to Jews, but many have now been sold. Jew Street once had three synagogues, but only one, the Paradesi Synagogue, is still in use. It was constructed, Halegua tells us, in 1334.

Though well maintained, Halegua's home is not museumised. This is surprising, given his popularity among scholars of Jewish history and anthropologists. There are a few artefacts that reflect the traditions of the house and the family, but they are not obtrusive. It looks very much the home of an easy, well-to-do middle-class family in Kerala, with its usual touch of austerity and Edwardian charm. The language of Cochin Jews is Malayalam and Halegua talks to his wife and the visitors who interrupt us in Malayalam. He calls it his mother tongue. It is a bit of a shock to some visitors to Cochin when they first hear two whites talking among themselves in Malayalam. However, Halegua speaks to us in fluent English.

Halegua himself seems well entrenched in Cochin. He has grown up in Jew Street and, as he once said in an interview to the BBC, it was like being brought up in a joint family. He starts by reminding me that different Jewish communities in India came at different times and, to that extent, their experiences and bonding with India are different. For instance, the Baghdadi Jews first came to India in the late eighteenth century, whereas the Bene Israelis have a history stretching into myths, folklore, and memories transmitted over generations. The various Jewish communities also differ in socio-economic and cultural status. Halegua's own community is well placed economically; they are a part of Cochin's élite.

When discussing the 2000-year-old history of the Jews in Cochin, Halegua mentions the even older connection between ancient Israel and India. The Talmud, written nearly two thousand years ago, mentions pepper from India as free from ritual pollution. There are also similarities between old Tamil and Hebrew; certain words in the two languages are close to each other. He implies that even these ancient links centred round Cochin. He probably means Cranganore but then, to him too, Cochin is only a reincarnation of

Cranganore. However, he acknowledges that most White Jews probably came into India from Spain as late as the seventeenth century, via the Ottoman empire, which had welcomed them after their expulsion from Spain in the late fifteenth century. The earliest available data on the White Jews of Cochin belongs to the seventeenth century.[23] The Bene Israelis, on the other hand, though probably an older community, are less well off. Culturally, too, they have no liturgy of their own, whereas the Cochin Jews, especially the White Jews, do. The latter have also maintained closer links with Hebrew. Over the centuries, some of them have written poems and songs in Hebrew. Halegua's own grandfather wrote songs in Hebrew.

Halegua is proudly Jewish. Like many Cochin Jews, and unlike most Bene Israelis I have met, he bears a slight ambivalence in relation to Christianity. Christ was born a Jew, and he lived and died a Jew, he says, but persecution and discrimination against Jews has been typical of Christian Europe. In Islamic countries they have been treated better. Though large parts of his family have settled in Israel, Halegua maintains a certain distance from the present-day problems of the Israeli State. He is committed to Israel, but not blindly. He certainly does not sound like an Israeli nationalist. The distance may be due to the Israeli attitude towards the Arabs. He likes the Arabs because of their excellent past treatment of Jews. This may also have something to do with Cochin's Arab connection.

Halegua is also a trifle distant from conventional interpretations of the Holocaust. He has read much on the subject and, naturally, feels strongly about genocide. But he has self-consciously tried not to be bitter. He finds it difficult to hate a 'whole nation' for the crimes of a regime and system. Apparently, in this respect, geographical distance and Indian experiences have played a role. While

[23] The Halegua family itself came to India from Spain via Alleppo and, hence, they have always maintained their links with the Yemeni and Aden Jews.

the ideas of religious and ethnic hostility and violence have a place in his world, the industrialisation of homicide—the cattle trains and chimneys of the Holocaust—remain alien to him. For that matter, he even found the 1984 riots against the Sikhs in Delhi 'unbelievable'.

Halegua is a proud Malabari and Indian too. 'I never wanted to live anywhere else,' he has more than once said. This is not merely nationalism; he is deeply attached to the Malabari, particularly Cochini Jewish traditions. His self-definition is that of a custodian of these traditions. They include everything from the distinctive liturgy and marriage rites of the region to Jewish versions of pancake called pastelle, and hot chicken curry. They also seem to include his interest in cricket while living in football-crazy Kerala. He strongly disagrees with Hanna Arendt, whom he identifies as an 'American sociologist'. According to him, Arendt has argued that persecution and discrimination have ensured the survival of Jewish culture. 'Arendt is wrong', Halegua says. 'We have not been persecuted or discriminated against, yet we have retained our identity.'[24] He agrees with the news item published in a journal given to us by a resident of Cochin:

> The only safe haven in the history of the Jewish Diaspora is disappearing. . . . India has been uniquely free from anti-Semitism . . . According to oral history, Jews arrived in Shingly, Cochin, in the year of 72 (Common Era), shortly after the destruction of the Second Temple in

[24] He does not know that, living with the culture of Israeli politics, partly organised around competitive histories of discrimination, sections of the Cochin Jews in Israel seem to have developed a sense of loss for not having a 'proper' history of oppression. At least a few of them have invented a less peaceful history of the community at Cochin. Some expatriate Malabari Jews there spoke of harassment and discrimination against the Jews at Cochin. To the dismay of the anthropologist known for her work on Indian Jews, who had taken me to meet the group, one of them talked with some relish about how St Thomas in the first century brought anti-Semitism to Kerala and precipitated a first-class conflict between the 'Jacobites' and the 'Catholics'.

Jerusalem. In the fourth century the Maharaja of Cochin granted them royal rights for 'as long as the world and the moon exist.'[25]

In 1492 the Jews were expelled from Spain, a few years after that from Portugal. But the Ottoman Empire welcomed them. Many came from Spain to India, after spending some time in various Arab societies. Portuguese rule in Cochin, however, was a tough time for the Jews (AD 1505–1663). 'We have known religious intolerance only from the Portuguese,' Halegua says; the inquisition in India was crueller than in Portugal. Dutch rule between AD 1664–1773 was slightly better. The synagogue constructed in AD 1334 remains the centre of community life in Cochin. Halegua sometimes leads the prayers there. The Cochin kings used to visit the synagogues, often carrying gifts, another Jewish informant tells us; prayers were said for them there.

For Halegua the major problem of the Indian Jews is 'numbers'. Between 1950 and 1960 more than a thousand Jews left for Israel: that was the major exodus. Around 1700 and 1800 Jews were now left. Migrants return off and on to Cochin, mainly at festival times; all have 'strong attachments' to India, Halegua claims. There are between four and five thousand Indian Jews in Israel.

This last remark of Halegua acquired certain poignancy over our last day at Cochin, when we were invited by his mother-in-law, Mrs Koder, at an evening get-together at the beginning of Sabbath. She is the oldest member of the community in the city. Her husband is dead and her children and most other relatives have migrated to Israel. She stays in a palatial house stretching over two blocks, with a retinue of about twenty. When we joined her in the

[25] *Rotunda* 16 (1), December 1991. See also the documentary film *Two Thousand Years of Freedom and Honor: The Cochin Jews of India,* Director: Johanna Spector (212) 666.9461. Halegua says that the Jews were given their rights in the fourth century and the engraved copper plates, which formalised these rights, were given to them in the fifth century. Others claim that the plates were actually given to the Cochin Jews in the tenth century.

evening, there were a few others there, who seemed to represent Cochin's past more than its present. Most of the invitees were in their seventies and eighties. Among them were a retired British business executive, a successful elderly Indian businessperson, an English journalist who stays permanently in the city, and a retired government servant. Most of them seemed regulars at Mrs Koder's place. Mrs Koder, hard of hearing, presided over the get-together in regal style—talking loudly, deciding who would come and sit next to her or have the privilege of speaking to her. It was a charming but exceedingly sad evening. For the entire atmosphere seemed to anticipate the moment of death of a proud, self-confident culture, dying perhaps for no reason other than the passage of time. The servants staying in the ground floor of Mrs Koder's house were probably waiting for her to die so they could occupy the elegant house. The costly, antique furniture and other artefacts in the house seemed waiting to be vandalised. We visitors at the party seemed to know that time was against us. As I talked to the guests I could almost see they were all haunted by the thought that it could well be the last such evening there. Their gaiety seemed to be of the forced kind often associated with a particularly painful farewell.

Malabari Jews, also known as Black Jews, are a shadowy presence for many scholars and historians who have studied the culture and history of Cochin's Jews. According to some accounts, fiercely disputed by others, Black Jews are freed slaves who were converted to Judaism and given a synagogue.[26] In recent decades White Jews have dominated the public imagination of the Cochin Jew. Self-confident and articulate, most White Jews also speak excellent English. Black Jews, on the other hand, give the impression of being

---

[26] *The Cochin Synagogue: 400th Anniversary Souvenir* (Cochin: 1968); see also Daniel and Johnson, *Ruby of Cochin*.

ordinary, middle- and low-brow Cochinis. Yet, for that very reason, they have an especial place in the city's culture. White Jews are a part of Cochin's élite; Black Jews are their more accessible, everyday version. However, a slight resentment has grown among Black Jews towards White: not so much because of the latter's wealth, influence and social salience, but because of the feeling that, during the last fifty years or so, White Jews have tried to distinguish themselves from Malabari Jews and become more strictly endogamous. (This came out even in some of my conversations with ex-patriate Malabari Jews near Jerusalem. They complained that only in recent times have White Jews claimed cultural distinctiveness and laid stress on their greater acquaintance with Jewish culture and rituals.) The complaint, however, has its other side. Samuel Hale-gua claims that White Jews tend to be endogamous not because of colour prejudice but because they are protective about their liturgy. They find Yemeni Jews fully acceptable even though they are darker than Malabaris.

Eliavoo Abraham may not be old, but he looks elderly. Soft spoken, exceedingly polite (in the way people in Indian public life often are), he gives the impression of being nondescript not by default but by choice. His son, Sam, has an automobile garage in Ernakulam, which also sells luxury cars. It is located in Ernakulam's Jew Street. Like the other Jew Street in Fort Cochin, this one too is identified with a proud community that shows no sign of defensiveness. It is a community that has felt protected against most of the humiliating experiences of the Jewish Diaspora. We met Eliavoo and Sam Abraham at the garage for the first time. Hospitable and friendly, they invited us to their home for a chat.

During the first visit we found out that Eliavoo himself had moved to Kiriyathyovel, Israel, twenty-five years ago, in 1973. His other son lives there. Sam stays at Ernakulam and looks after the garage. Eliavoo now comes every year to Cochin to visit his family and is also active in community affairs in the city. The Abrahams are a reasonably well-to-do family that has had a long interest in

Jewish culture. Eliavoo's uncle was a Hebrew teacher. His father, however, had less exalted interests; he supplied vegetables to the maharaja's palace for twenty-nine years. In appreciation of his services the maharaja gifted him a gold chain.

Eliavoo's grandfather died in 1940. He had been instrumental in laying the foundation stone of a grand synagogue the same year. Eliavoo was then very young. He does not remember his grand-father but remembers the days when both synagogues of Black Jews were active. They are now closed. His grandfather used to tell him that the Abraham family had stayed in Cochin for 600 years, but Eliavoo himself had not taken much interest in the history of his family nor ever asked his grandfather about the history of the Cochin Jews. Eliavoo now seems to regret that lapse.

Eliavoo remembers his childhood with a touch of nostalgia. He studied in Maharaja's School, with the princes and princesses of Cochin, even though he himself was of a modest background. He married in 1950. Like him, his wife was born on Jew Street. The 1980s were a bad decade for him. His father died in 1980, his mother and wife in 1984. That past pulls him to Ernakulam's Jew Street every year and he has to repeatedly affirm that he was very happy in India. He had been a successful Class-I PWD contractor for seventeen years—from 1954 to 1971. Though he claims he is also happy in Israel, he seems to feel his job in India gave him more prestige and dignity.

In Israel, he worked at first in a post office. Now he is an accoun-tant in an ambulance service, a semi-government job. He faced many difficulties at the beginning because he had to take care of everyone from his family who migrated to Israel. He also had to spend two years learning Hebrew in a government language centre. His parents, sister and brother-in-law, who joined him in Israel, never learnt any Hebrew. Eliavoo also had to work as a watchman for a while. Now, he is better off, but there is something in his tone which suggests that, like many first-generation immigrants, he is ambivalent about his adopted country.

That ambivalence has many sources, the most important of

them being the youth culture of Israel. Like the sexton of Cochin's main synagogue, Eliavoo is uncomfortable with that culture, which he sees as amoral and decadent. He distinguishes himself sharply and sometimes aggressively from the many Israelis who come to India as tourists. He does not believe they are genuinely interested in India or Indian culture. They come to Goa mainly to smoke hashish, he claims. Of the 300 odd Cochini Jews who come to Cochin from Israel every year, he estimates that roughly 40 per cent are interested in Cochin's Jewish traditions; 60 per cent are not.

Yet he is pretty certain that the remaining Jewish families in Cochin will also move to Israel. (According to him, there are about eleven Black Jewish families left in greater Cochin.) This is because of the problem of marriage. In Cochin there are just not enough marriageable boys and girls among Jews. Also, the heavy migration that took place has taken its toll. Now they have to make an effort to assemble the quorum of ten for prayers. For his prayers, Eliavoo joins White Jews at the synagogue at Fort Cochin, where Samuel Halegua serves as priest. The synagogues of the Malabari Jews remain closed.

As we talk and Eliavoo relaxes, his ambivalence about Israel becomes clearer. He starts by saying that the Jews had various problems in India, such as those faced by schoolgoing children in the family. They could not observe many of the rites and rituals of Sabbath. They had to go to school on Saturdays, and that was hard on the community.[27] Also, the better schools in greater Cochin were Christian missionary schools; members of the community constantly feared that their children would be taught the principles of Christianity or inducted into the Christian worldview and would lose respect for their own faith. As with many others of his community, Eliavoo Abraham's image of the local Christians is

---

[27] There is obviously a difference in the self-confidence of the Haleguas and the Abrahams. Samuel Halegua speaks of a cousin who joined the Indian navy and was finding it difficult to go through the usual drill on Sabbath. When the cousin complained to Samuel's father-in-law, the latter directly wrote to the prime minister. The rules were quickly changed.

split. He remembers the amicable relationship the Jewish communities had with Christians, but he also remembers the Portuguese
violence against the Jews as a defining moment in the life of the
community.

Yet, now that he is in Israel, he says, he constantly remembers
Cochin in Israel, and Israel in Cochin.[28] As he says this, Eliavoo
warms to the subject and is no longer as defensive or protective
towards Israel. He says, 'We always tell our grandchildren that
Cochin is the best place in the world, if you want to live peacefully.'
Suddenly he blurts out, 'I regret I went to Israel.' He adds that even
people with money in India cannot go and buy a shop or a house
in Israel. 'Israel is not an easy country.' But then, when they migrated, many Malabari Jews were poor; some 80 per cent of them,
he estimates, 'lived below the poverty line.' That was why they emigrated. Many of them are millionaires today.

It now transpires that in India Eliavoo took part in active politics. He remembers those days with much nostalgia and gives the
feeling that he regrets going to Israel mainly because he does not feel
efficacious in that society. Perhaps he also feels humiliated by his
inglorious low-skill jobs in Israel after his stint in Cochin's local
politics. Moreover, he and his family had 'very close relations' with
all the other communities of Cochin, particularly with the Brahmins and the Nairs among the Hindus and the Muslims. That had
helped him in his political career. The Muslims lived near Jew
Street and within Jew Street was a Muslim house. Malabari Jews,
he adds, are usually close to Muslims. Even in Israel they feel close
to Moroccan and Yemeni Jews. They are 'like the Malabari Jews
even in colour and orthodoxy.' From the context it appears he feels

[28] Eliavoo's case is not isolated, nor individual whimsy. I remember Ichak
Nehamia, a Malabari Jewish immigrant at Moshav Nevatim near Jerusalem,
telling me on behalf of his community, 'We like to live as if we were in Kerala.'
Indeed, Nehamia and his friends made it a point to serve us typical Malayali
food and claim that the Malayali food the Cochin Jews prepared in Israel was
better than that available in Cochin.

close to them also because of their similarities with Muslim neighbours he knew at Cochin. A touch of sadness creeps into his voice as he distinguishes himself from other Israelis, and he says, 'Israeli Jews and Muslims quarrel every day.' He adds proudly that some Israeli political leaders publicly say that Israelis should learn how to live with Muslims from Indian Jews. Eliavoo also grudges, though not explicitly, the compulsory military service in Israel.[29]

Three generations of the Abraham family stay in a beautiful house in the suburbs of Cochin. Sam, the son who runs the garage, is 48 years old. He, too, had emigrated to Israel, but came back after thirteen years to Cochin in 1985, because 'it was a quiet place.' The move also probably had something to do with his war experiences. He had fought in the Yom Kippur war in 1973 and the Lebanon war in 1984.

[29] Evidently, despite his long stay at Israel, Abraham has not picked up the anti-Muslim slant that occasionally intrudes into Daniel's account. While herself giving examples of the good relations between Jews and Muslims at Cochin (Daniel and Johnson, *Ruby of Cochin*, pp. 7, 97, 100–1, 145, 181) and even having an index entry on the subject, at one place she generalises: 'The Muslims and Christians as well as the Jews have stamped the Hindus as idolaters. But if you want to know what is humanitarianism you must go to them. You must look at a group of Jews who lived under the regime of these Hindu rajas for the last two thousand years without knowing discrimination. The Hindu rulers protected them when they came under attack by the Portuguese and Muslim rulers. In his petition to Oliver Cromwell before 1655 for the resettlement of Jews in England—from where they were driven away in 1290—Manasseh Ben Israel pleaded and gave the example of the tolerance enjoyed by the Jews of Cochin under the Hindu regime. The Jews of Cochin should be grateful to those Hindu rajas and the people of Cochin for their very existence as Jews in their country forever and ever.' Daniel and Johnson, *Ruby of Cochin*, p. 123. As with many Malabaris, Daniel's favourite villain of history is Tipu Sahib (1751–99). She tells the story of how a Jewish friend of Tipu's father, Hyder Ali, pleaded for Tipu's life when Hyder Ali had drawn his sword to kill his son for some act of cruelty. Hyder Ali gave in to his friend, but also warned him that his death would be at the hands of Tipu, and so it happened, ibid., p. 127.

Sam's wife, who served us tea and shortcakes, is indistinguishable from an upper-caste, Hindu woman, what with her elegant sari, *bindi* on the forehead, and easy Malayalam. Sam's son Anil Abraham—Sam had another son who had died some years ago in an accident—is even more aggressively a Cochini. Self-confident and articulate, he says he wants to go to Israel to see things for himself. He knows his grandfather wishes him to go and settle there, but he is clear his trip will only be exploratory. From his stray comments it appears he is also toying with the idea of running his father's business at Ernakulam. Sam, too, perhaps apprehensive about his surviving son being drafted by the Israeli army, seems to agree with his son rather than with his father.

The Abrahams are finding out the hard way what Basil Elias, a Jewish urologist at the General Hospital, Ernakulam, articulates openly. Elias tells us he is attracted to Cochin because it is a city of immigrants. 'Nobody here actually belongs to this place. It is built by immigrants.' Obviously, he looks at his community as one of those that have built Cochin over the centuries. Cochin belongs to the Jews as much as it belongs to the others. Elias' grandfather left for Israel in 1954 and he himself visited Israel in 1985. He now expects his children to go first to Israel and find out things for themselves. He himself is ambivalent about the idea of immigration.

Other Cochinis see the future as less open. Many of those we met seem prepared for the loss of the city's Jewish community. But they are not reconciled to the idea. Some years ago, in BBC's radio programme, 'The Last Jews of Cochin', the secretary of the city's spice traders' association compared the departure of the Jews with a daughter's marriage. One knows 'she may be doing well, but there is a sense of loss.'

Two 'Immigrants' Speak

Cochin introduces itself to you in unexpected ways. I remember the first afternoon of my first visit to the city for this study. We were having lunch at a seaside restaurant. Two people, one with a vermilion mark on his forehead, came and sat at a nearby table. They immediately ordered rum and Coca-Cola. My associate, an anthropologist, guessed they were BJP functionaries and predicted they would order beef preparations. They did. After lunch we joined them uninvited at their table and had a chat. They were exceedingly friendly and told us they were organising a BJP rally that evening. They were fortifying themselves for the job and were perfectly frank about what they were eating and drinking. They had to be strong, they claimed, as if mimicking BJP critics who accuse the party of being pathologically masculinity-seeking.

Communalism has reached Cochin but failed to make deep inroads. Hindu nationalist pamphlets in Malayalam, directed against Christians and Muslims, are occasionally published from Cochin and distributed in some of the other cities of Kerala. I am told they are not easily available in Cochin itself. This has something to do with the warp and weft of Hindu-Muslim relations in the city, particularly their social perceptions of each other. Ostensibly, neither sees the other or itself as a monolithic community. Nor do the others see them as such. Despite the entry of modern categories and attempts to delegitimise older categories like caste, most Cochinis with whom we talked continue to see generic terms, such as Hindus, Muslims and Christians, as representing confederations of living, identifiable communities. Many who claim to have risen above the traditional divisions of castes and sects slip into the use of these divisions when off-guard. As a result, there is no minority complex in the majority community, the sort that one finds in large parts of North India. The Hindus are a majority and the Muslims and Christians are minorities only theoretically. Two of those who told us the story of Cochin were Hasan Nasar and Muhammad Iqbal.

Hasan Nasar is a Malayali novelist in his late fifties. His grandfather migrated from Southern Yemen to Cochin. Their tribal surname was ba-Nasir. Nasar knows the names of seven generations of his ancestors. His grandfather made him learn the names. However, he has not taught his own children any family genealogy: 'I want to mingle', he says. He adds that, over the generations, his family has lost some of its older characteristics. Previously, there was a surfeit of Arabic words in the Malayalam his family spoke. That is no longer the case. He does not say so directly, but his experience of working in Riyadh in Saudi Arabia has something to do with the erosion of interest in his Yemeni roots. He is still proud of his origins, but not of 'those people'—probably meaning the Arabs whom he came to meet at Riyadh. His discomfort with Riyadh bears a relationship with the lifestyle and consumption patterns in that city. Presumably, he did not like them. That sojourn has made him more proud of being a Cochini and strengthened his sense of belonging to the Cochini Muslim community.

Nasar proudly says, 'Nowhere in the world will you find a community like this. Walk one kilometre and you will find more than one language and religion.' He quickly enters into a comparison between the cosmopolitan cultures of Dubai and Cochin. He does not like the former. 'Dubai has taken too much from the West; they spend their holidays in Europe.' On the other hand, Cochin has retained something of its Self. It is still, Nasar feels, a city of communities and, despite many recent changes, the city itself remains a community. There are not many instances of separate living or ghettos at Cochin; most of the localities are mixed. Yet the differences are not ironed out. 'If you go even ten kilometres away from Cochin, they speak perfect Malayalam, whereas there are so many dialects in the city. They add richness to its culture.'

In Cochin there is a custom, also found elsewhere in India, of people speaking one language at home, another at work, and using still another for creative self-expression. Nasar proudly mentions Kunal Jussawala, a Gujarati journalist who has become a well-known writer in Malayalam.

Of course, there are inter-communal distances in the city. Nasar gives the example of Kutcchi Memons who do not allow the use of their cemetery even to other Muslims. But these distances are more than compensated for by Cochin's tradition of mutuality. Even in the fourteenth and fifteenth centuries, Nasar says, India was known for its tolerance; so was Cochin. Indeed, he claims that the Spanish and Portuguese Jews tempted Vasco da Gama with money and other incentives to find a sea route to India. For the Iberian Jews, da Gama's fateful trip to India in 1498 was a means of accessing Cochin's legendary ecumenism and generosity.

At this point Mohammed Iqbal, a journalist and writer, intervenes. He is approximately sixty and is a Kutcchi Qazi, whose forefathers migrated from Kutch in north-west Gujarat. He speaks Kutcchi, too. From his tone it seems he feels that Nasar has not been fair and assertive enough about the culture and traditions of Cochin. (Iqbal, I suspect, thinks me to be a journalist, probably on a mission to dig out instances of Hindu-Muslim conflicts in the city. We are meeting soon after the Bharatiya Janata Party Government has come to power and the party's Hindu chauvinism is a much-debated subject in the newspapers. He seems to assume that I want to join the debate in my columns.)

Iqbal points out that not only in Cochin but in the whole of Kerala there has flourished a 'rich heritage of hospitality, since the time of King Solomon.' He has read somewhere that King Solomon's palace was adorned with teak wood and ivory. He is convinced that the wood and ivory went from Kerala. He claims that even a community of slaves from Mozambique has played a role in the history of Cochin, not as slaves but, strangely enough, as a cultural symbol. The practice of *Kappirri Muthappan* (kafir grandfather) involved what could be called slave worship among low-caste Hindus, as a system symbolically analogous to that of *Yaksha* in Eastern India, for the protection of hidden wealth of a person or a family.

Apart from these transcontinental connections, the city itself, according to Iqbal, is a remarkable testimony to communal coexistence. Apart from the communities usually mentioned, there are the Swetamber and Digamber Jains with their own functioning temples; Parsis, Sindhis, Dawoodi Vorahs, Maharashtrians, Konkanis (who have separate temples for Brahmins and Vaishyas, and even a special temple for Konkani goldsmiths); Bengalis, Kudumbis, Telugus, Tulus; and two sects of Tamil Brahmins, of whom Palghat Iyers are particularly conspicuous. He proudly adds that Cochin is a mosaic of communities. I have heard Cochinis speak of their diversity on a number of occasions. All Indian metropolitan cities have hundreds of communities; in none of them have I found people speaking as proudly of their diversity and the 'different histories' of their people, as if diversity itself was a value, and by itself constituted the first marker of the uniqueness of a city.

Mattancherry, at one time, Iqbal says, was settled by a large number of Muslims. They are still there but, proportionately speaking, their numbers have dwindled. They celebrate Deepawali, like the Hindus. 'My father was a pious man. He used to take me for the Deepawali celebrations.' Every community has examples of how it went out of its way to acknowledge or interact with other communities. He gives example of the *Coonan Kurish* (Bent Cross) oath that the Christians took to defend the Cochin kingdom against European powers. There were nine synagogues at Cochin at one time. As opposed to this, 'see, what is happening in Northern India.' Actually, North India seems to haunt Iqbal. 'There is no threat to the culture of Cochin,' he says confidently at one point and then quickly adds, 'but we are concerned when we see the national scene.'

Iqbal too believes that the Cochin maharajas had much to do with Cochin's ecumenism. They were, he seems to suggest, Brahmins, but not purists. Ten days before Onam they used to have a festival called Athachamayam. Technically, it was a Hindu festival and involved taking out a large procession. Invariably, the Naina

Muslims were in the front row of the procession. Even low-caste Hindus, Iqbal adds, had a place in the procession.

The unique feature of the city, according to Iqbal, is that nobody has 'abandoned' his or her cultural background, and yet everyone can appreciate other cultures. Even 'the advent of faiths like Christianity and Islam have been perfectly peaceful' in the city. The Arabs have maintained connections with Malabar since pre-Islamic days; one of the first groups to carry the message of Islam outside the Arabic tribes came to Cochin. It was led by Malik Ibu Deenar al Habeeb, a direct disciple of the prophet. Earlier the Arabs lived in a settlement in southern Cochin. The Chinese, too, lived in peace in a settlement at Fort Cochin and they built some pagodas there. Ma Huan was a Chinese Muslim. In 1963 when a ship hit the Malabar coast, some evidence of this settlement accidentally became available.

Cochin's ecumenism, Iqbal claims, extends to the humbler domains of life. Though they are exposed to Carnatic music, Cochinis can appreciate Ravi Shankar, Pankaj Mallik and ghazals. He also talks of the 'Pottey Ramayana' of the Konkanis and the way it has influenced other communities. Indeed, Iqbal believes that Cochin's diversity has allowed the influence and customs of communities to act as forms of cultural criticism of other communities. Thus, many of the 'regressive elements' in the culture of the Saraswats, such as the Devadasi system, have broken down under the influence of Christianity and the social status of Saraswat women has improved.

III

This is not the full story of Cochin. It is an exploratory peep into its strange charms. The scraps of conversations I have strung together are parts of a much larger narrative, and I have not told the story of the communities that may provide a glimpse of what both communalised and secular India would call, Hindu Cochin. A few things, however, are relatively clear even from this incomplete story.

Seemingly, Cochin does not offer any unique theory of communal amity or religious tolerance. It is multicultural not by design but by being itself. As we have seen, the city does not ooze with brotherly love: its easy communal amity includes communal distances and hostilities. But these distances and hostilities, because they operate within a widely shared psychological universe, have certain in-built checks against mass violence and nihilistic rage. Cochin, all said and done is a community where distances and hostilities, like closeness and friendship, have specific, culturally defined meanings. Resembling an annual Ramlila that cannot do without its demonic anti-hero Ravana, in Cochin one has to relive one's self-definition as much through one's enemies as through one's friends. For within Cochin's psychological universe one needs one's enemies to define oneself and one is aware every moment that one is incomplete without them.[30] This need to have enemies (to spite psychoanalyst Vamik Volkan) never acquires a passionate, homicidal edge. There is a certain optimality about Cochin's loves and hates.

The beehive-like organisation of communities endorses this optimality. The communities in Cochin do not swim together in a steamy melting pot. Indeed, their lifestyles, while being intertwined, are also partly autonomous. These sectors of autonomy, which can be called community affairs, subsume under them 'legitimate' differences in religion, caste and sect. These differences in the city have not lost their meanings, value and sense of continuity with the past, either in the communities or in their neighbours. As a result, after a point, despite ideological pretences, nobody seems particularly disrespectful towards or defensive about them. Communities can afford to take on the moderate hostilities of others because their self-esteem has not been badly damaged. Such

[30] Vamik D. Volkan, *The Need to Have Enemies and Allies* (New York: Jason Aronson, 1988).

hostilities do not constitute what psychoanalysts call a narcissistic wound.

'The future,' Jim Hicks reaffirms while reviewing Bruno Latour and Ivan Illich, 'may ultimately be found in our premodern past.' Perhaps because in the high noon of modernity that past, uncontaminated by modernity, allows a freer space for imagining a future less shackled by the present. Indeed, along with Mangalore and Calicut, Cochin is a window to a once-flourishing and now-forgotten alternative—probably threatened—culture of cosmopolitanism. That culture, I may have said at the beginning, refuses to die. However, I am more aware now that the refusal may end up guaranteeing an ugly, slow, painful death. In our times, the dice seems to be loaded against cultures dependent on the survival of communities and community ties. Cochin is constantly bombarded by ideologies that have little respect for the city's distinctive style of dialogue of cultures; it is subject to steam-rolling development and a style of random urbanisation that has become the hallmark of Asian and Latin American economic growth. The only saving grace may be that Cochin is still terribly habit-forming. It seems to socialise one very quickly to its algorithm of life, which is probably a way of subtly inducting one into the city's community-based normative frame. As sections of its Jewish population are finding out, just when you begin to feel you have washed Cochin out of your system, the city begins to haunt you like a friendly, persistent ghost.

Is that too shifting and fragile a base on which to build? The question troubles one because, as we have frequently seen in this century, when proximity sours, it releases strange demons. The Hutus and the Tutsis, the Bosnian Muslims and the Serbs—and in South Asia itself, the Punjabi Sikhs, Muslims and Hindus in the 1940s, and the Sinhalas and the Sri Lankan Tamils—they all are witnesses to the pathology of nearness rather than that of distance.[31]

[31] Ashis Nandy, 'The Invisible Holocaust and the Journey as an Exodus: The Poisoned Village and the Stranger City', in *The Ambiguous Journey to the*

Neighbourliness, Don Miller has again reminded us, always carries a load of ambiguity; neighbours themselves are—or can turn into—strangers.[32] Some sections of Cochin anxiously wait to hear the verdict of contemporary India on its version of neighbourliness.

One final word on the nature of this enterprise. In contemporary critical theory, criticism has been mostly unidirectional. The idea of systematic, durable, cumulative social knowledge in such theory has come to mean knowledge that demystifies manifest social realities hiding less palatable truths (realpolitik, class relations or psychosexuality, for example). In the mainstream global culture of knowledge, it is seen as an act of intellectual courage to unmask the manifest to unravel the hidden, the tacit or the latent in its full ugliness—in turn seen as closer to truth for that very reason. During the last hundred years, new certitudes have been built on such demystification. From Nietzsche to Marx to Freud, it has been the same story.

For a long while, this model has served the social sciences well. It has deepened the awareness of economic and political power and psychological and cultural defences that have hidden subtler forms of violence and dominance, which previously seemed natural or legitimate. However, with the knowledge industry gradually domesticating critical theory into a new domain of expertise, the theory's one-way style of demystification has not merely become a new source of certitude, but also a new means of legitimising the forced obsolescence for those marginalised by the world system. This study of Cochin once again suggests that the challenge is to

---

City: The Village and Other Sundry Ruins of the Self in Indian Imagination (New Delhi: Oxford University Press, 2001), pp. 98–139.

[32] Don Miller, *Neighbours and Strangers* (Delhi: Rainbow, 1999).

redefine what Philip Rieff calls the analytic attitude, and to exercise a new scepticism in the case of the defeated cultures in the tropics. This scepticism may involve challenging a series of ideas—among them progress, rationality, development and modern science—that, at one time, the victors of the world might have feared but have now come to adore. Critical theory will not be maimed if it borrows something from the idea of unending criticism or criticism of criticism implicit in Buddhist dialectics in general, and Nagarjuna in particular. In such criticism the unsightly that underlies the apparently trivial can also be further demystified to reveal a 'truth' that signposts alternative ways of organising a humane society.

The story of Cochin also suggests that multiculturalism need not be merely a political or social arrangement, nor even be a principle of citizenship that tolerates or celebrates disparate lifestyles. Multiculturalism may sometimes imply a culturally embedded identity in which the others are telescoped into the self as inalienable parts of the self. In that case, they survive not merely as fragments of a negative identity, but also as temptations, possibilities and rejected selves. Such internalisation is not unknown to psychoanalytic psychology though there is in it, in this instance, a larger cultural dimension. The internalisation need not be of significant individualised others; it can be of culturally significant collective others.[33] This, in turn, means that the communities do not usually need any painful rite of exorcism, because the spirits that populate the inner world of the Cochinis are no strangers. They are more like friendly ghosts who occasionally become unfriendly enough to haunt one.

[33] This is a process vaguely parallel to the one Sudhir Kakar describes in folk therapeutic contexts in his *Shamans, Mystics and Doctors* (New Delhi: Oxford University Press, 1993).

CHAPTER 7

Violence and Creativity in the Late Twentieth Century

Rabindranath Tagore and the Problem of Testimony

This essay—which was once a keynote address on Rabindranath Tagore—demands that I supply two caveats, one patently trivial, the other less obviously so. First, my childhood and teens in Calcutta were the golden days of keynote speaking. Keynoting everywhere is a ritual; it was doubly so in Calcutta in the 1950s, especially when it involved a symposium or conference on Tagore. We feared them. Keynotewallahs were then called inaugural speakers or chief guests and were seen as something like village elders. Wisdom was imputed to them, but also a degree of intellectual infirmity. I am told that Kalidas Nag, a permanent fixture as a keynote speaker at the time, went on the day of his daughter's marriage to the wrong wedding. As he was buttonholed by admirers and never went close to the real ceremony, he never found out his mistake. He got busy playing the keynote speaker and explaining the symbolic meaning of Indian marriage to some non-Indian invitees he had spotted. Only after his family informed the police was he restored to them. Keynoting, I learnt early in life, was not an unmixed blessing. It could be even more hazardous in the case of a person like Tagore, whose iconic presence in Indian cultural life tends to preclude any radical revaluation of his life and work.

Secondly, as you well know, all Bengali intellectuals are automatically Tagore scholars. I am not. I have merely read Tagore with pleasure and learnt from him. I would not dare give him a testimonial or recommend him to the Western academic world as an interesting Asian voice. I would find that humiliating.

The origins of this essay lie elsewhere. Years ago, I used to toy with the idea of writing a book on the culture of poverty without once mentioning the word 'poverty'. Indeed, by doing an empirical study of the super-rich and their lifestyle, I wanted to tell the story of the poor. I never quite acquired the self-confidence to execute the idea, but off and on I have played with similar ideas. Thus, I *have* tried to write on M.K. Gandhi without invoking his name. 'The Discreet Charms of Indian Terrorism', included in my book called *The Savage Freud,* was given in 1988 as a Gandhi Memorial Lecture; it uses Gandhi's vision and categories but with hardly any reference to him or his work. I shall make a similar effort here and try to liberate Tagore from Tagore himself and from his admirers, bypassing his formidable public presence as a defender and marker of Bengali self-esteem. Instead, I will deploy some of his insights and sensitivities to explore aspects of the relationship between violence and creativity in our times. I dare to do so because of Tagore one can say, echoing Auden's famous comment on Freud, that he was not merely a person or an institution but also a climate of opinion. If so, it is not necessary to always work on Tagore; it should be possible to work with him. Unfortunately, that also means acknowledging that Tagore, like Gandhi, may not be the best representative of his own worldview in all respects. Some aspects of his worldview might have been better represented by others before and after him, by people as diverse as Gandhi and Satyajit Ray in India, and Henry David Thoreau and Thomas Mann outside. I shall invoke Tagore here primarily as a climate of intellectual inquiry.

To do so, I shall focus on two aspects of Tagore's response to our times: his sensitivity to the specific forms of violence in which the twentieth century has specialised, and his attempt to transcend limitations on the creative imagination that the dominant concepts of creativity and the global order of cultures have imposed.

I

All efforts to talk about the future are a way of talking about the present and past. Talking the language of the future only forces us to look at our times and our pasts differently. Thus, if we look at the twentieth century from the point of view of the next, we are quite likely to conclude that ours is the century when human destructiveness reached its creative pinnacle. We might even admit that the ultimate symbols of the century are not space probes and computers but gas chambers and Hiroshima. The slaughter in the two world wars, the pogroms, the various holocausts starting with the Armenian and the Jewish ones and ending with the Cambodian and the Rwandan, the Stalinist terror, the carpet bombings and the fire bombings in various wars—they all constitute a rather impressive performance. Twentieth-century science may have produced many wonderful discoveries and miracles, but the gas chambers and the mushroom clouds remain its most resilient symbols. Years ago, I had started with a conservative, cautious estimate of something like 85 million people killed in the last century in avoidable, man-made violence. Despite the caution, the figure went on rising. Within a year or two it rose to nearly a hundred million. Today it is higher than 200 million. For I have now taken into account, in addition to the usual list of infamy, things like the avoidable Bengal famine of 1943 that killed at least two million, the two invisible famines in China that were Mao Tse Tung's immortal contribution to world civilisation, and casualties of more than forty, mostly forgotten, wars fought since 1945. Others have mentioned even higher figures.

This awesome destructiveness has killed not only individuals, but communities, cultures, ideologies, and worldviews. It has affected us, our children and grandchildren, perhaps even our imagination. For this violence has found a way of lodging itself in the less accessible parts of our consciousness and influencing us without our being any the wiser. Certainly, I am not surprised when I find that information-loaded mass societies in the West, living with their magnificent record over the last four hundred years in the Southern world, are getting more and more brutalised and seeing incredulously an element of psychopathic violence creeping into their public culture and even into the culture of their children and youth. During the last few years in the United States, the annual rates of homicide are said to have remained consistent around 30,000 and that of rape at around 100,000 a year. Without the benefit of numbers, George Orwell diagnosed the same malady in the 'Politics of the English Language' and identified in the 1940s a change in the quality of violence in Britain in his 'The Decline of English Murder.'[1]

One can now write similar essays about a number of societies. For the same change is now infecting the cultures of societies eager to mimic the societies they consider more wealthy, powerful and successful, possessing the 'normal' pathologies that go with success, including high levels of everyday violence. The rise in violence in a number of Indian cities has in recent years been spectacular. The South Asian euphoria over the nuclear tests, however short-lived and however limited in geographical spread, can be also read as an example of the same story of brutalisation and necrophilia. It reflects not merely deep feelings of inferiority, masculinity-striving and parity-seeking, but also a certain nihilism and vague, almost free-floating genocidal rage. I am not sure what came first in Europe in the 1930s: the Jews as a people who had to be hated or a free-floating, genocidal hatred looking for a target. Certainly,

---

[1] George Orwell, 'Politics and the English Language', in *Inside the Whale and Other Essays* (London: Penguin, 1957), pp. 143–57; and 'Decline of the English Murder', in *Decline of the English Murder and Other Essays* (Harmondsworth: Penguin, 1968), pp. 9–13.

the format of the holocaust had been already worked out in the tropics by the colonial powers; Europe in the 1930s only established some continuity between its domestic and international politics. A touch of that same diffused anger can be found in urban India, Brazil and Russia today, even if in attenuated form, for it is a natural consequence of the destruction of communities, cultures and worldviews that have taken place during the last fifty years. Hannah Arendt recognised the nature of this pathology when she saw European fascism as an attempt to build a compensatory pseudo-community.

This widening scale of violence and our sudden face-to-face confrontation with it in the age of *Homo psychologicus* have redefined our concept of what is creative and what is not. Because one by-product of the massive destruction of human beings and cultures in this century has been the destruction of social norms, cultural values, and the artistic and disciplinary conventions identified with certain cultural groups. These once shaped many distinctive styles of creativity but also, in the process, bridled some forms of creativity. In this sense, nothing probably has 'freed' the arts more than the two world wars. What we have done or not done with that freedom is a different matter. On this level, our passionate affair with dispassionate, professional, technicised mass murders *have* shaped our concepts of creativity and creative freedom. We know the source of our creative freedom, but we do not want to know it. The colossal destruction that we have inflicted on our fellow humans has made us wary of our new unbridled creativity. That destructiveness has also made us terribly insecure; we are afraid that the same laboratory principles that have helped us kill millions in this century might be applied to us some day. Our destructiveness has brought us face to face with our deep fears of transience, but without the benefit of the theories of transcendence that made such fears bearable in earlier centuries.

This is only part of the story. The anxiety of self-confrontation has been, perhaps understandably, matched by carefully nurtured forgetfulness or, as the presently fashionable expression goes, erasures.

Some psychoanalysts believe that human creativity is essentially restitution; it seeks to compensate for feelings of anger and hatred that we nurture within us, and the moral anxieties these feelings trigger. From this point of view, creativity is a form of atonement; it is born in our innate destructiveness and our fear of and guilt about such destructiveness. There has been ample reason for us to atone in this century and, if we take seriously what some of the early psychoanalysts ventured, our creativity should have not only flowered but also borne the stamp of this massive guilt. Perhaps, to some extent it does. However, it seems that we have been so brutalised, so exposed to and benumbed by the wanton, gratuitous violence in this century, either directly or through the media, that our creativity does not really carry the full imprint of the violence we have seen. Our creativity is built not on the ego defence of restitution and symbolisation but on massive, cultivated intellectualisation and on the more primitive defence of denial.[2]

I have a favourite story which I have told elsewhere but cannot help repeating. It seems that in 1945 three of the greatest scientists of our times calculated the level at which the nuclear bomb had to be exploded over Hiroshima, a city that had no military significance whatsoever, to maximise damage and casualties. All three—Enrico Fermi, John von Neumann and Richard Feynman—lived and died as highly respected scientists, recognised for their creativity all over the world, including Japan, which they so disdainfully devastated. Few have stopped to ponder what kind of persons they might have been, given what they were computing. The distinguished scientist A.K.N. Reddy, who told me this story, also added that when the three took their computations, which were to doom 140,000 non-combatants at Hiroshima, to Norbert Weiner to

[2] One version of this denial could be the numbing that is so central within the works of Robert J. Lifton, such as *Nazi Doctors: Medical Killing and the Psychology of Genocide* (New York: Basic Books, 1986).

check, he refused to collaborate. So the defences of rationalisation and denial of the three did not go unchallenged: Weiner's reaction must have breached the wall to some extent. Yet, so formidable were the defences, that ultimately, the self-righteousness of Fermi, von Neumann and Feynman triumphed, not the self-doubt of Weiner. Even without sympathising with the anti-intellectualism of the kind with which Mao Tse Tung and the cultural revolution went to town, one understands why moderate versions of such intellectualism have infected, at different times, so many cultural figures, from Tolstoy and Thoreau to Gandhi and Tagore. What looks like their stylised pastoralism is often an attempt to break out of the violence of rigid intellectual frames.

It is possible that our creativity, though an atonement, is also a defence against recognising the full might of the violence within us. We do not feel overburdened by the death of the millions we have killed in this century because in each case we have carefully chosen institutional and individual scapegoats, who, by themselves, are made responsible for the genocide: Hitler, Stalin, American hegemony, the military-industrial complex, capitalism, fundamentalism, Fascism, colonialism and neo-colonialism, and so on. We do not feel that the blood of millions is on our hands because we do not believe that our ideas of social engineering, evolution, progress, education, and development are complicit with the various versions of contemporary satanism. Even when finding scapegoats, we are cramped by contemporary sacred cows such as modern science and scientific rationality. At one time I had much hope that the post-Foucauldian sensitivity to the bonding between power and knowledge would somewhat correct this, but that initiative, too, I now notice, is getting increasingly formalised as another dispassionate, professionalised discipline within the mainstream culture of knowledge.

In sum, if our culpability in this century has been massive, that does not mean our sense of guilt has been commensurate and, unless it is so, atonement too cannot be adequate. To that extent our creativity has been dwarfed not by external limits but by internal ones. There is some indirect evidence for this. In Western literature, the deepest and most impassioned analyses of human violence and the moral issues it poses come arguably from Dostoevsky and Tolstoy, both of whom wrote before the two world wars, the Stalinist purges, the Nazi death camps, the fire bombing of Dresden, Hamburg and Tokyo, and the nuclear bombing of Hiroshima and Nagasaki. The true literary response to the violence of our times is yet to come. Chairing the jury to select a design of a memorial for Auschwitz, Henry Moore had to recognise this problem:

> The choice of a monument to commemorate Auschwitz has not been an easy task. . . . The crime was of such stupendous proportions that any work of art must be on an appropriate scale. But, apart from this, is it in fact possible to create a work of art that can express the emotions engendered by Auschwitz?
>
> It is my conviction that a very great sculptor—a new Michelangelo or a new Rodin—might have achieved this. The odds against such a design turning up . . . were always enormous. And none did.[3]

Faced with the problem, or perhaps the sheer scale of it, we seem to have lost the capacity to produce a *Crime and Punishment* for our times; we can only produce a *Heart of Darkness, One Day in the Life of Ivan Denisovich* and *Slaughterhouse Five*.

Indeed, after World War II the great theorists of violence have increasingly come from outside literature. They have come from psychiatry, psychology, philosophy, even biology and ethology. It is as if our literary imagination failed to grapple with the scope and

[3] Henry Moore, quoted in James E. Young, *The Texture of Meaning: Holocaust Memorials and Meaning* (New Haven: Yale University Press, 1993), pp. 134–5. I am not arguing that these defences are the only sources of our inability to cope with the full range of human violence. There are certainly more 'mundane' sources in operation, too. See for instance, Mick Broderick (ed.), *Hibakusha Cinema: Hiroshima, Nagasaki and the Nuclear Image in Japanese Film* (London: Kegan Paul, 1996).

range of violence in our life; as if we had to set up a second line of defence by further professionalising the issue. If the twentieth century saw a new form of expertise in violence, it also had to cope with the double meaning of this expertise. One of the two meanings is represented by the person who, unlike the warrior in earlier times, is an industrial tycoon of violence—often without any hate, any open ideology of violence, and any conspicuous touch of the millennialism that many scholars such as Robert J. Lifton consider an unavoidable part of genocidal ideologies.[4] The other meaning is personified by the expert who studies violence all through life and becomes perfectly blasé about it.

Have our experiences cramped or frozen our creative imagination? Have we literally become a bit speechless when facing the scale of violence in recent times? It is not impossible, but it is unlikely. Even a simple bibliography on violence will run to thousands of titles. Once, while planning to re-review the work of Theodor Adorno and his associates on the authoritarian personality, I came up with a preliminary listing of some four hundred items. Had it been the whole area of violence, the list would have had to include at least a few thousand books and papers.

Our imagination may not have been stifled or fettered, but it reflects a conspicuous asymmetry. While our cognitive sense has been challenged by our exposure to large-scale violence, our emotional and intuitive selves have been more numbed than challenged. Bureaucratised, dispassionate, calculated violence has often produced quasi-bureaucratic, dispassionate, calculated analytic ventures. Stanley Milgram's studies of human heartlessness are quite heartless themselves. I am not surprised when I hear rumours about the Nazi connections of Martin Heidegger and Konrad Lorenz.

In recent years I have come to suspect that this style of studying and talking about violence may have something to do with the

---

[4] Robert J. Lifton and Erik Markusen, *The Genocidal Mentality: Nazi Holocaust and Nuclear Threat* (New York: Basic Books, 1990), p. 98.

West's genocidal record outside the West during the last four hundred years. The extermination of millions is not easy to live with; it cries out for elaborate intellectualisation and rationalisation. Even the best-studied genocide in the world, the European holocaust, bears the mark of that cultivated forgetfulness. To trust psychoanalyst Henry Ebel, A.J.P. Taylor was the first to notice the extent to which the statesmen of the major European powers, in the 1930s, seemed to give Hitler cues concerning the areas in which he should push.[5] Ebel adds:

> The fact that the Western powers, before the Second World War, seemed to be sending out encouraging signals to Hitler—including encouragement for his anti-Semitic policies—is perfectly understandable, however, once we acknowledge the extent to which Hitler and Nazism were 'acting out' their own suppressed impulses; indeed, the extent to which they were able to suppress these impulses only *because* he was acting them out.[6]

I have often asked myself if the denial of that record of genocide and collusion with genocide has imposed a particularly onerous responsibility on our conceptual grids and categories, mostly produced and honed in the modern West. In the modern world does one have to handle gingerly all the violence that comes as part of a grand project of reason, progress and disenchantment? Certainly the great figures of the Enlightenment, from Vico to Voltaire, were garrulous on the subject of reason and taciturn about nonviolence as a guiding principle of social and intellectual life: as if reason in public affairs had nothing to do with nonviolence. Has the dominant idea of metropolitan civility, grounded in the vision of the European Enlightenment, itself been in league with that hidden record of violence? Have we somehow sensed that the neighbourhood

[5] Henry Ebel, 'How Nations Use Each Other Psychologically', in Howard F. Stein and William G. Neiderland (eds), *Maps from the Mind: Readings in Psychogeography* (Norman and London: University of Oklahoma, 1989), pp. 117–32; see pp. 128–9.

[6] Ibid., p. 128.

police has all along been in the pay of the thugs and, to further mix metaphors, have we all along been making intellectual protection payment to the cultural history of our social knowledge? The abstraction and reification of violence, I have come to suspect, might itself have become an elaborate, ornate ploy against recognising only some kinds of violence and denying or de-recognising others. Even the classical liberals and the Left Hegelians have not been able to face that record; even Marx had to impute to some forms of violence progressivist implications and a creative historical role.

Our creativity is partial, I suspect, because our atonement is partial. Our atonement is partial, in turn, because it does not acknowledge the full range of the violence on which the modern, disciplinary knowledge of violence is founded.

However, I am not pessimistic. This limited creative understanding of violence is not the last word on the subject. At the moment, we are benumbed not only by the scale of violence but also by the destruction of many of the conventions and codes that held together the world of creativity till the inter-war years. One reason why some of the finest creative minds engaged with the problem of human violence have shifted to science and the social sciences could be that conventions and norms still have a place in these sciences. Such conventions not only allow you to define conformism but also dissent. That is much less true of the arts. Till the inter-war years, in the case of virtually every great artist or writer in Europe, it was possible to more or less precisely state what convention or norm he or she had broken to mark out a place for himself or herself in the world of creativity. What was true of the great artists and writers was also more or less true of major art movements. That is now less true of the world of humanities, literature, and even music. Norms and conventions have already been broken with such impunity and ease in these disciplines that even minor writers and artists have gleefully got into the game. Often, you have to pretend to break a norm that already lies in smithereens around you.

This is not a roundabout plea to return to traditions of the kind to which T.S. Eliot paid homage. There *are* some parallels between his position and mine, but this is mainly a plea to admit that the scale of destruction in this century has created an environment of inner exile and uprooting that has not allowed new conventions and traditions to crystallise in the world of creativity. Indeed, we have been so busy celebrating the freedom and the space that the absence of norms has given to individual creativity that the idea of destructive creativity is no longer an oxymoron to us. We have had no time to distinguish between the loss of norms and conventions which we should celebrate, and the loss of those that must be made good, those that need to be resurrected in new guises for us to transcend the intellectual fetters of the nineteenth century. Hence the remarkable paradoxes of freedom in the twentieth century: the expansion of individual freedom in our times has often gone hand in hand with the continuing bondage of communities, cultures and peoples and, within the same society, with the diminishing capacity of individuals to use that individual freedom. The expansion of choices has often coextended with the abridgement of the same choices through relentless, one-way, media communication and advertisements that constantly engineer new needs. In the United States, for which some indirect data are available, bilateral and multilateral communication now occupy a small proportion of all communication; that figure was much higher a few decades ago.

Rabindranath Tagore's creative self was a magisterial protest against the dominant theories of violence and counter-violence. He was probably the first to identify the banal, sanitised machine violence of our times and much before Gandhi had entered the Indian political scene, Sisir Kumar Das shows that Tagore had anticipated and welcomed the emergence of a figure like Gandhi.[7] And

[7] Sisir Kumar Das, 'The Great Victim: Gandhi and Bengali Literature', *Social Science Probings*, June 1985, 2(2), pp. 131–48. Das acknowledges his

when Gandhi entered Indian public life, few gave him such un-stinted sanction. From the character of Dhananjay Bairagi in *Prayaschitta* (1885) and *Muktadhara* (1922) to the song '*Oi maha-manava ashe*' to the self-discovery of Gora in *Gora* (1908), many of Tagore's creative works can be read, Das suggests, as attempts to envision the emergence of someone like Gandhi. Tagore *did* re-cognise that Gandhi represented forces larger than himself; that Gandhi did not have to be the best Gandhian on all issues. Those who get caught in the manifest contents of the various Gandhi-Tagore debates have access to only half the story. For tacit in those debates was a dialogue on the future of India's past. That dialogue presumed some basic agreements. Both believed that the principles of the modern state and nationalism and the theory of progress in its various incarnations had already established the new violence of our times as a significant cultural bridgehead within Indian civil-isation. Both believed that this new violence was framed in moral, rational, optimistic theories of progress and a latent theory of blood sacrifice. And, therefore, resistance to that violence would have to self-consciously take a position against mainstream universalism and scientific-secular rationalism. It might even have to require a new language of faith.[8] Even the idea of multiculturalism may have

---

debt to Pramathanath Bisi, '*Rabindra Sahitye Gandhi Charitrer Purbhabhash*', *Rabindra Bichitra* (Calcutta: 1945), pp. 89–103.

[8] The best known controversy between Tagore and Gandhi centred around the Bihar earthquake of 1933, which killed thousands. In an essay bound to provoke modern Indians, Gandhi said, 'I want you to be supersti-tious enough to believe with me that the earthquake is a divine chastisement for the great sin we have committed against those whom we describe as Harijans' (untouchables). Tagore vehemently protested and Gandhi gave a spirited reply. Sabyasachi Bhattacharya (ed.), *The Mahatma and the Poet* (New Delhi: National Book Trust, 1997), pp. 156–61. The best way to enter the debate is to look at it, firstly, as controversy over the viability of the concept of collective *karma* in Hindu, Buddhist and Jain theologies or, alternatively, as a debate on the idea of collective guilt. Neither of the two debates can be

to be rethought. For it should invoke not an inventory of cultures but a multi-layered self, constantly in dialogue with others, conceptualised not as distant strangers but as alien fragments of the self.

Central to that dialogue between Gandhi and Tagore was also an agreement on the position one must take on the idea of sacrifice in politics—about who and what could be sacrificed, with whose consent and with what kind of sanction for the distant, impersonal, sanitised violence associated with modern sacrificial rites. Those who think that this awareness first emerged in *Char Adhyay* and *The Crisis of Civilisation* will do well to re-read Tagore's early work, *Sacrifice* (*Rajarshi*), which probably set the context of Tagore's moving tribute to Gandhi:

> He stopped at the thresholds of the huts of the thousands of the dispossessed, dressed like one of their own. He spoke to them in their own language; here was a living truth at last, and not quotations from books. For this reason the 'Mahatma', the name given to him by the people of India, is his real name. . . . At Gandhi's call India blossomed

---

settled through easy coffee table discussions and easy answers, as Ramchandra Gandhi's work on the subject and the still-raging debate on collective German guilt for the Jewish holocaust show. See particularly, Ramchandra Gandhi, 'Earthquake in Bihar: The Transfiguration of Karma', in Ramchandra Gandhi (ed.), *Language, Tradition and Modern Civilisation* (Poona: Indian Philosophical Quarterly, 1983), pp. 125–53. Arguing that a 'morally inquiring and unafraid man often says things the implications of which he himself is not fully aware,' Ramchandra Gandhi seems to argue that Mohandas Gandhi's claim was a variation on Simone Weil's belief, 'When we have sinned by injustice it is not enough to suffer what is just, we have to suffer injustice' (p. 151). 'The "unscientific" and "absurd" (in Kierkegaard's sense) character of his [Gandhi's] remark invites us to envisage the truth that continuing great or small moral wrongdoing on our part deeply roots sinfulness in human moral reality and by reason of a reciprocity more mysterious than causality, which could be called *karma,* makes others, quite arbitrary others, suffer . . .' (p. 134).

forth to new greatness, just as once before in earlier times, when Buddha proclaimed the truth of fellow-feeling and compassion among all living creatures.[9]

Tagore's attitude to Gandhi might have been influenced by his commitment to reason, but it was framed by his diagnosis of the violence of our times. That is why before his death he bequeathed his visionary rural university at Shantiniketan to Gandhi.

II

I now move to the other part of the story that I have only touched upon till now: the changing landscape of individual creativity and its relationship with institutionalised violence. Let me start with an example from my own life. Forty years ago when I first began working in the area of psychology of personality—the twentieth century's incarnation of the ancient human curiosity about the self—I was particularly interested in the personality correlates of human creativity, mainly creativity in science. At the time, much work was being done in the area. The sputniks had made the United States nervous that the Russians might leapfrog into the twenty-first century, leaving the Americans behind. Whether as a consequence or not, a number of major scholarly attempts were sponsored in North America to identify scientific or academic talent at an early age. Many of these attempts focussed on the personology of creativity, as Henry Murray might have put it.

There were a few recurrent themes in these studies.[10] Three of the main ones could be very crudely summarised as follows: First,

[9] Rabindranath Tagore on Gandhi, quoted at Sannidhi, Gandhi Smarak Nidhi, New Delhi.

[10] Some random instances that give a flavour of such studies are Ernst Kris, *Psychoanalytic Explorations in Art* (New York: International Universities Press, 1952); Anne Roe, *The Making of a Scientist* (New York: Dodd, Mead, 1952); B.T. Eiduson, 'Artist and Non-Artist: A Comparative Study', *Journal of Personality*, 1958, 26, pp.3–28; D.W. Mackinnon, 'The Personality Correlates of Creativity' (1962), in P.E. Vernon (ed.), *Creativity* (Harmondsworth:

a number of studies showed that, as compared to the highly competent, the highly creative were more androgynous. If they were men, they displayed qualities more associated with femininity and if women, qualities more associated with masculinity. Second, the personality of the creative had a more 'childlike' mix of the rational and the irrational, as compared to that of the academically highly competent but less creative. Borrowing a term popularised by Ernst Kris at around the time within the psychoanalytic literature on creativity, 'regression at the service of the ego', one could say that the highly creative had greater access to their primitive, irrational self and had a richer fantasy life than the less creative. Thus, the highly competent but less creative scientists seemed to have greater mastery over their disciplines; the more creative tended to be less organised and disciplined in their knowledge. The highly creative showed, as compared to the highly competent, less command over the technical literature of their subject; their readings, too, were less systematic. Often they showed ignorance of research directly relevant to their disciplines. Third, the highly creative consistently showed greater tolerance for ambiguities, chaos and open-endedness, and avoided premature psychological closure. When encouraged to choose between different kinds of graphic patterns, for instance, they chose the more complex, less symmetrical ones.

Over the years, I had moved away from the study of creativity and almost forgotten these works. Then, in the late 1970s, I began to work in a new area: psychology of colonialism and, especially, the crisis of the Indian self as it grappled with the experience of colonialism. I had to now read a mass of work by Western authors who, from Catherine Mayo of *Mother India* to John Strachey and James

---

Penguin, 1970), pp. 289–311; Frank Barron, *Creativity and Psychological Health* and *Creativity and Personal Freedom* (Princeton: Van Nostrand, 1968); and 'The Psychology of Creativity', in *New Directions in Psychology* (New York: Holt, Rinehart and Winston, 1965), pp. 1–134; C.W. Taylor and Frank Barron (eds), *Scientific Creativity: Its Recognition and Development* (New York: Wiley, 1963).

and John Stuart Mill, whose work was well known to historians but, to a clinical psychologist like me, mostly new. I found to my utter astonishment that their construction of the Indian self, too, showed certain running themes.

Once you ignore the likes of Mayo, the colonial theory of the Indian personality, I became aware, was not so much a product of hate as of dispassionate scholarly 'impartiality'. It was mainly a theory of sexual and cultural identity, coupled to a theory of necessary violence and re-education or resocialisation. It was certainly not standard racism. At least the basic assumption of much of the colonial literature, once it crystallised out as a distinct school in the mid-nineteenth century, was that there was no irreconcilable difference between India and Britain. Only India was what Europe had once been and, if India behaved, it would one day approximate its colonial master. The character traits that stood in the way of India becoming more like Britain, according to the colonial theories of Indianness, were, first, that most Indian men, particularly if they happened to be non-martial Hindus, tended to show a rather deplorable touch of the qualities of women and children. They were just not masculine and adult enough. Second, equipped with insufficient scientific spirit and organisational skills, Indians often showed a rather sad inability to distinguish between the mythic and the historical, the magical and the rational, the real and the unreal. Indians were often vague, indecisive, other-worldly, and abstruse. (Anyone interested in capsule versions of this entire gamut of traits should flip through the works of James Mill and Rudyard Kipling.) Suddenly, traits that in the early 1960s seemed identified with creativity had re-emerged in my life as markers of a different set of cultural and intellectual hierarchies; they come packaged as colonial explanations of Indian decadence and non-creativity.

There must be a moral to this story which I, for the moment, leave readers to decode. However, I cannot help remarking that here lies one possible clue to our inability to fully confront the violence of our times. To the extent that nineteenth-century social evolutionism remains a crucial component of presently dominant global culture, human creativity itself remains fettered.

The second possible approach to the intersection of human creativity and destructiveness lies in the changing meaning of creativity itself. Human creativity was once seen as not merely individual creativity. Bhasa, Bernini and Rumi, to give random examples, would have been horrified if told that their works were merely instances of great personal achievement, or smacked of a newness totally disjunctive with the past. They might not have considered that a compliment, for art was to them a ritual and a form of worship, partly a divine gift. The chances are that they even felt that they by themselves did not entirely sculpt or write their works; they were, partly, instruments through which the works were sculpted or written. When it seemed that they had done something spectacularly new, it was only in the sense that they had reinterpreted certain traditional texts, imageries and forms and these reinterpretations were truer to the original purposes of these texts, imageries and forms. Some of the stalwarts might even have said, as Sigmund Freud did after writing his *Interpretation of Dreams*, that such insights are *given to one* only once in a life time. Physicist E.C.G. Sudarshan tells me that, in some versions of the Mahabharata, Arjuna requests Krishna towards the end of the epic to repeat the Gita, for he has forgotten some of the teachings over the years. Krishna replies that, even for him, there is a right moment for everything; he himself can no longer recite the whole of the Gita. Even gods do not individually *possess* or *create* their wisdom or knowledge.

The idea of creativity as unalloyed individual achievement has been growing in the West for about four hundred years; in India for about two hundred. In Europe, however, the process of disenchantment that enfolds creativity is now complete; in India it is not. The idea of absolute individual creativity and the particular form of agency it presumes have spread, but do not yet enjoy unchallenged suzerainty. Even in the earlier decades of the twentieth century, exegeses and commentaries were still considered highly creative ventures and many thinkers, artists, musicians and creative writers proudly found fulfilment in them. Bankimchandra Chattopadhyay was convinced that his interpretation of Krishna was truer than the one in *Gita Govinda*, and more relevant to his times. Even those who were individuated or modern enough to believe that their works were disjunctive with the past, still felt driven by social, cultural and transcendental forces larger than them. Rabindranath Tagore was probably the last great representative of that dying culture of creativity. For that culture is now confined in South Asia to certain rural artisan castes, tribes, and families of traditional musicians, artists and craftspersons.

I have argued elsewhere that there are two languages of creativity: the language of disjunction or discontinuity, and that of continuity.[11] In the former, one speaks of creativity as a sharp break with the past and as something that stands on the ruins of the past; in the latter, creativity is primarily a hermeneutic adventure that reworks the past. They are not exclusive categories, because most societies seem to simultaneously live with both modes of self-expression, though the second language is admittedly becoming more marginal in many societies. However, while the language of continuity can include the language of discontinuity, the language of discontinuity cannot comfortably encompass the language of continuity. Note, for instance, the inner contradiction of all modes of self-expression that claim to be radical and revolutionary and which try to speak only the language of discontinuity. After claiming that a

[11] Ashis Nandy, *The Intimate Enemy: Loss and Recovery of Self under Colonialism* (New Delhi: Oxford University Press, 1983).

revolutionary break with the past has taken place, the rhetoric of revolution has to make enormous efforts to show that the break was not the break that it looked, for it was historically inevitable, a product of cumulative socio-economic, artistic or political changes taking place over a long span of time.

If one takes seriously the traditional idea of creativity, without altogether rejecting the idea of individual agency in creativity, one need not automatically arrive at a standard art-as-a-mirror-to-society or knowledge-as-disguised-self-interest model. One can probably propose that great literary visions as much as great scientific discoveries seem to speak on behalf of their times by reinterpreting past times and worldviews to meet the requirements of the present. They renegotiate the present by reaffirming it and also—this is probably more important—by critiquing it. If the quantum mechanics of Max Planck was partly a reflection of the chaos and uncertainties of the Weimar Republic in the inter-war years, as some historians and sociologists of science suggest, we should not have much problem seeing works of literature, art and music, too, as autobiographies of their times. At this level of discourse, the individual creator becomes a vehicle of a culture and of the anguish of an era.

I have now come to the end of the story. Rabindranath Tagore became the autobiographer of our times by grappling with the core discontents of modern civilisation and by oscillating between three sets of polarities. He spoke out against the violence built into India's traditional social order but also sensed that that violence was being overtaken in scale and range by the new violence of our times. He *had* to take a position against that new violence, too, even if it involved taking a position against the worldview encoded in what he had once thought to be the bedrock of a future, more humane world—the culture of modern Europe.[12] Elsewhere, I have traced his journey from the easy universalism of the Enlightenment vision to an alternative universalism more rooted in non-Western traditions.[13] His *Char Adhyay* and *Sabhyatar Sankat* (*Crisis of Civilisation*) stand witness to his sensitivity to the changing tonal quality of human violence, much before that change became the concern of sensitive Western scholars such as Martin Heidegger and, later, Hannah Arendt, Zigmunt Bauman and Robert J. Lifton. Tagore spoke for his times and for his civilisation, and he did so as a person who spoke both the languages of continuity and discontinuity.

Many of Tagore's fans would like to see him as a self-sustaining creative genius who, but for his family background, virtually created himself *ad nihilo*. Certainly, for many Bengalis, he is the last word in individual creativity. To them, any attempt to locate him in space and time becomes a threat and looks like destructive, if not nihilistic criticism. Tagore *has* become the defensive shield for a defeated culture. Defending Tagore is, for many Bengalis, defending one's own world and its distinctive modes of self-expression, now increasingly under threat.

Tagore does not need anyone's defence. He can defend himself. However, he serves as such a shield because, while representing the language of discontinuity, he also paradoxically invokes the language of continuity. His standard image, with which a large section of urban Bengalis have lived for at least four generations now, allows them to feel like dissenters while being conformists. They can interpret him systematically and formally, and at the same time informally and tacitly, to fit him in the *bhadralok* ideal of the rounded Edwardian gentleman, a polymath, and a Renaissance person. This automatically makes him the finest product of Bengali culture, because he is ultimately judged by standards set by him.

---

[12] Rabindranath Tagore, *Crisis of Civilisation* (Bombay: International Book House, 1941).

[13] Ashis Nandy, *The Illegitimacy of Nationalism: Rabindranath Tagore and the Politics of Self* (New Delhi: Oxford University Press, 1994).

Bengaliness itself is now partly defined by him. As one belonging to the culture that Tagore is supposed to shield from the vagaries of time and the changing visions of a desirable society, I should be the last person to complain against Tagore's present image as it survives in West Bengal and Bangladesh.

However, I am forced to recognise that the time has come to loosen our grip on Tagore and universalise him in a different sense, to grant him a location partly outside Bangladesh and West Bengal on the one hand, and West Europe and North America on the other.[14] Let us rediscover Tagore for other parts of India and the rest of South Asia before affirming the universality of his appeal from the housetops. To do that, we may have to accept two cardinal principles without which no new critical assessment of him is possible and without which his creative genius cannot cross the borders of urban Bengal and the Anglo-Saxon world.

First, everything that even a transcendent genius produces does not and should not survive. Nor does it deserve continuous, serious, intellectual attention, though even his marginalia can be rightfully the concern of specialised scholarship. All of Bach's works are not valued equally by music lovers, all the plays of Shakespeare are not read with equal ardour, even though Shakespeare wrote much less than Tagore. Certainly, all the 3000 songs and 2500 poems of Tagore are not masterpieces and to claim so is to discourage many readers genuinely interested in him. Yet, despite hundreds of books

[14] It is probably an index of the sense of defeat that afflicts the Calcutta-centric culture of Bengali babus that it is perfectly comfortable with the popular acceptance that once greeted Tagore in the West. Yet, that recognition was primarily one of a mystic poet vending Eastern spirituality in an increasingly materialistic world. See for example Ketaki Kushari Dyson, 'Rabindrottar Bangla Kavitar Ingreji Anubad: Udyoger Paschatbhumi Sthapan", *Jijnasa*, 1999, 19(4), pp. 419–33; p. 426. Tagore's Bengali admirers do not even care that Tagore's range of creativity was much better appreciated in some of the cultural regions of South Asia and that these neighbouring cultures produced much better translations of Tagore and put him to much more creative use intellectually.

on Tagore, I have not discovered a single work in recent decades that supplies a critical frame to help the next generation of South Asians or, for that matter, serious readers of Tagore outside the region who have no direct access to Bengali culture and taste. This makes it difficult to know which Tagore to read and which Tagore to avoid. Some of Tagore's novels and plays are mediocre and many of his essays have been overtaken by time. There has been no serious effort to warn first-time readers of Tagore even about these. By trying to sell Tagore in his entirety, Bengalis have only managed to provincialise him, all the while dishonestly—indeed possessively— calling him a universal poet, a *vishvakavi*. A leaner and less flabby Tagore has a better chance of survival as a relevant creative mind in the rest of the world in the coming years. This leaner Tagore may have to have many incarnations, for translatability is something that differs from language to language. The Tagore of *Gitanjali* may be terribly dated in the Anglophone world, but the Tagore of *Sonar Tari, Sheshlekha,* and *Raktakaravi,* to give random examples, may still have much to say to the coming generations. Large parts of the portfolio of Tagore the painter and the writer of short stories will almost surely survive. Tagore as an author of textbooks or as an educationist might have been a rewarding read at one time, but should now have a less audible voice. Tagore as a translator of his own work should be banned; despite a certain quaint charm, to most a contemporary readers, he looks like a literary assassin.

Second, it is time that scholars, artists, musicians and writers be allowed greater liberties with Tagore's works. The defensive, quasi-fundamentalist stranglehold of orthodoxy over the corpus of Tagore's work, exercised by an ageing coterie, diminishes him. More than fifty years ago, Dilip Kumar Roy—the gifted singer, musicologist and composer—passionately pleaded for the right to improvise while singing Tagore's songs. I also know of at least one highly respected classical vocalist, Amir Khan, who felt that he should have been allowed to re-score some of Tagore's songs. Such ideas are still considered blasphemous by many. Yet Tagore in this respect was more lenient than his disciples. His correspondence with Roy shows that he was not closed to the idea of improvisation and that he quite enjoyed Roy's liberties with his songs. He was afraid of less talented musicians fiddling with his scores. Even more revealing is that he personally permitted singer-composer Pankaj Kumar Mallik, certainly not a time-transcending composer, to turn one of his poems into a song for Pramathesh Chandra Barua's film *Mukti* (1936).

Finally, access to Tagore should be more direct, less mediated by his literary estate managers. Tagore belongs to everyone, not to Tagore experts and those who 'correctly' understand and interpret him. I have always been embarrassed by Satyajit Ray's defensive, insecure response to those who criticised him for not being true to Tagore in his various films based on Tagore's works.[15] I would have preferred Ray to be arrogant and say that his medium was not Tagore's and he had the complete right to decide what to do with any story that he, as a film director, turned into a film. The fear that uncontrolled, direct access to Tagore will lead to bad translations, interpretations, transliterations, and transcreations is misplaced. Somerset Maugham once said that no one should be too embarrassed about the works one would like others to forget; they would be forgotten in any case.

I am aware that both these steps will be difficult to take, for they seem to contradict the dominant iconography of Tagore in his homeland. If I may end this essay on a personal note, I have gained much from Tagore, but that is because I have not used him as a crutch; rather, I have dared to stand disrespectfully on his frail shoulders. Frankly, I have found them not that frail after all, and I suspect that he has been pleased that, thanks to this vantage ground he offered me, I have been able to take a more panoramic view of the nastier side of our times. I in turn believe that I have not

[15] See for instance Satyajit Ray, *Bishaya Chalacchitra* (Calcutta: Ananda, 1976).

hurt him by my audacity and, in fact, have established a lively if somewhat combative friendship with him.

This friendship has taught me that great writers occasionally display an eerie, posthumous ability to climb down from the bookshelves and open conversations with us at odd moments. That ability does not necessarily make them greater writers or thinkers, but it certainly makes them more open-ended. In our times, Shakespeare has not remained the same after opening a conversation with Akiro Kurosawa through *Ran* and *Throne of Blood* and even with the makers of popular films such as *West Side Story*. Vyasa's Mahabharata, too, has acquired new shades of meaning after being a constant target of reinterpretations during the last hundred years: some of them brilliant, like Tagore's *Karna-Kunti Samvad*, Heisham Kanhailal's *Karna* and Shyam Benegal's *Kalyug*, others staid or melodramatic, as in many popular Hindi films. George Steiner, I am told, captures something of the phenomenon when he distinguishes between books and texts, presumably the former more frozen in time and the latter more open to exegetic or hermeneutic ventures. Some books and authors have, however, the odd capacity to produce texts that a section of their dedicated admirers would like to read as books, not texts. Tagore may be one of them and, to that extent, he requires some freedom from his immediate cultural context so that those outside his bewitched circle of admirers can recontextualise him according to their needs.

Name Index

Subject Index

.